Corporate Liquidations

for the Lawyer and Accountant

Corporate Liquidations
for the Lawyer and Accountant

FOURTH EDITION

HOWARD A. RUMPF

Editor
Lecturer
Consultant

Prentice-Hall, Inc.   Englewood Cliffs, N.J.

Prentice-Hall International, Inc., *London*
Prentice-Hall of Australia, Pty. Ltd., *Sydney*
Prentice-Hall of Canada, Ltd., *Toronto*
Prentice-Hall of India Private Ltd., *New Delhi*
Prentice-Hall of Japan, Inc., *Tokyo*

First published as *Corporate Liquidations*
© 1960 by HAR PUBLICATIONS, INC.,
New York, N.Y.

Library of Congress Cataloging in Publication Data

Rumpf, Howard A
    Corporate liquidations for the lawyer and accountant.

    Includes index.
    1. Liquidation--United States.   2.   Liquidation--
Taxation--United States.   I.   Title.
KF1475.R8 1975   343.73'067   75-8929
ISBN 0-13-174417-8

Printed in the United States of America

To my wife—

Frances

ABOUT THE AUTHOR

Howard A. Rumpf is a distinguished tax attorney and consultant, a practitioner in the Tax Court of the United States, and a noted lecturer on corporation tax problems. He is a Charter Member of the Enrolled Public Accountants of the State of New York and has been awarded a bronze plaque to commemorate his 35 years of lecturing and advising the tax profession.

He is the author of several previous books, including the *CPA Tax Manual* and the *CPA Questions and Answers.* For many years, he was the Editor of the Prentice-Hall Federal Tax Course, and subsequently of the *Prentice-Hall Tax Guide.* Since establishing himself as an independent tax consultant in 1946, he has contributed to several symposiums on tax subjects, and he has written numerous articles for tax magazines and journals.

He has lectured at New York University and was for many years Chairman of the Tax Department of the Sobelsohn School. He is Chairman of the Tax Committee of the Enrolled Accountants Associations of New York, a member of the Board of Governors of the Accountants Association of New York, and is Past President of the Accountants Square Club of New York State. He is in active practice in New York City and Florida.

IN APPRECIATION

The author wishes to express his sincere appreciation to his partners, *Herbert Abrams,* C.P.A. (N.Y.) and *Irwin A. Steiner,* C.P.A. (N.Y.), for reviewing and supplementing the accounting features of this book, and to *Harry J. Winick, Esquire,* partner in the law firm of Winick & Schiffer, of New York City, for the suggested form of waivers, minutes and other legal documents.

INTRODUCTION TO FOURTH EDITION

In the past four years, more changes have occurred in the field of corporate liquidations and redemptions of stock than in the entire period since the enactment of the Internal Revenue Code of 1954. The changes resulted from many far reaching court decisions and several amendments to the specific sections of the Code affecting complete and partial corporate liquidations, redemption of corporate stock and Subchapter S corporations. The related problems of recapture of the investment credit and depreciation have been clarified, expanded and more clearly defined. In addition, the format of the forms for reporting the distributions in liquidation have been revised for 1974 filing purposes.

Among the many changes are the following important subjects, some of which were never applied to corporate liquidations and redemptions while others have been amended or revised:

- effect of non-compete agreements when included in a corporate liquidation
- effect of land leases
- constructive receipt of income and deductions as they affect the tax on a corporate liquidation
- treatment of advanced interest on the sale of corporate property involved in the corporate liquidation
- the separation of ordinary income in liquidations from capital gain
- how ordinary income can be converted into capital gain
- the totally new concept of the phrase "a mere change in the form of conducting the trade business" as it applies to the regular and to the Subchapter S corporate liquidation.

There was also a change in the concept of earnings and profits and basis. These changes have been woven into this practical book so that the accountant, lawyer, tax advisor and the business man can readily find the answers to the many problems involved in corporate liquidations and related distributions.

The tax meaning of liquidation and dissolution is not essentially the same. The dissolution of a corporation is the termination of its existence as a body politic.[1] Liquidation is defined as the "winding up of the corporate business."[2] Liquidating dividend is the receipt by the stockholders of the cash and other assets (and in some cases, the assumption of the liabilities) of the corporation in exchange or in redemption of the outstanding stock.[3]

The difference is most important since the gain or loss on a liquidating dividend is recognized only upon or at the time of the distribution of the assets by the corporation in complete or partial exchange or redemption of the outstanding stock of the corporation;[4] not at the dissolution of the corporation, unless occurring simultaneously.

Thus, the process of liquidation and dissolution for tax purposes may cover four distinct steps: (a) liquidation—the winding up of the affairs of the corporation, i.e. payments of debts, etc.; (b) computation of gain taxable to corporation under the receptive depreciation provisions and the adjustment of the surplus; (c) the dissolution of the corporation (if required by the method of liquidation); and (d) the liquidation distribution or liquidating dividend—the receipt by the stockholders of the net assets in exchange for or in redemption of their stock.

H.A.R.

---

[1] Black's Law Dictionary.

[2] W.E. Guild, 19 BTA 1186.

[3] Sec. 331(a), IRC 1954; Langstaff v Lucas, CB June, 1926, pg. 164, 9 F 2d 691, aff. 13 F 2d 1022; Benjamin H. Read, 6 BTA 407; Romie C. Jacks, 19 BTA 559.

[4] Sec. 1001, 1002, IRC 1954; OD 343, CB 1919, pg. 80; OD 461, CB June 1920, pg. 85; J.C. Bradford et al., 22 TC 1057.

CONTENTS

Chapter One.

General Rules of Corporate Liquidations

Chapter Two.

Valuation—Basis

Chapter Three.

   Recapture of Depreciation—Personal Property—Section 1245

Chapter Four.

   Recapture of Depreciation—Real Property—Section 1250

Chapter Seven.

Complete Liquidation: Specimen Problem

Chapter Eight.

Calendar Month Liquidation—Section 333, IRC 1954

Chapter Nine.

Calendar Month Liquidation: Specimen Problem

Chapter 10.

Liquidation Under Section 337

Chapter Eleven.

Section 337—Specimen Problem

Chapter Twelve.

Partial Liquidations—Section 331(a) (2)

Chapter Thirteen.

Redemption of Stock—Section 302, IRC 1954

Chapter Fourteen.

Complete Liquidation of Subsidiary—Section 322, IRC 1954

Chapter Fifteen .

Liquidations of Corporations—Sections 1361 and 1371 Elections

Chapter Sixteen:

Subchapter S Corporations—Basic Rules

SYLLABUS OF TERMS
AND ABBREVIATIONS

Acq . . . . Acquiescence by Commissioner
Adv. Rev. Proc. . . . . .Advance Revenue Procedure
Adv. Rev. Rul. . . . . .Advance Revenue Ruling
Aff . . . . .Affirmed
AFTR . . . . American Federal Tax Reports (Prentice-Hall, Inc.)
Ann. . . . . .Announcement
ARM . . . . .Committee on Appeals and Review Memorandum
ARR . . . . .Committee on Appeals and Review Recommendation
BTA . . . . Board of Tax Appeals
CB . . . . Cumulative Bulletin—Internal Revenue
CCA . . . . .Circuit Court of Appeals
Comm. . . . . .Commissioner of Internal Revenue
Ct. D . . . . .Court Decision
Ct. Cl. . . . . Court of Claims
D.C. . . . . District Court
F. Supp. . . . . Federal Supplement
F. 2d . . . . Federal Reporter, 2d Series
FMV . . . . Fair Market Value
GCM . . . . .General Counsel's Memorandum
IR . . . . .News Release (by IRS)
IRC . . . . .Internal Revenue Code
IT . . . . Income Tax Unit Ruling
IR-Mim. . . . . Internal Revenue Mimeograph
LO . . . . Solicitor's Law Opinion
Mim. . . . . Mimeograph
NA . . . . .Non Acquiescence by Commissioner
O . . . . Solicitor's Law Opinion
OD . . . . Office Decision of Income Tax Unit
Op, AG . . . . Opinion of Attorney General
Rev. . . . . Reversed

Rev. Proc. . . . . .Revenue Procedure
Rev. Rul. . . . . Revenue Ruling
S. . . . . .Solicitor's Memorandum
SM. . . . . .Solicitor's Memorandum
Sol. Op. . . . . Solicitor's Opinion
SR . . . . Solicitor's Recommendation
Sup. Ct. . . . . Supreme Court (US)
TBM . . . . .Advisory Tax Board Memorandum
TBR . . . . .Advisory Tax Board Recommendation
TC . . . . Tax Court of the United States
TDO . . . . Treasury Dept. Order
TIR . . . . .Technical Information Release
TD . . . . Treasury Decision
U.S. . . . . United States Supreme Court

ONE

General Rules of
Corporate Liquidations

GENERAL RULE.

A distribution by a corporation of its assets, whether in partial or complete liquidation, results in no recognized gain or loss to the corporation despite an appreciation or a decline in the value of the assets as compared with their costs or other basis since acquisition by the corporation.[1] This is the general rule, regardless of which method of liquidation (as described in the following chapters) is selected.

EXCEPTIONS TO GENERAL RULE.

However, there are three important exceptions to the general rule (as described more fully in the following chapters). Two of these exceptions apply to the recapture of depreciation on the sale or disposition of (a) tangible and intangible personal property[2] and (b) real property and leaseholds.[3] Disposition includes not only a sale of such assets but also a distribution in redemption of the corporate stock and in liquidation of a corporation, regardless under what section the liquidation occurs. The third exception applies to installment obligations received on the sale of corporate assets and their distribution in liquidation.[4]

Tangible and Intangible Personal Assets: Under Section 1245, the gain on the sale or other disposition of such assets is in part ordinary income (or gain) and in part gain under Section 1231 (usually resulting in long-term capital gain). The theory of this section of the Code is to tax to the corporation the depreciation allowed or allowable on such assets claimed by the corporation after December 31, 1961 and distributed in liquidation in any taxable year beginning after December 31, 1962 (as explained in the following chapters). Section 1245 does not apply where there is a loss on the sale or other disposition.

Example: A corporation acquired an asset in 1952 at a cost of $20,000 and adopted the straight line method for depreciation and a twenty year life (assume no salvage value). The asset was sold or distributed in liquidation under Section 331 (a) (1) at which time it had a fair market value (selling price) of $16,000.

The adjusted basis on 12/31/62 was, therefore, $9,000 (depreciation to 12/31/61 $10,000; for calendar year 1962 $1,000). The actual gain would be $7,000 ($16,000–$9,000). The actual gain would under Section 1245 be broken up between (a) ordinary gain (to the corporation) $1,000 and (b) Section 1231 gain $6,000 (subject to later discussion).

The recapture provision applies to all sections applicable to corporate liquidations except to a liquidation under Section 332 if the parent corporation carries over the subsidiary's basis as provided in Section 334 (b) (2). The rule of recapture does not apply if the parent corporation uses Section 334 (b) (1) in conjunction with Section 332. (See Chapter 14.)

Real Property and Leaseholds: As a result of the enactment of Section 1250 in the Revenue Act of 1964, and as amended in the Tax Reform Act of 1969, depreciation recapture applies to the sale or other disposition of real property and leaseholds at a gain in all taxable years beginning after December 31, 1963 as to the depreciation allowed or allowable after December 31, 1963. While the basic theory is the same as that which applies to personal property, the application of the recapture provisions is entirely different as fully described in the following chapters. Section 1250 does not apply to a loss on a sale or other disposition.

Installment Obligations: Under certain methods of liquidation, gain is recognized to the corporation at the time the installment obligations are distributed to the stockholders in exchange for or in redemption of the stock. The gain would likewise be taxable to the corporation if the installment obligations are distributed in liquidation of the corporation to a partnership or proprietorship which succeeded the corporation.[5] But where the assets (including installment obligations) are transferred to a liquidating trustee who represents the corporation and not the stockholders and the corporate life is extended over the period of collections by the trustee, the corporation, through its trustee, is taxable on the gain as realized.[6]

The amount of the gain to the corporation is the unrealized or deferred profit on the installment obligations at the time of the liquidation.[7]

Example: A calendar year corporation on July 1, 1969 sold a piece of real estate for $100,000, receiving at closing cash of $30,000 and a purchase money mortgage of $70,000, payable $10,000 a year, beginning July 1, 1970. The adjusted basis of the real estate at the time of the sale was $40,000. On February 1, 1971, the corporation liquidated, distributing—among the other assets—the purchase money mortgage.

The total gain on the sale was $60,000 ($100,000–$40,000) and the gross profit percentage 60%. In 1969 and 1970, the corporation reported for tax purposes recognized gains of $18,000 and $6,000, respectively. Thus, at the beginning of 1971, the unreported (deferred) gain was $36,000 (balance of mortgage receivable $60,000 × 60%). Upon liquidation, the corporation is required to include the $36,000 in its gross income for 1971, the year of liquidation.

As described in later chapters, the exception under Section 453 (d), IRC 1954, does not apply to corporate liquidations under (a) Section 332 (complete liquidation of subsidiaries) and (b) Section 337 (sale of corporate property during period of complete liquidation—the 12-month liquidation; but not as to sales on the installment basis made prior to the election under Section 337).

SALE v LIQUIDATION.

However, a corporation may elect to sell its assets prior to liquidation rather than distribute the assets in kind to the stockholders. In such cases, except where the special rules of Section 337, IRC 1954 are adopted and the exceptions above apply, the gain or loss is recognized by the corporation on all sales made by it.[8] Under certain conditions, it is advisable tax-wise to sell the assets in lieu of making a liquidating distribution.

For example, a corporation contemplating liquidation has a substantial net income for the year. The corporation's assets include certain machinery and equipment which have an adjusted basis of $65,000. The fair market value, based upon the actual current selling price for such machinery, is $25,000. Assuming no other transactions, the loss of $40,000 is an ordinary loss which is fully deductible against other income (since Section 1231, IRC 1954, does not apply). Thus, if the corporation was in the 52% bracket, it would save $20,800 by selling the assets instead of distributing them to the stockholders.

STOCKHOLDER v CORPORATION.

The corporation tax saving, after taking into account the depreciation recapture provisions, should be compared with the tax effect upon the stockholders. For example, if the general method of liquidating a corporation is selected,[9] the liquidating dividend to the stockholder is the net fair market value of all of the assets to be distributed as compared with the stockholder's cost or other basis of his stock. Thus, if in the above example, the corporation had other assets which had appreciated in value over their respective adjusted basis, the depreciated assets would be applied against the appreciated assets to compute the net liquidating dividend.

The election to sell or distribute the assets applies individually to each asset owned by the corporation. Hence, not only is the method of liquidation important tax-wise, but the election to sell or distribute in kind should be studied and compared for the tax effect on both the stockholders and the corporation.

LIQUIDATION AS A SALE.

Under the general rule, distributions in liquidation—more commonly known as liquidating dividends—are treated as a sale of the stock.[10] The stockholders recognize gain or loss upon the receipt of the corporate assets in exchange for their stock. As such, the gain or loss is a capital gain or loss (subject to the provisions of Section 1231). Whether the gain or loss is short-term or long-term depends upon the length of time the stock was held by the shareholder.[11] However, in addition to the general rule, special rules apply to each of the various methods of liquidation as described separately in the following chapters.

WHEN GAIN OR LOSS RECOGNIZED—CASH v ACCRUAL BASIS.

Gain on liquidation is taxable to a cash-basis taxpayer-stockholder in the year gain was received, whereas losses are deductible in the year when all the assets are distributed except the retention of nominal cash to meet specified liabilities. A stockholder reporting on the accrual basis should report gain or loss in the tax year in which all assets are distributed, despite the retention of some cash to cover liabilities, and the balance of the retained cash to be distributed in later years after the obligations have been paid.[12]

Where a liquidating dividend is received in cash, the gain from such distribution is included in gross income in the year of receipt. Where the liquidating dividend is in kind (assets other than cash), the gain, under the general rule, is determined in the year when the distribution of the corporate assets is made and the business and the property is actually transferred to the stockholders.[13] In some cases, the time depends on the provision of the state laws regarding the dissolution of the corporation.[14]

CONSTRUCTIVE RECEIPT.

The doctrine of constructive receipt of a liquidating dividend by a shareholder has been applied by the Courts.[15] A corporation adopted a resolution to liquidate in June 1963. The stockholder reported for tax purposes on the cash receipts basis and on the calendar year. The only asset of the corporation was securities. On December 30, 1963, the stockholder was informed as to the fair market value of the securities to be distributed. On the same date, the securities were delivered by the corporation to a broker for re-issue to the stockholder. The broker delivered the securities to the stockholder on January 9, 1964. The stockholder is required to report the liquidating dividend in the calendar year 1963 return.

WHEN LOSS RECOGNIZED.

A loss on liquidation is subject to the same general rules as are applicable to all tax losses. The loss must be evidenced by closed and complete transactions, fixed by identifiable events, and bona-fide, and actually sustained during the year.[16] Where the entire assets of a corporation are distributed in one year, the loss deduction is allowable for such year, despite the fact that the accounts of the liquidating trustees were not approved by the courts until the following year.[17] The Internal Revenue Service, the Regulations and the courts have generally recognized that a loss is deductible even though a negligible part of the assets is retained by the corporation to meet liabilities not determinable at liquidation.[18] The loss deduction is a capital loss and is subject to the limitations as provided in Section 1211, IRC 1954.

RETENTION OF ASSETS.

A corporation is considered in complete liquidation when all of its assets are distributed, except a nominal amount of cash which was deposited in a special account to cover current tax liability.[19] An amount which was set aside by a corporation in liquidation to cover the guarantee of accounts receivable is not a part of the liquidating dividend.[20]

LIQUIDATING DIVIDENDS IN INSTALLMENTS.

Where distributions in complete liquidation of a corporation are paid in installments, the stockholders do not report gain until they have recovered the cost or other basis of their stock.[21]

DIFFERENT DATES OF PURCHASE OF CORPORATE STOCK.

Under the general rule, the difference between the cost or other basis of the stock and the amount received in liquidation of the stock is the gain or loss. Where the stock was acquired on different dates, the gain or loss must be separately determined on each acquisition.[22] Thus, the stockholders may have a gain on one lot of stock and a loss on another. Similarly, the gain or loss may be short-term or long-term depending upon when each of the several lots was acquired.

This involves the specific identification of each lot acquired as to the date of acquisition or purchase and the cost or other basis.[23] Identification is usually accomplished by reference to the serial numbers on the stock certificates, the dates of issue or purchase and the financial records as to the price paid or, if acquired other than by purchase, the basis so established, i.e., acquisition by gift or bequest.[24] If this identity cannot be determined, the liquidating dividend will be charged against the earliest purchase.[25]

INCOME DURING LIQUIDATION.

Income and gain received by a corporation during the period of liquidation and prior to the actual distribution of the assets is taxed to the corporation.[26] If trustees are appointed to liquidate the corporation, the trustees are required to file corporate returns (not fiduciary returns) and report the income and deductions during the period of liquidation.[27] A corporation in the process of liquidation may not wait until the liquidation has been completed in order to see if a net profit resulted, but must report its income and deductions for each tax year encompassed in the period of liquidation.[28] A corporation, after liquidation and dissolution, distributed a Federal tax refund to the former stockholders. The refund received by the liquidated corporation is not income to the corporation but a part of the liquidating dividend.[29]

Expenses paid or incurred after the year of liquidation cannot be deducted in the year of liquidation.[30] Such expenses, if paid by the former stockholders after liquidation, are an adjustment to the liquidating dividend. Note, however, that in some of the methods of liquidation, the Regulations provide that the corporation should retain sufficient monies to pay contingent or unascertained liabilities.

CORPORATE TAX RETURN DURING LIQUIDATION.

A corporation which has adopted a resolution or plan to liquidate, ceased doing business, distributed all of its assets, except those retained to pay claims, including taxes, prior to the end of its regular tax year is required to file a short-period return before the 15th day of the third month following the liquidation (unless an extension to file was granted by the Internal Revenue Service).[31] But a corporation which has ceased doing business, retained no assets, and had no income may, upon presentation of the facts to the Internal Revenue Service, be relieved from filing a return for such period even though not formally dissolved.[32]

But where the business is continued until actual distribution in liquidation has taken place, a corporation is taxable as such until the charter is revoked,[33] or annulled,[34] or expired under the state law.[35] A corporation is required to file a return as long as it has the right to function.[36] Thus, a corporation was held liable for taxes for its full tax year where it remained in existence during such period.[37]

CORPORATION OPERATED BY RECEIVERS.

A corporation which continues to operate under the direction of receivers does not go out of existence and corporate returns are required.[38] If trustees in liquidation are not appointed by the corporate directors, the stockholders are required to file the returns since they are personally liable as transferees in equity for the tax of the corporation.[39] Before distributing the assets, a corporation contemplating dissolution should reserve sufficient funds to cover the estimated tax liability.[40]

SHORT TAX YEAR—LIQUIDATING CORPORATION.

A dissolving corporation is required to file a return for the period from the beginning of its calendar year or fiscal year to the date of dissolution. Thus, if a corporation which reports for tax purposes on the calendar year basis is dissolved on September 16, a return is required for the short period from January 1, the first day of its regular tax year to the date on which the corporation goes out of existence, i.e., September 16th. This short period is the final return for the corporation and should be clearly marked "Final Return" on the top of page one of the corporation tax form 1120. The income shown on the return for the short period of a dissolving corporation is not annualized for the purposes of computing the final tax, if any, on the return.[41]

Ordinarily, a corporation is not in existence after it ceases business and dissolves, retaining no assets, whether or not under the state law of incorporation it may be treated as a continuing corporation while winding up its affairs.[42] If the corporation has retained valuable claims for which it is bringing or intends to bring suit, it has retained assets and continues in existence. A corporation that is operated by receivers does not go out of existence.

CORPORATE LIQUIDATIONS A QUESTION OF FACT.

All corporate liquidations are a question of fact.[43] The mere adoption of a resolution by the stockholders authorizing the directors to take the necessary action to liquidate is merely a technical status. The adoption of the resolution to liquidate must be substantiated by affirmative action, namely, the winding up of the corporate business.[44] On the other hand, the fact that the stockholders have not passed a resolution authorizing the directors to proceed to liquidate or dissolve the corporation does not of necessity mean that the corporation is not in the process of liquidation,[45] or prevent the distributions from being liquidating dividends.[46]

Action alone by the stockholders in winding up the corporate affairs and the business may result in liquidating distributions.[47] The increasing technical requirements of the Code would seem to dictate that the proper resolutions should be passed authorizing the liquidation and, thereafter, distributing the assets as provided by the various liquidating sections of the Internal Revenue Code described in subsequent chapters.[48] However in certain family corporations, i.e., husband and wife, informal discussions were upheld as satisfying the requirements.[49]

DEPRECIATION AFTER LIQUIDATION.

Under Section 167 (b), IRC 1954, the cost of certain assets acquired after December 31, 1953, can be written off at a more rapid rate than under the prior Code.[50] The accelerated rates, i.e., the double declining balance (200%) method and the sum-of-the-years-digits method, apply only to real and personal tangible property with a useful life of at least three years used in the taxpayers trade or business or held for the production of income. Special rules apply to property if acquired after the effective date of the Tax Reform Act of 1969. The new methods do not apply to intangible assets such as patents, leases or copyrights.[51]

Two prerequisites applicable to the accelerated methods are important to a corporation contemplating liquidation and dissolution. The accelerated methods may be used only if property is new (original use) in the hands of the taxpayer. Thus, if a corporation had elected the accelerated methods under the 1954 Code, the stockholders, either as individuals or as a partnership, who received a liquidating dividend, may not continue to use these methods after the liquidation and dissolution.

However, this rule does not apply to the 150% declining balance method, known also as the limited declining balance method or 1½ times the straight line rate, or method. Thus, the successor entity to the liquidated corporation may adopt the limited declining balance method (150%) in its first return filed after the receipt of the corporate assets in liquidation.[52] It should be noted, however, that if adopted by the successor entity, a change to the straight line method may only be made with the permission of the Commissioner of Internal Revenue.[53]

The sum-of-the-years-digits method and the declining balance method (150%), once elected, result in a binding election. However, with respect to depreciable personal tangible assets which are classified as Section 1245 assets (depreciation recapture), the depreciation method may be changed in the taxpayer's return for the first taxable year beginning after December 31, 1962.[54] Also, the amount of estimated salvage value may be reduced to an amount which does not exceed 10% of the basis of the property.[55] The above rules do not apply to Section 1250 property, i.e., real property and leaseholds subject to recapture of depreciation.

ORGANIZATION EXPENSES.

Organization expenses of a corporation are not deductible at the time of incorporation but are required to be capitalized. However, at the election of the corporation the capitalized expenses may be treated as deferred expenses and deducted rateably over a period of not less than sixty months. The corporation may elect such a deduction beginning with the month in which the corporation begins business; not in the month of incorporation, necessarily.[56]

Where a corporation completely liquidates and dissolves, the amount of the organization expenses, or the unrecovered organization expenses if the corporation elected to deduct the expenses pro-rata, is deductible in full as an ordinary expense to the corporation in the year of liquidation and dissolution.[57]

LIQUIDATION AND DISSOLUTION EXPENSES.

Legal, accounting, valuation, appraisal, brokerage and other fees and expenses of liquidation and dissolution are deductible in the year of dissolution.[58] The deduction is allowed even though the liquidated assets are transferred to a new corporation.[59] Where there is a partial liquidation, an allocated part of the expenses is allowable as a deduction.[60] Under a Section 337 liquidation, legal fees and commissions in connection with the sale of the assets are offsets against the selling price and are not deductible as ordinary and necessary expenses.[61]

STATE FRANCHISE TAX.

In computing the tax-cost under the various methods of liquidation, the attorney and/or the accountant should determine the dissolution tax, if any, payable to the state in which the corporation was incorporated.

CITATIONS

[1] Sec. 336, IRC 1954; Reg. Sec. 1.336–1.

[2] Sec. 1245, IRC 1954.

[3] Sec. 1250, IRC 1954.

[4] Sec. 453 (d), IRC 1954; Reg. Sec. 1.453–9.

[5] Rev. Rul. 55–672, CB 1955–2, pg. 551.

[6] First Nat'l Bk. of Greeley, Colo. v U.S., 86 F 2d 938, aff. 9 F. Supp. 28.

[7] Reg. Sec. 1.453–9; IT 3586, CB 1942–2, pg. 65.

[8] Reg. Sec. 1.336–1.

[9] Sec. 331 (a), IRC 1954.

[10] Sec. 331 (a), IRC 1954.

[11] Sec. 1222, IRC 1954.

[12] GCM 22822, CB 1941–2, pg. 126.

[13] National Grocery Co. v Comm., 111 F 2d 328; Pierce Oil Corp., et al., 32 BTA 403.

[14] Rex Brugh, 32 BTA 898.

[15] Byrne, 54 TC No. 160.

[16] Reg. Sec. 1.165–1 (d).

[17] John F. Braun, 23 BTA 536.

[18] Comm. v Winthrop, 98 F 2d 74, aff. 36 BTA 314; GCM 21966, CB 1940–1, pg. 130.

[19] Colonial Enterprises, Inc., 47 BTA 518.

[20] Cushing, et al., v U.S., 18 F. Supp. 83.

[21] J.C. Bradford, et al., 22 TC 1057; Susan J. Carter, 9 TC 364, 170 F 2d 911.

[22] GCM 20826, CB 1938–2, pg. 202; Norman Cooledge, 40 BTA 110 (Acq.).

[23] Reg. Sec. 1.1012–1 (a).

[24] Wood v Comm., 197 F 2d 859, aff. TC Memo 1950; Davidson v Comm., 305 U.S. 44.

[25] John P. Elton, 47 BTA 111.

[26] OD 231, CB 1919, pg. 213; IT 2016, CB June 1924, pg. 29; Williamson v U.S., 155 Ct. Cl. 279; Susan J. Carter, 9 TC 364.

[27] OD 821, CB June 1921, pg. 279; Mrs. Grant Smith, et al., 26 BTA 1178.

[28] American Industrial Corp., 20 BTA 188.

[29] Mente & Co., Inc., et al., 29 BTA 804, aff. 76 F 2d 965.

[30] Hirst & Begley Lindseed Co., 4 BTA 1160; J. Gilmore Fletcher, et al., 16 TC 273.

[31] Rev. Rul. 215, CB 1953–2, pg. 149; Rev. Rul. 56–483, CB 1956–2, pg. 933.

[32]IT 3871, CB 1947–2, pg. 62; Kamin Chevrolet Co., 3 TC 1076 (Acq.).

[33]Ralph G. Wootan, et al., Memo TC 1955.

[34]OD 365, CB June 1920, pg. 222.

[35]Sol. Op. 93, CB June 1921, pg. 305; The Roe Stephens Mfg. Co., 12 BTA 1254.

[36]OD 882, CB June 1921, pg. 307.

[37]Neil v Phinney, 245 F 2d 645.

[38]U.S. v C.T. Loo, Trustee (C. & M. McCarthy, Ltd.) 248 F 2d 765.

[39]Homer S. Warren, et al., 31 BTA 1041; Bates Motor Transport Lines, Inc., 17 TC 151, aff. 200 F 2d 20.

[40]Brady v Anderson, 240 Fed. 665.

[41]Sec. 443 (a), IRC 1954; Reg. Sec. 1.443–1 (a) (2).

[42]Consult local state law; IT 1416, CB Dec. 1922, pg. 199.

[43]John Milton, 33 BTA 4; C.M. Menzies, Inc., 34 BTA 163.

[44]W.E. Guild, 19 BTA 1186.

[45]GCM 8623, CB Dec. 1930, pg. 164.

[46]Holmby Corporation v Comm., 83 F 2d 548, aff. 28 BTA 1092.

[47]Benoit v Comm., 238 F 2d 485, aff. 25 TC 656.

[48]Whitson v Rockwood, DC, ND, 2/13/61. 7 AFTR 2d 677; Intercounty Development Corp., TC Memo 1961–217.

[49]Alameda Realty Corp., 42 TC 273, Acq.

[50]Sec. 23 (1), IRC 1939.

[51]Reg. Sec. 1.167 (c)–1.

[52]Rev. Rul. 57–352, CB 1957–2, pg. 150.

[53]Rev. Rul. 57–510, CB 1957–2, pg. 152. See also Sec. 167 (j) (1) (4).

[54]Sec. 167 (e) (2), IRC 1954.

[55]Sec. 167 (f) (1), IRC 1954.

[56]Sec. 248, IRC 1954; Reg. Sec. 1.248–1.

[57]Shellabarger Grain Products Co., 2 TC 75, aff. 146 F 2d 177; Wayne Coal Mining Co., Memo TC 1953, aff. 209 F 2d 152.

[58]Neurer Steel Barrel Co., Inc., Memo TC 1943.

[59]U.S. v Arcade Co., et al., 203 F 2d 230, aff. 97 F Supp. 942; Rite-Way Products, Inc., 12 TC 475.

[60]Mills Estate Inc. v Comm., 206 F 2d 244, rev. 17 TC 910.

[61]Alphaco, Inc. v Nelson, 385 F 2d 244.

TWO

Valuation –
Basis

BASIC PROBLEM—VALUATION.

One of the basic problems in corporation liquidations is the valuation of the assets. While more important in some of the liquidation methods than in others, the question of valuation appears in some form in all of the methods of liquidation and dissolution. For example, in some methods, the valuation provides a basis for computing the recognized gain or loss; in others, a basis for the determination of ordinary income as in the case of receivables. Valuation—the value of the corporate assets—is most important in determining which of the various methods of liquidation and dissolution should be selected to accomplish the desired result, particularly with respect to a stepped-up basis for the assets, the amount of the gain or loss, the amount of the tax liability and whether the gain is capital gain or ordinary gain.

FAIR MARKET VALUE.

For tax purposes, the assets which are received in liquidation are valued at "fair market value." Judicially, "fair market value" is defined as "the price which property will bring when it is offered for sale by one who is willing but who is not obliged to sell it, and is bought by one who is willing or desires to purchase, but is not compelled to do so."[1] In other words, a price or value determined at arm's length. It is not necessary that the property shall be for sale, nor that there shall be a known buyer for it before it can have a market value.[2]

BURDEN OF PROOF.

The determination of value by the Commissioner is presumptively correct. This rule applies unless the taxpayer can produce affirmative evidence to disprove the Commissioner's determination.[3] Opinion evidence offered by the taxpayer may be sufficient to substantiate the taxpayer's burden of proof.[4] However, the Court can ignore this testimony.[5] The Court can substantiate its own value provided it had knowledge and experience with respect to the subject matter to be valued.[6]

DETERMINATION OF VALUE—GENERAL RULE.

The value of the assets distributed in liquidation is the fair market value on the date of receipt[7] determined on the basis of the selling price,[8] appraisal[9] or by expert testimony,[10] or by other methods summarized later in this chapter. In order to establish fair market value, competent evidence is necessary. The value may not be established by formula alone.[11] In the determination of the fair market value, the facts and circumstances as they exist on the date of receipt of the liquidating dividend must be considered plus the reasonable prospects for the future.[12] The depreciated cost of the property is some evidence of fair market value but is not conclusive. The book value of the assets will be acceptable as the liquidating value only if it coincides with the fair market value,[13] or if there is an absence of other evidence as to the value.[14] However, if other evidence as to value is available and offered as proof by the Internal Revenue Service, the book value or depreciated cost will not be acceptable.[15] These rules have been applied to the cost of reproduction when offered as evidence of fair market value. Offers made in good faith and the opinions of intelligent men experienced in the business are acceptable in the establishment of the fair market value of assets received in liquidation.[16]

VALUE A VITAL FACTOR.

Extreme care is required in determining the fair market value of the assets received since the amount of the gain or loss to be reported and recognized for tax purposes is solely dependent upon this figure in some sections of the Code covering liquidating dividends.[17] Furthermore, the amount reported on the income tax return as the value of the property at the time received as a liquidating dividend by the stockholders has been held not conclusive (in the absence of satisfactory proof) as to the value of the property for purposes of determining gain or loss on the later sale or other taxable disposition of the property.[18] Hence, it is vital that the value of the property at liquidation be correctly determined, otherwise the subsequent sale or other disposition could be attacked as to the amount of the gain or loss reported.

GOODWILL.

Property distributed in liquidation includes both tangible and intangible property.[19] In many corporate liquidations, the Internal Revenue Service has attempted to include as part of the liquidating dividend the value of goodwill (and other intangibles) where the corporation liquidates, dissolves, and the business is continued by a proprietorship or by a partnership. For example, goodwill was determined in one case where a stockholder who owned 101 shares out of a total of 190 shares, purchased the other 89 shares and then liquidated the corporation and continued as a sole proprietorship. The Internal Revenue Service contended that the amount paid for the 89 shares was indicative of goodwill after giving effect to the book value of the stock (without regard to goodwill). The Tax Court reduced the amount determined above by the Internal Revenue Service, based upon the testimony of witnesses.[20]

Usually, goodwill does not attach where the success of the business depends solely on skill, ability, integrity, or other personal characteristics of the stockholder—owner.[21] The following rule has been adopted by the Tax Court of the United States in connection with the problem of whether goodwill existed at the time of the liquidation of a corporation: "Ability, skill, experience, acquaintanceship, or other personal characteristics or qualifications (of an officer or employee) do not constitute goodwill as an item or property; nor do they exist in such form that they could be the subject of transfer."[22]

Accounting and tax-wise there are no uniformly accepted rules for the determination of goodwill or for its valuation thereafter. The circumstances and history of the business must be considered.[23] The taxpayer has the right to value the goodwill, if any, under the methods and rules which have been generally accepted. Furthermore, expert opinion will be given consideration and weight in the determination both of whether goodwill exists and the value thereof. The opinion, however, must be by qualified persons[24] whose qualifications must be proven before they testify[25] and whose reasoning is sound and logical based upon the facts at the time[26] and must be founded on actual knowledge of the situation or the property involved.[27]

DETERMINATION OF GOODWILL—FORMULA.

In the absence of other data necessary to establish goodwill, the Internal Revenue Service has applied a formula involving a fair return on the average tangible assets over a period of not less than five years. The surplus earnings (in excess of ten percent) will be capitalized at not more than five times. However, where the business to be valued is of a less hazardous nature, the Internal Revenue Service may reduce the return from 10% to 8% or 9% of the average value of the tangible assets and the rate of capitalization from 20% to 15%.[28]

Average tangible assets	$200,000
Average earnings	$ 35,000
10% of average tangible assets	20,000
Excess or surplus earnings	$ 15,000
Capitalized at 20%—goodwill	$ 75,000

The fair market value of the tangible assets at the date of liquidation would be increased by $75,000, the value of the goodwill of the business.

In computing the average tangible assets, the total tangible assets should be reduced by the current liabilities.[29] The Federal income tax liability reduces the earnings of the corporation before the earnings are averaged.[30] In other words, the Federal income tax liability is considered an expense of the business for this purpose. The cost of the tangible assets is essential in order to value the intangible goodwill in the production of income.[31] A three-year average has been held not sufficient to determine a fair average.[32] Abnormal years such as war years or other inflationary years, should be eliminated in determining the average tangible assets and the earnings.[33] Depending upon the industry and other circumstances, the courts have established various percentages in addition to those established by ARM 34 above (percent of average tangible assets and the capitalization rate, respectively—8% and 15%;[34] 10% and 15%;[35] 10% and 20%;[36] 6% and 20%).

The courts in upholding the formula method for computing goodwill stated, "Goodwill may be defined by the following formula: Goodwill equals a-b, where 'a' is capitalized earning power and 'b' is the value of the assets used in the business. Goodwill, then, is an intangible consisting of the excess earning power of a business. A normal earning power is expected of the business assets, and if the business has greater earnings, then the business may be said to have goodwill."[37]

Goodwill cannot be reduced by so-called negative goodwill. For example, a group of corporations used 20% in computing goodwill. However, some of the corporations in the group earned 10% or less. In computing the total goodwill, the group goodwill was reduced by the goodwill of those low earning corporations, i.e., negative goodwill.[38]

PATENTS—COPYRIGHTS.

There is no hard and fast rule for valuing patents. It is a question of the particular facts in each case.[39] As in most tax matters, the burden of proof is upon the taxpayer.[40] In valuing patents, the courts have taken into account the savings accruing to the taxpayer, the user of the patent, due to the use of the patent. In other words, the excess earnings due to the use of the patent as against its non-use.[41] However, the savings or excess earnings should be adjusted by such items as the interest expense on the money invested in the patent.[42]

Value of the patent is not necessarily equal to the par value of the stock issued for the patent[43] nor is the selling price of the stock of a corporation conclusive or the dividend payments during the period of use.[44] The value of a patent has been established by the position the owners occupy in the industry as the result of the patent, the earning power and expert opinion.[45] In another case, the value was based upon the contribution which the patent made to the success of the corporation in its business group.[46]

The sinking fund method by applying the Hoskold formula has been used extensively in valuing patents.[47] It is based upon the discounted present worth of anticipated income from the patent. A theoretical formula, however, was not held conclusive.[48] Valuation is a matter of giving proper weight to all of the pertinent facts in a particular case: (a) the appraisal of the corporate directors as men of experience in the industry; (b) expert testimony; (c) the purchase for cash within the first year of organization by persons familiar with the industry of the corporate stock which was preferred as to the assets in the event of corporate liquidation; (d) the superiority of the patented item measured by the simplicity of construction, facility of repair, greater accuracy and lower up-keep cost.[49]

Patent license contracts and copyrights are determined as to their value in liquidation under the rules outlined above.[50]

LAND AND BUILDINGS.

The "fair market value" of property is the fair value of the property in money as between one who wishes to purchase and one who wishes to sell, and is the price at which a seller willing to sell at a fair price and a buyer willing to buy at a fair price will trade, both having reasonable knowledge of the facts.[51] Fair market value means "exchangeable value."[52] A fair value at arm's length is always the basic test.

Valuation is based upon the testimony of experienced real estate owners and dealers who were acquainted for many years with the property of the taxpayer and the property in the city (area) in which the property was located.[53] Reputable appraisal of the value of the land and building is acceptable as against comparable sales prices.[54] Valuation based upon city or county assessment records is not considered proof unless corroborated by other evidence.[55]

The appraisal is competent evidence of value as of that date. If the date is other than the date of liquidation, it must be adjusted to that date. The Internal Revenue Service will, however, accept retrospective appraisals,[56] which meet certain requirements.[57] Reproductive value, unless supported by testimony from experienced realtors, will not be accepted by the Internal Revenue Service.[58] The Tax Court of the United States will usually determine value only when it is based upon conclusive evidence.[59]

Where depreciable and non-depreciable property is acquired in liquidation of a corporation, the basis of the land and buildings must be separately determined in order to establish the basis for depreciation in the hands of the successor entity.[60] Thus, where land and building is distributed to the stockholders of a corporation in liquidation, separate value must be secured for the land and the building. The lump sum value must be allocated between the land and the building based upon the value of each to the total. In some cases, the ratio of the assessed value will be accepted.[61] Unless the basis is properly determined and supported, the Internal Revenue Service may disallow or adjust the depreciation claimed, with the hardship upon the taxpayer.[62]

LEASEHOLDS.

The fair market value is the amount which a purchaser having a choice of acquiring the lessee's interest or entering into negotiations for acquiring a lease of some other comparable property would be willing to pay to acquire the lessee's interest.[63] A purchase would expect to recover not only the purchase price but also a reasonable return upon the money invested over the unexpired term of the lease.[64] The courts have upheld valuations based upon the testimony of qualified persons familiar with the particular properties or the area where the property is located.[65]

LIFE INSURANCE.

The value of life insurance policies at the date of liquidation is the interpolated terminal reserve value of the policy adjusted by the last premium paid.[66] For practical purposes, the value to be used at liquidation is the cash surrender value. This value should be acquired from the insurance company in writing.

ACCOUNTS AND NOTES RECEIVABLE.

In general, the value depends chiefly upon the following three factors or any combination of them: (a) economic conditions; (b) age of the accounts and notes receivable; and (c) expert testimony.[67] Accounts and notes receivable received in liquidation have been valued at various percentages of face value. In one decision, the Court valued the notes receivable at 50% and the accounts receivable at 65% of face value.[68] Based upon expert testimony, the Court set the value of the accounts receivable at 45% of the face value[69] and in another case at 72%.[70] Accrued interest must be considered when valuing notes receivable distributed in liquidation.[71]

INVENTORY.

The question of the value of the inventory at the date of liquidation of a corporation is generally based upon the books of account and economic conditions existing at that date. The relative time of purchase of the articles in the inventory as compared to the date of liquidation (age of the items in the inventory) and the current market price must be considered in the valuation with adjustments for older purchases, seasonal items, discontinued models, unsaleable articles, odd lots, broken or incomplete articles. In certain fields, current demand as determined by fashion trends should be considered.[72]

SECURITIES.

The fair market value of property is generally a question of fact which should be established by competent evidence. In determining the fair market value of stock or other securities of a small or closely owned corporation, the fair market value of the assets and the liabilities of the corporation must be taken into account as of the date of liquidation. Where securities are traded in on the public exchanges or on the over-the-counter exchanges, the actual sales on or near the basic date of liquidation afford evidence of the fair market value. In general, the fair market price or value is not determined by a forced sales price or by an estimate of what the block of securities would bring if placed on the market, but rather the unit price established by all of the facts and the elements of value (as discussed more fully below).[73]

Actual sales executed on the basic date (date of receipt by the stockholder of the securities owned by the liquidating corporation) are generally considered the best evidence as to the fair market value. Thus, if the securities are listed on one of the stock exchanges, the selling price on the contract date is used as the measure of the fair market value.[74] The price paid for full shares more properly reflects the true fair market value than the price paid for fractional shares.[75] Actual sales prices were held acceptable as a measure of fair market value instead of the determination of the Internal Revenue Service based upon the books and other facts.[76]

Representative sales at or close to the date of liquidation are considered better evidence than the value determined on the book value of the net assets.[77] However, sales under the following circumstances and conditions do not always prove the fair market value solely on the basis of the market price: (a) sales in small lots;[78] (b) sales of stock restricted by trust or other agreements;[79] (c) resale restricted for a definite period of years;[80] (d) sales restricted to certain specified buyers;[81] (e) sales restricted to a certain specified price;[82] and (f) sales encumbered by an option.[83]

The fair market value of restricted shares is determined on the basis of the price for unrestricted shares and other financial data.[84] Where a large block of stock is to be valued, the "blockage rule" has usually been accepted as a basis for holding that the stock exchange quotation is not conclusive as to the value of the stock. This rule is based upon the theory that if a relatively large block of stock is suddenly thrown upon the market within a short period of time, the quoted price is not a proper value for a unit share.[85]

Where there are bid-and-ask quotations, the value may be determined by taking the average between the two prices although the mean price is not in itself conclusive.[86] Bid-and-ask prices standing alone are of no value as evidence.[87] The value, based upon the bid-and-ask price may be adjusted by expert opinion.[88]

Closely held stock, despite the fact that none of it may be sold in the open market, has a market value.[89] Valuation of closely held stock is based upon the following factors: nature of the business, history since inception, economic outlook generally and in specific industry, book value, financial condition, earning capacity, dividend paying capacity, goodwill and other intangible value, sales of stock, size of block to be valued, market value of other corporations in same or similar line of business whose stocks are actively traded. While goodwill is based primarily on earning power, the Internal Revenue Service also considers prestige, renown of the business, ownership of a brand or trade name and the record of operations over a prolonged period of time. The rate of earning power cannot be standardized but depends upon the industry, the particular company and current economic conditions. The averaging of several factors such as book value, capitalized earnings and capitalized dividends is not acceptable.[90]

Where stock is subject to an option price, that price is usually acceptable to the Internal Revenue Service and the courts.[91]

Based upon the principles in Revenue Ruling 59-60, above, the book values of the assets have been used in determining the value for liquidation purposes.[92] In the absence of other evidence to the contrary, the book value and the earning power have been upheld as the basis of fair market value.[93] The fair market value in such cases does not mean the replacement cost of the assets[94] nor the depreciated cost of the assets.[95]

The Internal Revenue Service in capitalizing the earnings to compute value has used the formula in ARM 34.[96] The method of computation was described as follows: "The net annual earnings of the company for the years (at least 5 years), inclusive, were taken and a net average was computed therefrom as being the average earnings of the company for the years in question.*** The average thus computed for the years in question is $232,850.30. Taking the figure of $1,650,465.60 as the value of the tangible assets, the Department computed 8% upon this sum as the amount of the average earnings attributable to the tangible assets. This gives the figure of $132,037.25, which, subtracted from the average annual earnings of $232,850.30, leaves the sum of $100,813.05 as the amount of average earnings attributable to intangibles. The last mentioned sum was then capitalized at 15%, which gives the sum of $672,087.00, which the Department took as its appraised figure of the value of the intangible assets and which added to the amount of the physical or tangible assets gave a total sum of $2,322,552.60 as being the total value of the company's property and business upon which to base the value of its capital stock****."

MORTGAGES.

The fair market value of mortgages depends largely upon economic conditions. When business conditions are generally good, the collection ratio is normal whereas in times of speculative activity, the collection may be somewhat doubtful. In such cases, discounts vary from 40-50%. [97] Extended terms adversely affect the value of notes and mortgages.[98] Extended prepayment provisions will adversely affect the value.[99] However, evidence that the obligations will be paid warrants a valuation of face value.[100]

CONTRACTS.

The fair market value is usually determined upon expert testimony.[101] Such factors as limited duration of contract[102] and partial completion of contract[103] must be considered in determining the fair market value.

CITATIONS

[1] Metropolitan Street Railway Co. v Walsh, 197 Mo. 392, 94 S.W. 860; Grace N. Williams Est. v Comm., 256 F 2d 217, aff. Memo TC 1956–239.

[2] Chicago Railway Equipment Co. v Blair, 20 F 2d 10, rev. 4 BTA 452; Doric Apartment Co. v Comm , 94 F 2d 895, aff. 32 BTA 1189.

[3] Kernachan v U.S., 63 Ct. Cl. 592; George L. Castner Co., Inc., 30 TC 1061.

[4] Anita M. Baldwin, 10 BTA 1198.

[5] Tracy v Comm., 53 F 2d 575.

[6] P.C. Tomson & Co., Inc. v Comm., 82 F 2d 398.

[7] Louis F. Timmerman, 42 BTA 188.

[8] Berg v U.S., 167 F. Supp. 756.

[9] J.H. Dean, Memo TC 1948.

[10] Rose L. Simmons, Memo TC 1950.

[11] Kinsman Transit Co., 1 BTA 552.

[12] Art Metal Construction Co., 4 BTA 493.

[13] Wilson E. Schmick, 3 BTA 1141; Wessel, et al. v U.S., 48 F 2d 137.

[14] Heller Bros. Co., et al., 9 BTA 1328.

[15] J.A. Bentley, et al., 5 BTA 314.

[16] Heiner v Crosby, 24 F 2d 191; Edward W. Payne, 12 BTA 781.

[17] Sec. 331 (a); Sec. 337, IRC 1954.

[18] Jesse D. Otley, Memo TC 1954.

[19] SR 2099, CB June 1925, pg. 92.

[20] Estate of Ben R. Henderson, et al., Memo TC 1952.

[21] Ruth M. Cullen, 14 TC 368; Floyd W. Eates et al., Memo TC 1947, aff. 168 F 2d 68.

[22] The Danco Co., 14 TC 276; Vita-Food Corp. v Comm., 238 F 2d 359, rev. Memo, TC 1954.

[23] Mossman, Yarnelle & Co., 9 BTA 45.

[24] Boggs & Buhl, Inc. v Comm., 34 F 2d 859, rev. 11 BTA 612.

[25] J.A. Bradley, 4 BTA 1179; W.H. Batcheller, 19 BTA 1050.

[26] H.H. Blumental, 21 BTA 901.

[27] Pruett v U.S., DC, Texas 1952; Esther Firestone, 2 BTA 309.

[28] ARM 34, CB June 1920, pg. 31.

[29] Plaut v Smith, 82 F. Supp. 42, aff. Plaut v Munford, Adm. (Smith), 188 F 2d 543.

[30] ARR 2954, CB Dec. 1923, pg. 202.

[31] International Consolidated Chemical Co., 2 BTA 407.

[32]The White & Welles Co. v Comm., 50 F 2d 120, rev. 19 BTA 416.

[33]SR 5545, CB Dec. 1925, pg. 242; Plaut v Smith, 82 F. Supp. 42, aff. Plaut v. Munford, Adm. (Smith), 188 F 2d 543; Est. of A. Bluestein, 15 TC 770.

[34]John Q. Skunk, et al., 10 TC 293.

[35]W.M. Ritter Lumber Co., 30 BTA 231.

[36]Corning Glass Works, 9 BTA 771.

[37]George J. Staab, et al., 20 TC 834.

[38]General Outdoor Adv. Co., Inc., 137 Ct. Cl. 607, 149 F. Supp. 163.

[39]National Pneumatic Co., 5 BTA 637.

[40]Central City Chemical Co., 3 BTA 1306.

[41]Westclox Co. v U.S., 68 Ct. Cl. 758, 37 F 2d 191.

[42]R. Hoe & Co., Inc., 7 BTA 1277.

[43]Hershey Mfg. Co. v Comm., 43 F 2d 298, aff. 14 BTA 867.

[44]Leggett & Platt Spring Bed Mfg. Co., 8 BTA 61; The Owens Bottle Co., 8 BTA 1197; see also Deck Clamp Tank Co., 10 BTA 191.

[45]Hyatt Roller Bearing Co. v U.S., 70 Ct. Cl. 443, 43 F 2d 1008.

[46]Kraft Foods Co., 21 TC 513.

[47]St. Louis Screw Co., 2 BTA 649; S. Marsh Young, 2 BTA 457.

[48]Tyler and Hippach, Inc. v Comm., 6 BTA 636; Appeal of Keller Mechanical Engineering Corp., 6 BTA 990; Simmons Co. v Comm., 33 F 2d 75.

[49]Gamon Meter Co., 1 BTA 1124.

[50]Owens Bottle Co., 8 BTA 1197; J.M. & M.S. Browning, 6 BTA 914; Est. of Sam Marsack, TC Memo 1960–75, aff. 288 F 2d 533.

[51]TBR 57, CB 1919, pg. 40; Halbert K. Hitchcock, 4 BTA 273.

[52]Walls v Comm., 60 F 2d 347, aff. 21 BTA 1417.

[53]Esther Firestone, 2 BTA 309; Amos L. Beaty & Co., Inc., 14 TC 52.

[54]General Outdoor Advertising Co., Inc., v U.S., 137 Ct. Cl. 607, 149 F. Supp. 163.

[55]William A. Daly, 1 BTA 933; Tabor Mfg. Co. v Comm., 34 F 2d 140, rev. 10 BTA 1197.

[56]ARR 747, CB June 1922, pg. 353.

[57]Mim. 3209, CB Dec. 1924, pg. 339.

[58]Georgia Railway Co. v Comm., 262 U.S. 625.

[59]James Couzens, 11 BTA 1040.

[60]Reg. 1.167 (a)–5; Nat. Pub. Co., Memo TC 1965–271.

[61]2554–58 Creston Corp., 40 TC 932.

[62]Pittsburgh & West Virginia Ry. Co., 30 BTA 843; 32 BTA 66; W.B. Mayes, Jr., 21 TC 286.

[63]Northern Hotel Co., 3 BTA 1099.

[64]Kaufman-Strauss Co., 2 BTA 718.

[65]August Belmont Hotel Co., 18 BTA 643.

[66]Rev. Rul. 59–195, IRB 1959–23; See either Form 938 (used for gift tax purposes) or Form 712 (used for estate tax purposes) Valuation of Life Insurance.

[67]Calvin Crouse, 11 BTA 1327; Richard Powers, 14 BTA 701.

[68]Kib H. Warren, 7 BTA 293.

[69]S.L. Becker, BTA 65.

[70]J.L. Harris, et al., 14 BTA 1259.

[71]Howard Cook, 5 TC 908.

[72]Kib H. Warren, 7 BTA 293; Albert E. Davison, Ex., 11 BTA 493; Sec. 312 (b) (1) (2) (A), IRC 1954; Sec. 471, IRC 1954; Reg. Sec. 1.471–2; 1.471–3; 1.471–4.

[73]Sec. 1053, IRC 1954; Reg. Sec. 1.1053–1.

[74]ARR 4837, CB June 1924, pg. 39; First National Bank of Birmingham, Trustee, 29 BTA 352.

[75]Charles F. Ayer, 7 BTA 324.

[76]Amos L. Beaty & Co., Inc., 14 TC 52.

[77]ARR 2771, CB Dec. 1923, pg. 18; Supplee-Biddle Hardware Co., Memo TC 1943, aff. 144 F 2d 711.

[78]Walter V. Duffy, 287 Fed. 41; Est. of Paul M. Vanderhoeck, et al., 4 TC 125.

[79]Helvering v Tex-Penn Oil Co., 300 U.S. 481; Heiner v Crosby, Heiner v Anderton, 24 F 2d 191, aff. 12 F 2d 604.

[80]IT 2308, CB Dec. 1926, pg. 114; Junior Amusement Co., Memo TC 1956.

[81]Helen S. Delone, 6 TC 1188; Harold Kuchman, et al., 19 TC 154.

[82]Phil Kalech, 23 TC 672.

[83]Society Brand Clothes, Inc., 18 TC 304.

[84]Durant Insulated Pipe Co., Memo TC 1946.

[85]Safe Deposit & Trust Co. of Baltimore, Ex. (Walters), 35 BTA 259, aff. 95 F 2d 806; F.J. Sensenbrenner, Memo BTA 1935; Dean Babbitt, et al., 23 TC 850.

[86]Ralph A. Applegate, Ex. (Holmes), 10 BTA 705; Robert E. Dowling, 8 BTA 676; William C. Sampson, 1 BTA 73.

[87]Wiget v Becker, 84 F 2d 706.

[88]Great Northern Railway Co., 8 BTA 225.

[89]George M. Wright, et al., 9 BTA 541, aff. 50 F 2d 727; Crowell v Comm., 62 F 2d 51, aff. 21 BTA 849.

[90]Rev. Rul. 59–60 CB 1959–1, pg. 237, Superseding Rev. Rul. 54–77, CB 54–77, CB 1954–1, pg. 187. The cited ruling deals with estate and gift tax valuation of closely held stock but its principles are equally applicable to valuation in connection with corporate liquidations.

[91]Kathleen I. Gibbs, et al., TC Memo 1959–58.

[92]Maco Stewart, Exec., 32 BTA 442; Est. of W.R. Bassick, et al., Memo TC 1944.

[93]Roger W. Pope, Memo TC 1956; Benjamin E. May, et al., 35 BTA 84.

[94]R.H. Soaper & James E. Rankin, Sr., 3 BTA 701.

[95]Est. of John J. Hessian, Memo TC 1944; Seymour Mfg. Co., 19 BTA 1280.

[96]ARM 34, CB June 1920, pg. 31; ARR 252, CB Dec. 1920, pg. 46; Boyd v Heiner, DC, Pa. 1924.

[97]Calvin Crouse, 11 BTA 1327; Richard Powers, 14 BTA 701.

[98]John Q. Skunk, et al., 10 TC 293, aff. 173 F 2d 747.

[99]Michelin Corp. v McMahon, 137 F. Supp. 798.

[100]Whitlow, et al., Adm. v Comm., 82 F 2d 569, aff. Memo BTA 1934.

[101]Murray Thompson, et al., 21 TC 448, aff. 222 F 2d 893.

[102]George M. Newcomb, 23 TC 954; Maurice A. Mittleman, 7 TC 1162.

[103]Ida Ambrose, et al., Memo TC 1956.

THREE

Recapture of Depreciation
Personal Property Section 1245

INTRODUCTION.

Prior to the Revenue Acts of 1962 and 1964, if a taxpayer sold or exchanged a depreciable asset the recognized gain was, in most instances, capital gain under Section 1231.[1]

Example 1: Taxpayer acquired by purchase a depreciable asset in January 1966 at a cost of $20,000. If the taxpayer estimated a ten year life for the asset and adopted the straight line method of depreciation, each taxable year, the taxpayer would deduct depreciation of $2,000 (ignoring, for example purposes only, salvage value and the 20% additional first year depreciation). If the asset were sold in December 1970 for $16,000, the recognized capital gain would be $6,000, computed as follows:

Selling Price		$16,000
Cost	$20,000	
Depreciation (5 years at $2,000)	10,000	
Adjusted Basis		10,000
Recognized Capital Gain (Long-term)		$ 6,000

If, in Example 1, the taxpayer had elected the 20% additional first year depreciation[2] and an accelerated depreciation method,[3] i.e., double declining balance, the adjusted basis at the date of the sale would have been lower with a resultant higher recognized capital gain. The establishment of a shorter life at the time of acquisition would also have the effect of increasing the recognized capital gain at the time of the sale.

THEORY OF RECAPTURE.

The effect of the 20% first year depreciation allowance, the accelerated depreciation rates and the shorter life elected by the taxpayer was to convert ordinary income by way of an ordinary depreciation deduction into capital gain at the time of disposition by sale or exchange. The adoption of the recapture provisions applicable to personal property[4] limits the amount of capital gain by providing that the total recognized gain to the extent of the depreciation allowed or allowable after December 31, 1961 shall be taxed as ordinary gain and the balance, if any, as Section 1231 gain (capital gain).

It should be noted that the method of recapture as it applies to personal property is different from that of real property (see Chapter 4).

HOW RECAPTURE OPERATES.

The recapture provisions of the Code as they apply to personal property are illustrated in the following basic example.

Example 2: Corporation purchased machinery on January 2, 1960 for $50,000. Depreciation was computed on the basis of a 10 year life under the straight line method (ignore possible salvage value). Corporation did not elect the 20% additional first year's depreciation. On December 30, 1964 the corporation sold the machinery for $45,000.

Cost of Machinery 1/2/60		$50,000
Depreciation to 12/31/61 (2 yrs. at $5,000) . .		10,000
Adjusted Basis at 12/31/61		$40,000
Depreciation—1/1/62 to 12/30/64 (date of sale)		15,000
Adjusted Basis—Date of Sale		$25,000
Selling Price		45,000
Actual Gain on Sale		$20,000
Adjusted Basis 12/30/64	$25,000	
Plus: Depreciation Allowed or Allowable since 12/31/61	15,000	
Recomputed Basis	$40,000	
Selling Price	$45,000	
Recomputed Basis or Selling Price, whichever is lower	$40,000	
Adjusted Basis 12/30/64	25,000	

Ordinary Gain	15,000
Section 1231 Gain (Capital Gain)	$ 5,000

Example 3: If the selling price in Example 2 was $35,000, the entire recognized gain would be ordinary gain.

Actual Gain on Sale		$10,000
Recomputed Basis or Selling Price, whichever is lower	$35,000	
Adjusted Basis 12/30/63	25,000	
Ordinary Gain		10,000
Section 1231 Gain (Capital Gain)		$ 0

Example 4: Corporation purchased machinery for $50,000 on January 2, 1962. Depreciation was computed on the basis of a 10 year life under the straight line method (ignore possible salvage value). Corporation did not elect the 20% additional first year's depreciation. On December 30, 1964 the corporation sold the machinery for $55,000.

Cost 1/2/62		$50,000
Depreciation to 12/30/64 (date of sale)		15,000
Adjusted Basis 12/30/64		$35,000
Selling Price		55,000
Actual Gain		$20,000
Adjusted Basis 12/30/64	$35,000	
Plus: Depreciation Allowed or Allowable since 12/31/61	15,000	
Recomputed Basis	$50,000	
Selling Price	$55,000	
Recomputed Basis or Selling Price, whichever is lower	$50,000	
Adjusted Basis 12/30/64	35,000	
Ordinary Gain		15,000
Section 1231 Gain (Capital Gain)		$ 5,000

Example 5: If in Example 4, the selling price was $45,000, the entire gain of $10,000 would be ordinary gain.

DEPRECIATION AND AMORTIZATION.

The recapture provisions apply to (a) depreciation allowed or allowable under the provisions of Section 167, IRC 1954 and (b) amortization under the provisions of

Section 168, IRC 1954. Depreciation subject to recapture includes the amount deducted under the provisions of Section 179–the 20% additional first year allowance.

Where the amount of depreciation allowed for any tax year was less than the amount allowable, the amount to be added back in computing the recomputed basis is the amount allowed.[5] In other words, the amount to be used is the amount which was actually deducted each year since December 31, 1961.

EFFECTIVE DATES.

The recapture provisions apply to "Section 1245 property" which is disposed of during a taxable year beginning after December 31, 1962[6] at a gain. The section does not apply to losses. Thus, the first year to which the rules apply would be the calendar year 1963 and to fiscal years beginning in 1963 and ending in 1964 and thereafter. The provisions also apply to a short year beginning after December 31, 1962.

While the date of disposition of the Section 1245 property is on or after January 1, 1963, the recaptured depreciation is the amount of depreciation allowed or allowable for tax years or periods after December 31, 1961[7] as illustrated in the examples above.

With respect to elevators and escalators, the effective date is June 30, 1963.

DISPOSITION.

For the purpose of corporate liquidations, the definition of the term "dispositions" is vital. Under the Code,[8] the definition includes not only a sale or an exchange in the narrow sense but also involuntary conversions, corporate liquidations, partnership distributions, exchanges of like kind and many other transactions.[9]

Specifically, in respect to corporate liquidations, Section 1245 supersedes the provisions of Section 336 which provide that no gain or loss shall be recognized to a corporation on the distribution of its property in partial or complete liquidation. As explained in later chapters, a corporation will be taxed on the ordinary gain as computed under the recapture provisions, upon the distributions in liquidation under Section 331 (the general method of liquidation, both complete and partial), under Section 333 (the calendar month liquidation), under Section 337 (the 12-month liquidation) and under Section 332 (parent-subsidiary liquidation) unless the parent carries over the subsidiary's basis under Section 334 (b) (2).[10]

GENERAL RULE–ORDINARY INCOME.

A separate rule or basis is used in the computation of the ordinary income attributable to the recapture of depreciation depending upon whether the transaction is a sale, an exchange, an involuntary conversion, a corporate distribution in complete or partial liquidation or other distribution.[11]

In computing the ordinary gain, the excess of the lower of either (a) or (b) over the adjusted basis equals the ordinary gain; the balance, if any, is Section 1231 (Capital Gain)–

   (a) Recomputed Basis, or

(b) (1) in case of a sale, exchange or involuntary conversion–the amount realized

(2) in case of any other disposition, i.e., corporate liquidation–the fair market value of the property.

The application of the recapture provisions as they apply to each method of liquidation is illustrated in the succeeding chapters.

"SECTION 1245 PROPERTY."

Section 1245 property includes any property (other than livestock) which is or has been property subject to the allowance for depreciation and which is either (a) personal property (tangible and intangible); (b) other tangible property (but excluding a building or its structural components) which is used as an integral part of manufacturing, production, or extraction or of furnishing transportation, communications, electrical energy, gas, water or sewage disposal services, or constitute research or storage facilities used in connection with any of the previous listed activities; or (c) an elevator or an escalator.[12]

The most common example of Section 1245 property is machinery and equipment, which includes production machinery, printing presses, transportation and office equipment, refrigerators, counters, testing equipment, display racks and shelves, and neon and other signs and similar assets used in trade or business. Patents and copyrights are common examples of intangible personal property. Many forms of property are classified as fixtures by local law and, therefore, constitute real property under local law. However, for purposes of Section 1245, many of such assets are subject to recapture since they are classified as personal property for this purpose, i.e., gasoline pumps, lifts, vending machines and individual air conditioning and heating units.

Real property consisting of a building and its component parts is not subject to Section 1245 but it is subject to Section 1250 as discussed in Chapter 4. For the purposes of Section 1245, central air conditioning and heating systems, including ducts, wires and pipes, paved parking areas, wharves and docks, and bridges and fences are classified as real property. However, if the air conditioning and humidification equipment is used solely for the purpose of manufacturing or storage of the products manufactured, it is Section 1245 property.

SALVAGE VALUE.

Salvage value is required to be estimated under Section 167 under certain methods of depreciation. Where a depreciable asset with an estimated life of three years or more was acquired after the enactment of the Revenue Act of 1962, the salvage value may be disregarded up to 10% of the cost.[13]

Example 6: Asset cost $10,000. Salvage value $1,500. Basis for depreciation $8,500. Under the amendment by the Revenue Act of 1962, the basis may be increased to $9,500.

DEPRECIATION—YEAR OF SALE.

Prior to the enactment of Section 1245 which provides for a recapture of depreciation as described above, the Commissioner of Internal Revenue issued a Revenue Ruling[14] concerning the deductibility of depreciation in the year of sale of depreciable personal assets. Under the ruling, the depreciation deduction of a depreciable personal property asset used in trade or business or in the production of income is limited to the amount (if any) by which the adjusted basis at the beginning of the tax year in which the asset is sold or otherwise disposed of, exceeds the amount realized from the sale or exchange of the asset. The adjustment is based upon the theory that the salvage value of an asset is the selling price or value received in exchange. In other words, the taxpayer either did not estimate a salvage value at the time of acquisition or underestimated the salvage value. Thus, under the ruling no depreciation is allowed as a deduction in the year of the sale.[15]

However, as a result of a Supreme Court decision, the effect of the ruling has been all but eliminated.[16] The Court upheld the deduction for depreciation in the year of sale even though the sale price exceeds the adjusted basis at the beginning of the year.[17]

The Supreme Court, however, pointed out that its decision was based upon the fact that the original estimate of the salvage value by the taxpayer was reasonable and had been proven accurate. If the taxpayer's original estimate of the salvage value is challenged by the Commissioner, it must be proven.[18]

Following the above Court decisions, the Commissioner ruled that the allowable depreciation deduction for any open year, including the year of sale or other disposition, may be adjusted if in light of all relevant facts which are known or are fairly ascertainable as of the end of the tax year or the date of sale or other disposition it appears that the estimate of the useful life or the salvage value on the basis of the depreciation claimed is unreasonable.[19]

CITATIONS

[1]Sec. 1222, IRC 1954; Sec. 1231, IRC 1954.

[2]Sec. 179, IRC 1954.

[3]Sec. 167 (b), IRC 1954.

[4]Sec. 1245, IRC 1954.

[5]Sec. 1245 (a) (2), IRC 1954.

[6]Sec. 1245 (a) (1), IRC 1954.

[7]Sec. 1245 (a) (2), IRC 1954.

[8]Sec. 1245 (a) (b) (i) (ii), IRC 1954.

[9]Sec. 1245 (b) (1)–(6), IRC 1954.

[10]See Chapter 13.

[11]Sec. 1245 (a) (1), IRC 1954.

[12]Sec. 1245 (a) (3) (c), IRC 1954.

[13]Sec. 167 (f), IRC 1954.

[14]Rev. Rul. 62–92, CB 1962–1, pg. 29.

[15]Cohn v U.S., 259 F 2d 371.

[16]Fribough Navigation Co. Inc. v Comm., 383 U.S. 272 (1966), rev. 335 F 2d 15.

[17]The Motorlease Corp. v U.S., 383 U.S. 573.

[18]Durfee's, Inc., Memo TC 1966–111.

[19]Rev. Rul. 67–272, CB 1967–2, pg. 99.

FOUR

Recapture of Depreciation
Real Property Section 1250

INTRODUCTION.

The recapture provisions as regards personal property apply to the total amount of depreciation allowed or allowable after a definite date regardless of which method of depreciation has been elected, i.e., straight line or one of the accelerated methods. Furthermore, there is no time limit at which time the recapture provisions do not apply. These are the two principal distinctions between the recapture provisions applicable to personal property as against real property and leaseholds.[1]

Briefly, the recapture of depreciation allowed or allowable with respect to real property and leaseholds does not apply where the property was held more than ten years and, in general, only to the excess depreciation claimed under an accelerated method over the amount allowed or allowable under the straight line depreciation method. Thus, if the corporation elected the straight line method, the recapture provisions do not apply (except for the first year as explained below).[2]

EFFECTIVE DATES.

The original recapture provisions as applicable to real property and leaseholds apply to all dispositions after December 31, 1963. The amount of the recapture depends upon the depreciation allowed or allowable since December 31, 1963 under the rules described below.[3]

However, for tax years ending after July 24, 1969 and a sale or a disposition occurring after December 31, 1969, the Tax Reform Act of 1969 amended the original provisions by eliminating the applicable percentages as illustrated below.[4] Where property was acquired prior to 1963 and sold or otherwise disposed of after December 31, 1969, both the original and the amended provisions of the Internal Revenue Code are applicable for the respective periods.

FORMULA FOR COMPUTING GAIN.

The amount of the ordinary gain is based upon the following formula:[5]

The Lower of—
(a) Additional Depreciation

or

(b) Recognized Gain on Disposition × Applicable Percentage

Briefly, "additional depreciation" is the excess of the depreciation claimed over the amount as determined under the straight line method for computing depreciation. The section does not apply to a loss on a sale or other disposition.

Example 1: Taxpayer sold depreciable real property at a recognized gain of $50,000. The "additional depreciation" as later defined amounted to $30,000 and the "applicable percentage" was 40%. The ordinary gain reportable on the sale is $12,000; gain subject to Section 1231 is $38,000.

"ADDITIONAL DEPRECIATION."

Additional depreciation means in respect to real property and leaseholds the depreciation claimed by the taxpayer over the amount which would have been allowed under the straight line method times the applicable percentages.

"APPLICABLE PERCENTAGES."

The applicable percentages are based upon the date of acquisition of the real property and the date of sale or other disposition. The applicable percentages, therefore, may be based upon (a) the original provisions which were in effect from 1964 to 1969, inclusive; (b) the amended provisions under the Tax Reform Act of 1969 which eliminated the percentages; or (c) a combination of both (a) and (b) if the acquisition occurred before 1969 and the sale or other disposition occurred after 1969.[6]

ORIGINAL RULES OF RECAPTURE.

The original recapture rules may be summarized under four headings:

(a) If the real property or the leasehold is sold within 12 months after acquisition, the recapture is the total depreciation claimed after December 31, 1963 regardless of what depreciation method was used—straight line, declining balance methods, sum of the years-digits or other methods elected. It should be noted that the first 12 month method is different from that applicable to periods in excess of 12 months (see [b] and [c] below).

Example 2: Taxpayer purchased real property—land $10,000; building $50,000—on October 1, 1963. Depreciation rate 3%—straight line method elected (fiscal year ending 9/30/—). The property was sold on June 1, 1964 for $70,000 (land $15,000; building $55,000).

Annual Depreciation ($50,000 × 3%)		$ 1,500.00
Monthly Depreciation ($1,500 ÷ 12)		$ 125.00
Depreciation 10/1/63 to 12/31/63 .	$375.00	
Depreciation 1/1/64 to 6/30/64 . .	750.00	$ 1,125.00
Selling Price of Building		$55,000.00
Building Cost	$50,000.00	
Less: Depreciation	1,125.00	
Adjusted Basis		$48,875.00
Actual Gain		$ 6,125.00
Depreciation since 1/1/64—		
Ordinary gain		750.00
Capital Gain under Section 1231 . .		$ 5,375.00
Land—Selling Price		$15,000.00
Basis—Land		10,000.00
Capital Gain under Section 1231 . .		$ 5,000.00

(b) If the real property or the leasehold is sold between 13 months and 20 months, the recapture is 100% of the excess depreciation claimed by the taxpayer over the straight line depreciation.

Example 3: Taxpayer purchased real property—land $10,000.00; building $50,000.00—on October 1, 1963. Depreciation rate 3%—double declining balance method elected (fiscal year ending 9/30/—). The property was sold on March 31, 1965 for $70,000 (land $15,000.00; building $55,000.00).

Cost—Building	$50,000.00
Depreciation 10/1/63—9/30/64 (2 × 3% × $50,000).	3,000.00
Adjusted Basis—9/30/64	$47,000.00
Depreciation 10/1/64—3/31/65 (2 × 3% × $47,000 × ½)	1,410.00
Adjusted Basis—Date of Sale	$45,590.00
Selling Price—Building	55,000.00
Actual Gain	$ 9,410.00
Monthly Depreciation claimed since	

12/31/63

$250 × 9 mos (1/1/64–9/30/64) . .	$2,250.00
$235 × 6 mos (10/1/64–3/31/65) .	1,410.00
	$3,660.00

Depreciation on straight line $125 × 15 mos (3% per year × $50,000)	1,875.00
Excess Depreciation claimed over straight line method	$1,785.00

100% of Excess = Ordinary Gain . . .	$ 1,785.00
Capital Gain under Section 1231	$ 7,625.00
Sale of Land	$15,000.00
Basis of Land	10,000.00
Capital Gain under Section 1231	$ 5,000.00

(c) If the real property or the leasehold is sold between 21 months and 120 months after acquisition of the real property or the leasehold, the applicable percentage is reduced one per cent a month.

Example 4: Taxpayer purchased real property for $250,000.00–land $50,000.00; building $200,000.00 on January 1, 1963. Estimated life 40 years. Double declining balance method elected. On December 31, 1967, the property was sold. Recognized gain on land $20,000.00; on building $30,000.00 Calendar year basis.

Year	D/D/B	S/L
1963	$10,000.00	$ 5,000.00
1964	$ 9,500.00	$ 5,000.00
1965	9,025.00	5,000.00
1966	8,573.75	5,000.00
1967	8,145.06	5,000.00
	$35,243.81	$20,000.00

Additional Depreciation	$15,243.81	
Recognized Gain		$30,000.00
Ordinary Income (Lower × Applicable Percentage $15,243.81 × 60%)* . .		9,146.29
Gain Subject to Section 1231		$20,853.71
Gain on Land subject to Section 1231		$20,000.00

* 100% less 1% per month for the 40 months held in excess of the first 20 months.

(d) If the real property or the leasehold is sold more than 120 months after acquisition, there is no recapture, since the applicable percentage has been reduced to zero.

AMENDED RULES OF RECAPTURE.

The Tax Reform Act of 1969 eliminated the percentages shown in the original rules of recapture illustrated above, effective for depreciation attributable to periods after December 31, 1969. As already indicated, if the property was acquired before January 1, 1970 and sold or disposed of after December 31, 1969, the taxpayer will be required to use both the old percentage provisions for the period prior to January 1, 1970 and the new method for the periods after December 31, 1969.

Note: In computing the "applicable percentage" in accordance with the original provisions of recapture, the applicable percentage is based on the total period during which the real property was held before and after 1970. See Example 5–48%.

Example 5: The taxpayer acquired a building at a cost of $100,000 on January 2, 1967. Estimated life 40 years (disregard salvage value). The taxpayer elected the double declining balance method (5%). On December 31, 1972, the property was sold for $120,000. The ordinary gain from recapture was $7,974.31 and the Section 1231 gain was $38,516.50, computed as follows:

YEAR	D/D/B	S/L
1967	$ 5,000.00	$2,500.00
1968	4,750.00	2,500.00
1969	4,512.50	2,500.00
Total	$14,262.50	$7,500.00
Deduct S/L	7,500.00	
Excess	$ 6,762.50	
Applicable % (48%)	3,246.00	
Recaptured Depreciation (A)	$ 3,246.00	
1970	$ 4,286.88	$2,500.00
1971	4,072.53	2,500.00
1972	3,868.90	2,500.00
Total	$12,228.31	$7,500.00
Deduct S/L	7,500.00	
Excess	$ 4,728.31	
Recaptured Depreciation 100% (B)	$ 4,728.31	
Total Recaptured Depreciation (A) & (B)	$ 7,974.31	
Cost (1/2/67)		$100,000.00

Depreciation allowable	26,490.81
Adjusted Basis (12/31/72)	$ 73,509.19
Selling Price	$120,000.00
Total Recognized Gain	$ 46,490.81
Recaptured Depreciation (ordinary income)	7,974.31
Gain subject to Section 1231 (capital gain)	$ 38,516.50

DEPRECIATION—LEASEHOLD.

Under the general rule, depreciation of leaseholds is based upon the lease period including all renewal periods.[7] Renewal period is defined as any period for which the lease can be renewed, extended, or continued pursuant to an option exercisable by the lessee. However, under the exception to the general rule, the inclusion period may not be extended by more than two-thirds of the period on the basis of which the depreciation adjustments were allowed.[8]

Example 6: Original lease period was 10 years with a renewal period of an additional 9 years. The maximum period to take into account for purposes of depreciation subject to recapture is 16 2/3 years (initial period 10 years plus 2/3 of original period—6 2/3 years).

Example 7: Assume the same facts as in Example 6 except that the useful (depreciable) life of the depreciable asset was 15 years. The depreciable life to be taken into account is 15 years.

"SECTION 1250 PROPERTY."

Section 1250 property includes all real property which is or has been subject to the allowance for depreciation under Section 167, the section which covers depreciation generally. It includes all property except property included under the definition in Section 1245.[9]

Section 1250 property includes three types of depreciable real property:[10] (1) intangible real property, i.e., leaseholds; (2) a building or its structural components; and (3) all other tangible real property except fixtures as described in Section 1245 (see Chapter 3).

Section 1250 property may lose its character and become Section 1245 property. Thus, if property described in (3) above is held for three years and, thereafter, is converted as an integral part of the manufacturing process, the property becomes Section 1245 property. However, if property in the hands of the taxpayer is Section 1245 property, it can never become Section 1250 property in the hands of such taxpayer.

MAJOR IMPROVEMENTS.

Each major improvement must be considered as a separate element as a basis for recapture of the depreciation. The basic test of a major improvement is applied only if the sum of the improvements added to the asset account during the 36 month period ending on the last day of any taxable year exceeds the greatest of (1) 25% of the adjusted basis of the property; (2) 10% of the unadjusted basis of the property; or (3) $5,000.00[11]

However, there is an exception to the general rule. If the improvement in any tax year cost $2,000.00 or less, or not more than 10% of the unadjusted basis (cost), such improvements are to be disregarded.

The recapture percentage is applied separately to the Section 1250 property and the major improvements.

Example 8: Assume the actual gain is $10,000.00. Building was held for 60 months; improvement for 30 months. Additional depreciation, building, $7,000.00; improvement $1,000.00.

The percentage applicable to building is 60%; the improvement 90%. Since the gain is greater than the additional depreciation, the recapture is computed as follows:

$7,000.00 × 60% =	$4,200.00
1,000.00 × 90% =	900.00
Ordinary Income	$5,100.00
Gain subject to Section 1231	$4,900.00

CORPORATE LIQUIDATIONS AND DISTRIBUTIONS.

In the ordinary sale of depreciable real property the basic amount for computing the gain is the selling price. In the case of a corporate liquidation, distribution or redemption, the basis is the fair market value of the property.[12] The following chapters explain and illustrate the statute as it applies to each section.

DEPRECIATION—YEAR OF SALE.

As already explained in Chapter 3, the Supreme Court has decided on the issue of the depreciation deduction in the year of sale.[13] The decisions apply to both real property and personal property.[14] Thus, the recapture provisions will apply to liquidations as discussed in the subsequent chapters.

INSTALLMENT LIQUIDATIONS—RECAPTURE:

If the liquidation proceeds are payable in installments, the ordinary gain from recapture must first be reported until exhausted before any part of the Section 1231 gain is reported.[15]

CITATIONS

[1] Chapter 3.

[2] Sec. 1250, IRC 1954.

[3] Sec. 1250 (a) (2), IRC 1954.

[4] Sec. 1250 (a) (1), IRC 1954.

[5] Sec. 1250 (a) (1) (2), IRC 1954.

[6] Sec. 1250 (a) (1) (2), IRC 1954.

[7] Sec. 1250 (b) (2), IRC 1954.

[8] Committee Report–House General Explanation.

[9] Chapter 3.

[10] Committee Report–House General Explanation.

[11] Sec. 1250 (f), IRC 1954.

[12] Sec. 1250 (a) (1) (B) (i), IRC 1954.

[13] Fribough Navigation Co., Inc. v Comm., 383 U.S. 272 (1966), rev. 335 F 2d 15.

[14] Randolph D. Rouse, 39 TC 70, Acq.

[15] Reg. Sec. 1.1250–1 (c) (6).

FIVE

Recapture of
The Investment Credit

INTRODUCTION.

The 7% investment credit was introduced by the Revenue Act of 1962, repealed in 1969 and reinstated in 1971. Briefly, the investment credit is computed at the basic rate of 7 per cent of the qualified investment in new and used depreciable property (other than buildings). The credit so computed is subtracted from the tax liability. Under certain conditions, an unused investment credit may be carried back and/or forward.

For purposes of corporation liquidations, the provisions relating to the recapture of the investment credit claimed are important. Recapture of the investment applies to an early disposition of the qualified asset as later explained. Does the liquidation of a corporation constitute a disposition? If so, the liquidating corporation must repay the investment credit in whole or in part in the year of liquidation as an addition to the tax computed for that year.

The amount of the recapture must be computed based upon the provisions of the original Revenue Act of 1962 for tax years beginning in 1962 and ending at the temporary termination period from April 18, 1968 to tax years ending in 1971. The Revenue Act of 1971 reestablished the investment credit, applicable to assets acquired after August 15, 1971. Despite the termination of the investment credit, the recapture provisions were applicable to an early disposition during this period. Hence it is important to know the basic elements of the Code for each of the three periods.

QUALIFIED PROPERTY.

Eligible property, known as "Section 38 property," includes—

(1) depreciable, tangible personal property such as machinery, and equipment, automobiles, trucks and similar items; and

(2) other tangible property (excluding a building and its structural components) which is used in manufacturing, production, extraction or the furnishing of utility-like services, or constitutes a research or storage facility associated with manufacturing, production, extraction or utilities.[1]

Buildings and their structural components such as a central heating system, air conditioning, wiring and plumbing, are specifically excluded. Elevators and escalators qualify if constructed, reconstructed, or acquired after June 30, 1963.[2] Intangible property such as a patent, does not qualify. Livestock is also ineligible.

In order to qualify, the property described above must be subject to depreciation or amortization and must have a useful life of at least 3 years under the provisions of the Revenue Act of 1971 (4 years under the Revenue Act of 1962). If property is partly depreciable and partly nondepreciable, only the portion which is depreciable qualifies.

USEFUL-LIFE AND PERCENTAGE.

The basic credit is 7 per cent of the cost or the adjusted basis of the qualified asset.[3] However, the basic 7 per cent is reduced depending upon the useful life of the asset for depreciable purposes. Under the provisions of the Revenue Act of 1971, the class lives are—

(1) if the useful life is 3 or 4 years, multiply the cost or other basis by 33 1/3 per cent and resultant figure by 7 per cent;

(2) if the useful life is 5 or 6 years, multiply the cost or other basis by 66 2/3 per cent and the resultant figure by 7 per cent; and

(3) if the useful life is 7 or more years, multiply the cost or other basis by 100 per cent and the resultant figure by 7 per cent.[4]

Example: A corporation purchased for use in its business the following assets—

Eligible Asset	Useful Life	Cost or Other Basis
Machinery (1)	10	$20,000
Truck	3	9,000
Machinery (2)	6	12,000

The investment credit aggregates $2,170, computed as follows:

Eligible Asset	Cost	Applicable Percentage	Qualified Investment
Machinery (1)	$20,000	100%	$20,000
Truck	9,000	33 1/3%	3,000

Machinery (2)	12,000	66 2/3%	8,000
			$31,000
			.07
			$ 2,170

Under the Revenue Act of 1962, the class useful life for depreciation and credit purposes was as follows:

(1) if the useful life is 4 or 5 years, multiply the cost or other basis by 33 1/3 per cent and the resultant figure by 7 per cent.

(2) if the useful life is 6 or 7 years, multiply the cost or other basis by 66 2/3 per cent and the resultant figure by 7 per cent.

(3) if the useful life is 8 or more years, multiply the cost or other basis by 100 per cent and the resultant figure by 7 per cent.

LIMITATION ON CREDIT.

The investment credit in any tax year cannot exceed the computed tax liability. For taxable years ending after March 9, 1967, if the tax is more than $25,000, the maximum credit which is deductible is $25,000 plus 50 per cent of the tax liability over $25,000. For taxable years ending on or before March 9, 1967, the credit is limited to $25,000 plus 25% of the tax liability over $25,000.[5]

Thus, if the corporation has a tax of $12,000 and an investment credit of $12,000, the credit eliminates the entire tax for the year. However, if the tax was $12,000 and the investment credit was $15,000, the balance can be carried back and/or forward.

CARRYBACK OR CARRYOVER OF UNUSED CREDIT.

If the amount of the investment credit is in excess of the maximum allowable based upon the computed tax, the excess must first be carried back and then forward. For taxable years ending after December 31, 1966, the unused investment credit may be carried back for three years and forward for seven years. For taxable years ending before January 1, 1967, the period is three years back and forward for five years.[6]

For taxable years beginning after December 31, 1968 and ending after April 18, 1969, the carryover or carryback is *limited* to 20 per cent of the total carrybacks and carryovers to taxable years beginning after December 31, 1968.

RECAPTURE OF THE INVESTMENT CREDIT.

If a qualified asset is disposed of before the end of its estimated useful life, the investment credit must be recomputed and paid back as an addition to the tax liability for the year of recapture.[7]

Example: Corporation purchased machinery in 1967 for $50,000. The estimated useful life of the machinery was established at 10 years. The corporation deducted in 1967 an investment credit of $3,500. In 1969, the corporation disposed of the asset. In 1969, the corporation must repay the $3,500 (recaptured of the investment credit) since the investment credit must be recomputed on the basis of a two year life. No credit is allowed if the asset has a useful life to the taxpayer of less than four years.

DISPOSITION.

The word "disposition" in connection with the recapture of the investment credit is broadly defined. The most usual example of a disposition is the common sale of Section 38 property.

The Regulations specifically exclude the following transactions from the term "disposition" and, therefore, there is no recapture of depreciation:[8]

(a) transfer of qualified property because of the death of an individual taxpayer;

(b) destruction or damage of qualified property by casualty or loss of property by theft which is thereafter replaced;

(c) reselection of used property disposed of within the taxable year;

(d) a sale-and-leaseback transaction even though gain or loss is recognized to the vendor-lessee and the property ceases to be subject to depreciation to the vendor-lessee.

(e) a merger of a parent and a subsidiary corporation under Section 332;

(f) a statutory reorganization under the following categories—(1) a statutory merger or consolidation; (2) an exchange of stock solely for stock; (3) an exchange of stock for at least 80 per cent of the corporate property; (4) a transfer of assets to a corporation for at least 80 per cent of the issued and outstanding stock of another corporation; a recapitalization of a corporation and; a change in identity, form, or place of organization.[9] In such cases, the acquiring corporation takes the place of the acquired corporation with respect to the investment credit and eliminates recapture.

Disposition does not apply to a mere change in the form of conducting the trade or business. A mere change in the form of conducting the trade or business (whether through a corporation, the formation of a partnership, or otherwise) applies only to cases where the properties of a trade or business are transferred. Thus, the transfer of Section 38 assets to a newly formed corporation in a tax-free transaction under Section 351 will not fall within the exception unless the transaction also involves the transfer of the trade or business in which the assets are used.

There is no disposition due to a change in the form of conducting the trade or business unless all of the following conditions exist—

(1) the Section 38 property remains in the same business;

(2) the taxpayer retains a substantial interest in the business;

(3) substantially all the property (whether or not it is Section 38 property) is transferred in the change of form; and

(4) the basis of the Section 38 property is carried over (in whole or in part) in the change of form.[10]

The taxpayer is considered to have retained a substantial interest only if, after the change, the taxpayer's interest (a) is substantial in relation to the total interest of all the owners; or (b) is equal to or greater than his interest prior to the change.[11]

A common example of a mere change in the form of conducting the trade or business is the tax-transfer of the business and assets of a sole proprietor or of a partnership to a corporation in exchange for at least 80 per cent of its issued and outstanding stock at the time of the transfer.[12] An example of substantial and substantially the same interest before and after would be a 15 per cent partner who retains a 15 per cent interest in the corporation to which the partnership has transferred its assets and business.

A disposition does not refer to a change in the manner of reporting income or paying the tax on the income derived from the business but rather to a change in the form of conducting the business. For example, a corporation which changes its election from a regular corporation to a subchapter S corporation is not covered by the phrase "a mere change in the form of conducting the trade or business" and will be subject to the rules of recapture since the change is considered a disposition.[13]

By a process of inclusions and exclusions based upon the above analysis, the following transactions would be considered to be dispositions—

(1) gifts;

(2) trade-ins and exchanges;

(3) certain corporate liquidations, i.e. Section 337 liquidation;

(4) certain contributions of property to a regular corporation or to a subchapter S corporation;

(5) contributions to certain partnerships;

(6) involuntary conversions;

(7) sale of stock by a subchapter S corporation;

(8) sale by an interest in a partnership;

(9) sale by a beneficiary of an interest in an estate or trust; and

(10) retirement of property.

The succeeding chapters will discuss more specifically the application of the recapture provisions as they apply to the various types of corporate liquidation.

CITATIONS

[1]Sec. 48 (a).

[2]Sec. 48 (a) (1) (C); Reg. Sec. 1.48–1 (m).

[3]Sec. 46 (a) (1).

[4]Sec. 46 (c) (2).

[5]Sec. 46 (a) (2).

[6]Sec. 46 (b) (1); Reg. Sec. 1.46–2 (a) (1)–(3).

[7]Sec. 47 (a) (1) (C); Reg. Sec. 1.47–1.

[8]Reg. Sec. 1.47–3.

[9]Sec. 381 (a) (1) (A) (B) (C) (D) (E) (F).

[10]Reg. Sec. 1.47–3 (f) (1).

[11]Reg. Sec. 1.47–3 (f) (2).

[12]Sec. 351.

[13]Tri-City Dr. Pepper Bottling Co., 61 TC (No 56). See also Reg. Sec. 1.47–4 (b) (2)–stockholders liability for recapture eliminated.

SIX

The General Method of Liquidating a Corporation — Complete Liquidation

COMPLETE LIQUIDATION—BASIC RULE.

The general method for liquidating a corporation—Section 331, Internal Revenue Code of 1954—applies to both complete and partial liquidations (see Chapter 11—Partial Liquidations). The complete liquidation consists of an exchange of the corporate assets for the outstanding stock of the corporation. The exchange of the assets for the stock is the distribution in exchange—the liquidating dividend. Under the general rule— Section 331 (a) (1)—the distribution in liquidation is treated, in effect, as a sale of the stock from the stockholder to the corporation. Thus, such distributions fall under Section 1201, et seq., 1954 Code and the gain or the loss resulting therefrom is a capital gain or loss to the stockholders. Whether this gain or loss is short-term or long-term depends upon the holding period of the capital stock.

However, where the corporation distributes in complete liquidation, depreciable personal property and/or depreciable real property, the corporation under the recapture of depreciation provisions described in Chapters 3 and 4 may realize ordinary income in the year of the liquidation since the corporation is in effect selling the property for its fair market value to the stockholders.

FAIR MARKET VALUE OF ASSETS.

Under this method of liquidating, the assets are valued at their fair market value as of the date of the liquidating dividend. Deduct the liabilities unpaid at the date of distribution from the fair market value of the assets. The net fair market value of the assets so arrived at—the liquidating dividend—is considered in full payment for the stock owned by the stockholders. The following outline illustrates the general method of liquidating a corporation:

Fair Market Value of All Assets

minus

Liabilities (unpaid)

equals

Net Fair Market Value of All Assets

minus

Cost or Other Basis of Capital Stock

equals

Capital Gain or Loss (short or long term)

Example 1: Stockholder A paid in $12,000 cash for the capital stock of the corporation at the time of organization in 1956. The assets of the corporation were distributed to the stockholder in July, 1974 in complete liquidation under Section 331 (a) (1), IRC 1954. The book basis and the fair market value of the assets and liabilities were as follows:

ASSETS	Per Books	F.M.V.	LIABILITIES & CAPITAL	Per Books
Cash	$ 5,000	$ 5,000	Mortgage Payable	$50,000
Land	20,000	40,000	Capital Stock	12,000
Building (net of			Earned Surplus	8,000
depreciation)	45,000	80,000		
Total	$70,000	$125,000	Total	$70,000

Computation of gain on liquidation:

Fair Market Value—Assets	$125,000
Less: Liabilities (Mortgage Payable)	50,000
Net Fair Market Value of Assets—	
Liquidating Dividend	$ 75,000
Less: Cost or Other Basis of Capital St.	12,000
Capital Gain on Liquidation—long-term	
(1956 to July 1974)	$ 63,000

The gain or loss on a complete liquidation under Section 331 (a) (1), IRC 1954, is a capital gain or loss. The capital gain or loss is short-term or long-term depending upon the length of time that the capital stock was held (date of acquisition to date of liquidating dividend).[1] The gain in the above example is long-term (1956 to July, 1974).

Example 2: Assume the same facts as in Example 1 except that the stockholder sold his capital stock to X in June, 1974 for $75,000. X, in July, 1974, completely liquidated the corporation under Section 331 (a) (1), IRC 1954. Assume that the fair market value of the assets did not change between the date that X purchased the capital stock from A and the date of liquidation.

Stockholder A will have a recognized long-term capital gain of $63,000 ($75,000 minus $12,000) on the sale of the capital stock to X. Since (as assumed) the fair market value of the net assets has remained the same between the date of sale and liquidation, X will have no recognized gain or loss upon the receipt of the net assets in liquidation ($75,000 net fair market value upon receipt of the net assets in liquidation minus $75,000, X's cost of acquiring the capital stock from A).[2]

SALE—EFFECT ON BALANCE SHEET.

The sale of the corporate stock by the original stockholders to others does not change the capital stock on the balance sheet and the book value of the assets. The balance sheet in Example 2 above, both before and after the sale, would be as follows:

ASSETS		LIABILITIES & CAPITAL	
Cash	$ 5,000	Mortgage Payable	$50,000
Land	20,000	Capital Stock	12,000
Building (net of depreciation)	45,000	Earned Surplus	8,000
Total	$70,000	Total	$70,000

Thus, although X purchased the capital stock for $75,000, the book basis on the corporate books is still $12,000. Likewise, the assets continue the same basis. Despite the fact that the capital stock was purchased for the current net fair market value ($75,000) by X, the corporation cannot use the higher current fair market value for the basis for depreciation or a subsequent sale of assets by the corporation.

LIQUIDATION TO OBTAIN HIGHER BASIS.

The higher basis (current fair market value) can be obtained only by liquidation of the corporation under the general rule of Section 331 (a) (1), IRC 1954. Thus, if the corporation in Example 2 above was liquidated by X after the purchase of the capital stock and he operated the former corporation as a proprietorship, the books of accounts of the individual would be as follows:

ASSETS		LIABILITIES & CAPITAL	
Cash	$ 5,000	Mortgage Payable	$ 50,000
Land	40,000	X, Capital Account	75,000
Building (net of depreciation)	80,000		
Total	$125,000	Total	$125,000

HOLDING PERIOD.

The holding period of the assets received in distribution in liquidation of a corporation begins with the date of the receipt of the assets in liquidation. In the example above, the holding period of the land and the building for purposes of X as an individual would be July, 1974. Under Section 331 (a) (1), IRC 1954, the receipt of the assets in complete liquidation of a corporation is a closed transaction at which time gain or loss is recognized. For tax purposes, a closed transaction starts the running of a new holding period for the purposes of future recognition of gain or loss on a sale or other disposition of the assets.

Thus, if X sold the assets after the liquidation, the capital gain or loss would be short-term or long-term depending upon the date of sale as compared with the date of receipt of the liquidating dividend. If the date of receipt of the liquidating dividend was July 17, 1974, X, in order to have a long-term transaction, could not sell the assets until January 18, 1975 (more than six months; 12 months under the 1969 Act).[3]

COMPUTING THE PERIOD OF TIME.

The period of time is computed by excluding the day on which the asset is acquired and including the day on which the asset is disposed of.[4] Thus, for example, if a capital asset was acquired on May 1 and sold on November 1, the holding period begins on May 2 and ends on November 1. The asset was held for exactly six months and the gain or loss is short-term.[5] The period is not computed on a uniform 30-day month. Holidays, Saturdays and Sundays do not affect the holding period.[6] The computation of the holding period is computed by reference to the calendar month and fractions thereof rather than by reference to days.[7]

Example 3: (1) A security acquired on January 21 and sold on February 21 was held for exactly one month.

(2) A security acquired on January 28, 29, 30, or 31 and sold on February 28 (other than in a leap year) was held exactly one month.

(3) A security acquired on April 8 and sold on August 8 was held for exactly four months.

Warning: To insure the benefits of a long-term capital gain it is advisable to have a minimum holding period of 185 days.

RECAPTURE OF DEPRECIATION.

In general, the rule for recapture may be summarized as follows: where a corporation distributes in liquidation depreciable personal or real property which has a fair market value at the time of distribution greater than the adjusted basis (book basis), to the extent of the depreciation allowed or allowable after a specific date, the difference between (1) the lower of the fair market value and the recomputed basis and (2) the adjusted basis is ordinary income to the corporation.[8]

Example 4: The ABC Corporation elects to liquidate under Section 331 (a) (1) in

1964. Among the assets distributed to the stockholders was depreciable personal property which had a current fair market value of $20,000. The adjusted basis of the asset was $8,000 and the recomputed basis was $11,000 (depreciation allowed or allowable since 12/31/61—$3,000).

The corporation must report $3,000 as ordinary income in the year of liquidation (distribution of the assets computed as follows):

Fair market value ($20,000) or recomputed basis ($11,000), whichever is lower	$11,000
Adjusted basis in hands of corporation	8,000
Ordinary income taxable to corporation	$ 3,000
Gain subject to Section 1231	$ 9,000

The stockholders in computing the liquidating dividend will include the asset at its fair market value, $20,000.

The amount of the ordinary income must be computed separately for an asset which is subject to recapture under either Section 1245 or Section 1250.[9]

As already indicated in an earlier chapter, the enactment of the recapture provisions creates income to the corporation which elects the general method of complete liquidation. The effect is that the corporation not only has ordinary income but the stockholders pay a capital gain on the same basis as prior to the recapture provisions.[10] The fact that the corporation pays an additional tax in the year of liquidation does not reduce or affect the stockholder's capital gain with respect to that asset.

METHOD OF DEPRECIATION.

Under certain conditions, a complete liquidation under the general method will affect the depreciation deduction. If a corporation had elected to use one of the accelerated depreciation methods, i.e., the double declining balance or the sum of the digits method, the succeeding entity must adopt the straight line method for computing depreciation or, with permission of the Commissioner, the 150% (1½) declining balance method. It cannot continue to use the two accelerated methods provided for by the Revenue Act of 1954.

The two accelerated methods (the double declining and the sum of the digits methods) apply only to new assets and to the first user.[11]

Example 5: Corporation P acquired machinery in 1960 and adopted the double declining balance method. In 1964, the corporation liquidated and distributed its assets (including the machinery) and liabilities to its stockholders who continued to operate the business under a partnership form of entity. The partnership will be required to adopt the straight line or the 150% declining balance method and estimate the remaining life of the machinery.

Note: However, the basis of the machinery in the hands of the new partnership for depreciation purposes will be the fair market value at the date of liquidation.

RECAPTURE OF INVESTMENT CREDIT.

The Revenue Act of 1962 provided for an investment tax credit on the purchase, or other acquisition and, in some cases, the leasing of assets known as Section 38 assets.[12] The provision became effective for tax years ending after December 31, 1961 but only as to qualified investments acquired, constructed, or reconstructed after December 31, 1961. The estimated life established for the asset determined the amount of the investment credit.[13] If the asset was disposed of by the taxpayer prior to the established life, the law requires a recomputation of the allowed credit and, in some cases, the credit in whole or in part must be repaid as a tax in the year of disposition.[14] In other words, the credit previously allowed is recaptured in whole or in part. The tax for the current year is increased by the amount that the credit would have been decreased had the original credit been computed on the period of actual use instead of the estimated period of use.

The recapture provision applies to all sales, exchanges, transfers, distributions and involuntary conversions. The question is whether the investment credit is subject to recapture where there is a corporate liquidation under Section 331 (a) (1), the general method. The statute provides that there is no recapture where there is a mere change in the form of conducting the business and where such property is retained in the trade or business and the taxpayers' stockholders retain a substantial interest in such trade or business.[15] Thus, if a corporation liquidates and the stockholder or stockholders continue to operate the business as a proprietorship or partnership with substantially the same interest, the liquidating corporation is not subject to recapture. However, in other cases, the liquidating corporation with its final return must repay the investment credit as recomputed based upon the early disposition.

However, in a subsequent sale or other disposition, the recapture provisions will apply to such disposition.

COMPLETE LIQUIDATION IN INSTALLMENTS.

Where a corporation liquidates under Section 331 (a) (1), IRC 1954, in installments rather than in one liquidating distribution or dividend, gain is not recognized until the investment in the capital stock is recovered, i.e., capital recovery theory;[16] and the holding period of the stock exchanged in a complete corporate liquidation ends with the receipt of the total amount on which gain is recognized—the final liquidating distribution rather than the earlier date or dates of receipts in liquidation following the decision to liquidate as set forth in the resolution.[17]

Example 6: A calendar year taxpayer acquired 100% of the capital stock of the ABC Corporation on June 1, 1972 for $100,000. On June 16, 1972, the taxpayer received the first of the distributions in complete liquidation of the corporation of $75,000 and the second and final distribution on August 15, 1973 of $60,000. In 1972, the taxpayer should report no recognized gain ($75,000 value of assets received as against the cost basis of the capital stock $100,000). In 1973, the recognized capital gain to be reported is $35,000. This gain is long-term capital gain (June 1, 1972 to August 15, 1973).

The same rule applies (a) where the stockholders surrender part of their capital stock at the time each of a series of distributions is made; or (b) where the stockholders acquired their capital at different times. The basis must be aggregated in applying the capital recovery.[18]

Example 7: Taxpayer purchased 100 shares of the XYZ Corporation capital stock for $2,500 in May, 1972 and 200 shares for $6,000 in January, 1973. The corporation adopted a plan of complete liquidation on July 1, 1973 and made an initial distribution of $4,000. In February, 1974, the second and final distribution of $6,500 was paid.

The taxpayer would report no recognized gain in 1973, but he would report a recognized long-term capital gain of $2,000 in 1974.

Under the general rule,[19] where a payment is deferred for a year or more, interest will be imputed in such a payment if (1) no interest is payable or (2) if the interest rate is less by more than one per cent below the rate established by the Commissioner. However, this rule of imputed interest does not apply to corporate liquidations which are payable in installments.[20]

WHEN GAIN IS RECOGNIZED.

A cash basis stockholder will report the recognized gain at the time he actually or constructively receives the cash or other property in liquidation, whereas a stockholder on the accrual basis reports the gain as soon as the amount of the liquidating distribution is ascertainable and it is known that the payment will be made within due course.[21]

Where a corporation liquidates and transferred its assets and liabilities to a newly formed partnership by journal entry, each stockholder is required to include in his personal income tax return the gain on the liquidation. The recognized gain is measured by the difference between the net fair market value of the assets and the adjusted basis of the stock investment.[22]

WHEN LOSS IS RECOGNIZED.

Where the distributions in complete liquidation are paid in installments, loss will usually be recognized only when the final liquidating payment has been distributed to the stockholders. This rule is upheld despite the fact that the corporation has withheld sufficient money to pay unknown or ascertained (at liquidation date) liabilities. However, if the corporation, after the initial distribution, retains valuable tangible or intangible assets, the value of which is not then ascertainable, no loss will be allowed until the year of final disposition of such assets even though it is known that a loss will eventually be sustained.[23]

Example 8: Stockholder A sold capital stock to X for $75,000 in June, 1972 (at which date A had a recognized long-term capital gain—see Example 2). X continued to operate the corporation until October, 1972 at which time he completely liquidated the corporation. The book basis and the fair market value of the assets and liabilities at liquidation were as follows:

ASSETS	Per Books	F.M.V.	LIABILITIES & CAPITAL	Per Books
Cash	$ 2,000	$ 2,000	Mortgage Payable	$45,000
Land	20,000	45,000	Capital Stock*	12,000
Building (net of depreciation)	44,000	93,000	Earned Surplus	9,000
Total	$66,000	$140,000	Total	$66,000

Computation of gain on liquidation:

Fair Market Value of Assets	$140,000
Less: Liabilities (Mortgage Payable)	45,000
Net Fair Market Value of Assets	$ 95,000
Less: Cost of Stock to X	75,000
Capital Gain on Liquidation	$ 20,000

* Cost Basis to X $75,000 in June, 1972.

The capital gain of $20,000 is a short-term capital gain as measured by the period that the capital stock was owned—June, 1972, to October, 1972, the date of liquidation.

Example 9: Z subscribed to 100 shares of the capital stock at the time of the organization of the corporation on October 1, 1958. On June 1, 1960, Z purchased another 100 shares from another stockholder. The corporation was liquidated under Section 331 (a) (1), IRC 1954 on September 1, 1960.

The gain or loss on each lot must be computed separately. The gain or loss on the original 100 shares would be long-term capital gain or loss (October 1, 1958 to September 1, 1960); the gain or loss on the second 100 shares would be a short-term capital gain or loss (June 1, 1960 to September 1, 1960). (Note: See method of computation where distributions in complete liquidation are paid in installments— Example 5.)

Example 10: A, an individual who makes his income tax returns on the calendar year basis, owns 20 shares of stock of the P Corporation, a domestic corporation, 10 shares of which were acquired in 1951 at a cost of $1,500 and the remainder of 10 shares in December, 1954 at a cost of $2,900. He receives in April, 1955 a distribution of $250 per share in complete liquidation, or $2,500 on the 10 shares acquired in 1951, and $2,500 on the 10 shares acquired in December 1954. The gain of $1,000 on the shares acquired in 1951 is a long-term capital gain to be treated as provided in sections 1201 through 1223. The loss of $400 on the shares acquired in 1954 is a short-term capital loss to be treated as provided in sections 1201 through 1223.[24]

SURPLUS OR DEFICIT IMMATERIAL UNDER SECTION 331 (a) (1), IRC 1954.

The amount of the earned surplus in a complete liquidation is not a factor in the determination of the recognized gain or loss. As illustrated above, the amount of the recognized gain or loss depends solely upon the fair market value of the assets (after subtracting the liabilities) as compared to the cost or other basis of the capital stock. Similarly, a deficit has no effect upon the recognized gain or loss upon a complete liquidation.

Example 11: Stockholder paid in $10,000 cash for the capital stock at the time of organization of the corporation in 1966. The assets of the corporation were distributed to the stockholder in July, 1970 in complete liquidation under Section 331 (a) (1), IRC 1954. The book basis and the fair market value of the assets and liabilities were as follows:

ASSETS	Per Books	F.M.V.	LIABILITIES & CAPITAL	Per Books
Cash	$ 1,000	$ 1,000	Mortgage Payable	$57,000
Land	20,000	40,000	Capital Stock	10,000
Building (net of			Deficit	(5,000)
depreciation)	41,000	80,000		
Total	$62,000	$121,000	Total	$62,000

Computation of gain on liquidation:

Fair Market Value of Assets	$121,000
Less: Liabilities (Mortgage Payable)	57,000
Net Fair Market Value of Assets	$ 64,000
Less: Cost or Other Basis of Stock	10,000
Capital Gain (long-term) on Liquidation	$ 54,000

The holding period of the corporate assets for the purposes of short-term or long-term capital gain or loss on the complete liquidation of a corporation takes the same period as the date of the holding or ownership of the capital stock of the corporation.

Example 12: A corporation at date of liquidation (July, 1970) owned the following assets:

Land and building acquired May, 1970
Land and building acquired January, 1967

The corporation was organized in January, 1967. The assets as of the date of liquidation—July, 1970—had appreciated in value.

The gain on liquidation is a long-term capital gain to the organizing stockholder; measured by the holding period of the capital stock—January, 1967 to July, 1970—despite the fact that one of the assets had been acquired by the corporation less than six months prior to the date of liquidation (assuming that the corporation is not a collapsible corporation under Section 341, IRC 1954).

TRANSFER OF ASSETS TO ANOTHER ENTITY.

The Regulations under Section 331 provide that under certain conditions a liquidation which is followed by a transfer to another corporation of all or a part of the assets of the liquidating corporation or which is preceded by such a transfer may, however, have the effect of the distribution of a dividend or of a transaction in which no loss is recognized, and gain is recognized to a limited extent.[25]

Such transactions, in which a complete liquidation under Section 331 (a) (1) may be superseded, fall under two sections of the Code, namely, Section 301 and Section 356, IRC 1954. Thus, if in connection with a liquidation, there is a statutory reorganization, no loss would be recognized and gain would be recognized only to the extent of "other property" which is received in the transaction, i.e., boot (cash). Under certain conditions, if a distribution is substantially equivalent to a dividend under Section 301, the distribution would be taxable as an ordinary dividend instead of a capital gain.

However, the decisions supporting this sub-section of the Regulations must be read in the light of the changes made by the Internal Revenue Code of 1954, particularly Section 302 as it affects Section 301[26] (see Chapter 11). The Internal Revenue Service has announced that it will not issue advance rulings on the tax effect of a corporation which has adopted a plan of liquidation under Section 331 (a) (1) where a part or all of the business or the assets are transferred to a new corporation and the stockholders of the old corporation own more than a nominal amount of the capital stock of the new corporation. The Internal Revenue Service refers to such transactions as the "reincorporation of the previous business or assets."[27] The current announcement broadens the position of the Internal Revenue Service since under a previous ruling the request for a ruling was denied only where the stockholders of the liquidating corporations own at least 50 per cent of the voting stock of the acquiring corporation.[28] The current position is based upon a Supreme Court decision which held that it is necessary only that the stockholders continue to have a definite and substantial equity in the assets of the acquiring corporation.[29]

SALE OF ASSETS—RETENTION OF CHARTER.

Where a corporation sells or otherwise disposes of its assets following the adoption of a plan of liquidation, retains its corporate charter, and thereafter the former stockholders reactivate the corporation in another line of business, the distribution in liquidation constitutes a partial liquidation under Section 331 (a) (2), IRC 1954 (Chapter 9). In such cases, gain or loss on the sale or other disposition of the corporate assets, after the adoption of the plan of liquidation, will be recognized to the corporation.[30]

INFORMATION REQUIRED ON FORM 1040—STOCKHOLDER.

The Code and the Regulations require the stockholders and the liquidating corporation to report the facts and circumstances of the exchange of the capital stock for the assets received in liquidation. The stockholders must report on a schedule attached to their individual income tax returns the facts and circumstances of the liquidation unless the property is part of a distribution made pursuant to a corporate resolution reciting that the distribution is made in liquidation of the corporation and the corporation is completely liquidated and dissolved within one year after distribution.[31] Thus, if the entire liquidation and distribution in complete liquidation occurs within one taxable year, the stockholders are not required to report the details on their individual income tax returns. But if, for example, the liquidation extends over a longer period than a tax year, the stockholders' individual tax returns must disclose the nature of the liquidation, the distributions received and other pertinent information as to the number of shares, the cost and the date or dates of acquisition and the method of acquiring, i.e., by purchase, gift, etc.

Form 966: All corporations in complete liquidation are required to file certain information returns in addition to the execution of a resolution or plan of liquidation.[32] The information Form 966 must be filed in respect to all liquidations whether or not any gain or loss will be recognized to the shareholders.[33]

Within 30 days after the adoption of the resolution or plan for the liquidation and dissolution of the corporation, the corporation must file Form 966 with the Internal Revenue Service Center in which the corporation usually files its corporation income tax return. If any amendments are made to the resolution or plan of liquidation or any supplements are made thereto, an additional Form 966 is required to be filed within 30 days after such amendment or supplement.

All of the information on Form 966 must be given: (a) name and address of the corporation; (b) place and date of incorporation; (c) Internal Revenue Service Center in which the last corporation income tax return was filed and the taxable year covered; (d) date of adoption of the resolution or plan of liquidation and the date of any amendment of the resolution or plan or supplement thereto; (e) taxable year of final return; (f) total number of shares outstanding (common and preferred); (g) type of return filed; (h) type of liquidation (complete or partial); and (i) section of the Code under which the corporation is to be liquidated.

Form 966 must be signed in the corporate name, followed by the signature and title of a corporate officer empowered under the laws of the state or country where incorporated to sign for the corporation. The Internal Revenue Service does not require the corporate to be affixed to the Form 966.

Certified Copy of Resolution of Liquidation: A certified copy of the resolution or plan of liquidation must be attached to Form 966 when filed. In addition, if any amendments or supplements are executed in reference to the original resolution or plan, a certified copy of such amendment or supplement must be attached to an additional Form 966 when filed. Where, under certain state laws no corporate resolution to dissolve is necessary and a certificate of dissolution is executed and forwarded to the proper state officials, such action will be considered as the adoption of a proper resolution to liquidate for tax purposes.[34]

Form 1099 L: Every corporation making a distribution in liquidation of $600 or more to a stockholder during a calendar year must file for each such stockholder Form 1099 L.[35] The following information must be given on Form 1099 L: (a) number and class of shares owned by the shareholder at the time of the liquidating dividend; (b) the total amount of cash distributed to the stockholder; (c) the total amount of other assets distributed to the shareholder and a description of such assets; (d) name and address of the stockholder; and (e) name and address of the liquidating corporation.

The assets to be reported on Form 1099 L are the fair market value of such assets without reduction by the liabilities and the capital as of the date of the distribution attributable to each stockholder according to their proportionate interest in the corporation, i.e., an undivided interest in the total assets unless specific assets are to be distributed to each stockholder.

Form 1096 must be prepared and filed in duplicate. The original Form 1096 is filed with the Director, Internal Revenue Service Center at the applicable center[36] with no attachments, i.e. Form 1099 L, under separate cover. The duplicate Form 1096 with Forms 1099 L (one for each stockholder receiving a distribution in liquidation as described above) must be filed under separate cover with the Director at the applicable service center.[37]

The information forms (Form 1099 L) and the letter of transmittal (Form 1096) may be filed on computer processed magnetic tape in lieu of the government supplied paper forms.

ASSETS—NO ASCERTAINABLE VALUE AT LIQUIDATION.

Under the general rule, tangible and intangible assets which have no ascertainable value at date of liquidation will be considered as having a zero basis for the purposes of future use or disposition.[38] Thus, for example, upon the sale of such an asset, the gross selling price less the selling expenses and fees paid will be recognized capital gain; not ordinary income. The gain or loss will be short or long term depending upon the length of time that the capital stock was owned.

MORTGAGES, CLAIMS AND RECEIVABLES—
NO ASCERTAINABLE VALUE AT LIQUIDATION.

If a corporation distributes in complete liquidation under Section 331 (a) (1), IRC 1954, claims which at the date of liquidation had no ascertainable value, the stockholder will, upon receipt of any payment on such claims, have a recognized capital gain; not ordinary income.[39] For example, prior to liquidation, a corporation had claims on file to recover certain custom duties. The claims for refund, at the date of liquidation, had no ascertainable value. After the corporation was liquidated, the former stockholders received the refunds. These refunds are to be treated as capital gains in the hands of the stockholders.[40] The length of time that the stock was owned will determine whether the capital gain is long term or short term.

On the other hand, if claims and receivables have a value at the date of liquidation, the distribution of such claims or receivables having a value at the date of liquidation, the distribution is a closed transaction and gain or loss, whether capital or ordinary, must be computed. Thus, where a corporation distributed in complete liquidation insurance renewal commissions which had ascertainable value, the stockholders had a liquidating dividend equal to the fair market value. To the extent that the former stockholders received payments in excess of the basis, i.e., fair market value at liquidation, the stockholders received ordinary income; not capital gain.[41] The gain at the time of the liquidating dividend to the extent that the fair market value exceeded the cost basis of the stock was capital gain.[42] Royalties received by former stockholders under a patent licensing agreement distributed in complete liquidation of a corporation which had ascertainable value at that time were held to be ordinary income to the former stockholders receiving the royalties after the liquidation; not capital gain.[43]

CREDITOR v STOCKHOLDER.

A taxpayer acquired by purchase all of the capital stock of a corporation and a demand note of the corporation. Thereafter, the corporation was completely liquidated. The Court held that the distribution in liquidation was in payment of the note and that the stockholder received the payment as a creditor, not as a stockholder. The payment of the note was ordinary income to the creditor-stockholder. In another case, a taxpayer acquired by devise the capital stock of a corporation and a claim against the corporation. The corporation thereafter liquidated. The taxpayer-stockholder authorized the corporation to transfer the assets in liquidation in satisfaction of the claim. The Court held that such payment was not a liquidating dividend but a payment to a creditor and, therefore, ordinary income.[44]

CORPORATE LIABILITIES ASSUMED BY STOCKHOLDER.

Where the former stockholders of a liquidating corporation assume the corporate liabilities, the amount of such liabilities shall be deducted from the net assets received in liquidation. The effect of the assumption would reduce the net recognized gain on the liquidation. For example, a corporation had irrevocably voted a pension to two officers of the corporation who were non-stockholders, payable for a fixed number of years. At complete liquidation of the corporation, the stockholders assumed the payment of the pensions. The Court held that the present value of the pension reduces the net recognized gain on the liquidation.[45]

STOCKHOLDERS AS TRANSFEREES AFTER LIQUIDATION.

A stockholder reported a capital gain on the complete liquidation of a corporation. After the liquidation of the corporation, the stockholder was required to pay additional income taxes, claims, or other liabilities not ascertainable at liquidation assessed or collectible against the corporation. The payment by the former stockholder is treated as a capital loss in the year of payment.[46]

The enactment of Section 1341 of the Internal Revenue Code of 1954 did not overrule the Supreme Court decision allowing capital losses in the year of payment as described above, but did provide for relief to the taxpayer stockholder in certain cases where applicable. The relief section[47] applies only to a payment of more than $3,000 in any one taxable year of the former stockholder.

Example 13: In 1961, taxpayer, the sole stockholder in the XYZ Corporation, received a liquidating dividend upon the liquidation of the corporation which resulted in an actual long-term capital gain of $30,000. In addition, the taxpayer received a salary of $20,600. The taxpayer, single, had allowable deductions of $1,000.

1961 Federal Income Tax Return as Filed

Salary	$20,600
Long-term Capital Gain (liquidation) ($30,000 × 50%) . .	15,000
Adjusted Gross Income	$35,600
Deductions	1,000
Net Income	$34,600
Personal Exemption	600
Taxable Income	$34,000
Tax (alterate method)	$14,230

In 1963, the liquidated corporation was examined and received an additional Federal tax assessment of $4,000 which the taxpayer, the former stockholder, paid in 1963. The taxpayer had, in 1963, a salary of $12,600, long-term capital gain of $10,000 and deductions of $1,000.

1961 Federal Income Tax Return Recomputed with Deduction for Long-term Capital Gain—Assessment Paid in 1963.

Salary		$20,600
Long-term Capital Gain	$30,000	
Long-term Capital Loss	4,000	
	$26,000 × 50%	13,000
Adjusted Gross Income		$33,600
Deductions		1,000
Net Income		$32,600
Personal Exemption		600
Taxable Income		$32,000
Tax (alternate method)		$13,200
Difference in Tax ($14,230 − $13,200)		$ 1,030

1963 Federal Income Tax Return
(With Deduction for Assessment)

Salary		$12,600
Long-term Capital Gain	$10,000	
Long-term Capital Loss	4,000	
	$ 6,000 × 50%	3,000
Adjusted Gross Income		$15,600
Deductions		1,000
Net Income		$14,600
Personal Exemption		600
Taxable Income		$14,000
Tax		$ 4,260

1963 Federal Income Return
(Without Deduction for Assessment)

Salary	$12,600
Long-term Capital Gain	
($10,000 × 50%)	5,000
Adjusted Gross Income	$17,600
Deductions	1,000
Net Income	$16,600
Personal Exemption	600
Taxable Income	$16,000
Tax	$ 5,200

Limitation

1963 Tax computed without deduction for assessment.	$ 5,200
Less: Saving in 1961	1,030
	$ 4,170
1963 Tax computed with deduction for assessment	$ 4,260
1963 Tax payable under Sec. 1341	$ 4,170

CITATIONS

[1] Sec. 1222, IRC 1954; Reg. Sec. 1.1222–1.

[2] Reg. Sec. 1.331–1.

[3] Sec. 1222, IRC 1954; Reg. Sec. 1.1222–1.

[4] IT 3287, CB 1939–1, pg. 138; Kenneth Blanchard, Memo TC 1956.

[5] E.T. Weir, 10 TC 996, aff. 173 F 2d 222; S.H. Fogel, Memo TC 1951, aff. 203 F 2d 346. (See also Sec. 1223, IRC 1954; Reg. Sec. 1.1223–1.)

[6] IT 3705, CB 1945, pg. 174.

[7] IT 3985, CB 1949–2, pg. 51.

[8] Sec. 1245; 1250, IRC 1954; Reg. Sec. 1.1245–1 (c) (2); Chapters 3 & 4.

[9] Reg. Sec. 1.1245–1 (a) (1).

[10] Sec. 1245 (d); Sec. 1250 (h).

[11] Sec. 167 (c) (1) (2), IRC 1954; Reg. Sec. 1.167 (c)–1.

[12] Sec. 48, IRC 1954.

[13] Sec.46 (c), IRC 1954.

[14] Sec. 47, IRC 1954.

[15] Sec. 47 (b), IRC 1954; Committee Report, Rev. Act of 1962; Reg. 1.47–3 (f).

[16] Sec. 1001, IRC 1954; Doyle v Mitchell Brothers Co., 247 U.S. 179; Burnett v Logan, 283 U.S. 404; Letts, 30 BTA 800, aff, 89 F 2d 760.

[17] Alvina Ludorff, 40 BTA 32; Mattison v U.S. 163 F. Supp. 754.

[18] Florence M. Quinn, 33 BTA 412; Karl G. Von Platen, Memo TC 1953.

[19] Sec. 483, IRC 1954.

[20] Rev. Rul. 74-89.

[21] GCM 22822, 1941–2 CB, pg. 126.

[22] Rev. Rul. 69-534, superseding IT 1323 and SR 1240.

[23] Dresser v U.S., 55 F 2d 499; Karl G. Von Platen, Memo TC 1953.

[24] Reg. Sec. 1.331–1 (e).

[25] Reg. Sec. 1.331–1 (c).

[26] Est. of John B. Lewis, 10 TC 1080, aff. 176 F 2d 646; Est. of Elsie W. Hill, et al., 10 TC 1090; U.S. v The Arcade Co., 203 F 2d 230, aff. 97 F. Supp. 942.

[27] TIR 310, 3/3/61; Drummond v U.S., DC, Calif., 9/19/68; Kind, 54 TC 600.

[28] Rev. Proc. 60–6, CB 1960–1, pg. 880.

[29] John A. Nelson Co. v Helvering, 296 U.S. 374.

[30] Rev. Rul. 60–50, CB 1960–1, pg. 150; Rev. Rul. 61–156, 1961–2 CB, pg. 62.

[31]Reg. Sec. 1.331–1 (d).

[32]Sec. 6043, IRC 1954; Reg. Sec. 1.6043–1.

[33]Reg. Sec. 1.6043–1 (a).

[34]IT 3249, CB 1939–1, pg. 143.

[35]Reg. Sec. 1.6043–2 (a).

[36]2306 East Bannister Road, Kansas City, Missouri 64170; 310 Lowell Street, Andover, Massachusetts 01812; 1160 West 1200 South Street, Ogden, Utah 84405; 4800 Buford Highway, Chamblee, Georgia 30006; 11601 Roosevelt Boulevard, Philadelphia, Pennsylvania 19155; 201 West Second Street, Covington, Kentucky 41011; 3651 South Interregional Highway, Austin, Texas 78740; 1040 Waverly Avenue, Holtsville, New York 11799; 5045 East Butler Avenue, Fresno, California 93730; and 3131 Democrat Road, Memphis, Tennessee 38110.

[37]*Ibid*

[38]Sec. 1001, 1011, IRC 1954.

[39]L.H. Burnett, TC Memo 1956–210; Westover v Smith, 173 F 2d 90; Susan J. Carter, 9 TC 364, aff 170 F 2d 911; George J. Lentz, et al., 28 TC 1157; John H. Altorper, et al., TC Memo 1961–48; The Shea Company, 58 TC 135.

[40]H.D. McDonald v U.S., DC, WD Wash., 1881 F. Supp. 332.

[41]Anthony Campagna v U.S., 290 F 2d 682; aff. 179 F. Supp. 140; Burnett v Logan, 283 U.S. 404; William A. and Margaret K. Tomvari v Comm., 299 F 2d 889; aff. 35 TC 250; Osenback, 198 F 2d 235; aff. 17 TC 797, 42 AFTR 355.

[42]Est. of Abraham Goldstein, et al., 33 TC 1032, acq.

[43]Est. of Sam Marsack, TC Memo 1960–75; aff. 288 F 2d 533.

[44]Harriet Aldrich, et al., 1 TC 602; D.J. Jordan, 11 TC 914.

[45]Rev. Rul. 59–228, CB 1959–2, pg. 59.

[46]Arrowsmith v Comm., 344 U.S. 6, aff. Comm. v Bauer, 193 F 2d 734.

[47]Sec. 1341 (b), IRC 1954; Reg. Sec. 1.1341–1 (i).

SEVEN

Complete Liquidation:
Specimen Problem

THE ABC CORPORATION

of 6 Drue Street, New York, N.Y. 10010 was organized on May 2, 1960 under the laws of the State of New York by A. Adams (10 First Avenue, Scarsdale, N.Y.), B. Black (Hotel Royale, N.Y.), and C. Charles (Harbour Lane, Hicksville, N.Y.). At organization, each of the organizers subscribed for one-third of the capital stock of 300 shares no par common stock. Thereafter, each of the three individuals paid in $20,000 for each of the 100 shares subscribed to. The stockholders were also the directors of the corporation. The corporation adopted the calendar year for reporting its corporate net income for Federal income tax purposes, filing on Form 1120. The corporation files its return with the Internal Revenue Service Center at Holtsville, New York. Identification #13-1774568.

At 10 A.M. on August 10, 1974, the directors and the stockholders held a joint special meeting at the office of the corporation's attorneys, Law & Law of 50 Elm Street, New York, N.Y. At this special meeting, the directors and the stockholders adopted a resolution to completely liquidate the corporation under Section 331 (a) (1) as of the close of business on August 31, 1974.*

The assets and liabilities of the corporation were distributed in complete

---

*In some states, separate special meetings must be held by the directors and the stockholders; the directors adopting the resolution to liquidate and the stockholders thereafter approving the directors' action.

liquidation to the stockholders on August 31, 1974 and a new general partnership was organized effective September 1, 1974.

The corporation was legally dissolved on September 30, 1974 under the laws of the State of New York.

The balance sheet as of the close of business on August 31, 1974 was as follows:

ABC CORPORATION

Balance Sheet as of August 31, 1974

ASSETS		Per Books
Cash		$ 5,000
Accounts Receivable	$ 60,000	
Less: Reserve Bad Debts	3,000	57,000
Notes Receivable		12,000
Inventory		36,000
Land		25,000
Factory Building	150,000	
Less: Reserve Depreciation	30,000	120,000
Machinery	80,000	
Less: Reserve Depreciation	36,000	44,000
Deferred Assets		1,000
Total Assets		$300,000
LIABILITIES & CAPITAL		
Accounts Payable		$ 60,000
Mortgage Payable		100,000
Loans Payable—A. Adams		30,000
Capital Stock		60,000
Capital Surplus (paid-in)*		9,000
Earned Surplus 12/31/73	$ 35,000	
Net Income 1/1/74 to 8/31/74**	6,000	41,000
Total Liabilities & Capital		$300,000

Based upon expert appraisals, the assets of the corporation for purposes of complete liquidation were valued as follows:

ABC CORPORATION

Fair Market Value as of August 31, 1974

ASSETS	Fair Market Value
Cash	$ 5,000
Accounts Receivable	55,000

---

*In 1962, each stockholder returned $3,000 of their officers' salary in order to increase the working capital.

**Includes $2,000 ordinary income based upon the recapture of depreciation under Sections 1245 and 1250.

Notes Receivable	12,000
Inventory	36,000
Land	40,000
Factory Building	195,000
Machinery	84,000
Deferred Assets	1,000
Total Assets	$428,000

WAIVER OF NOTICE OF JOINT SPECIAL MEETING
OF STOCKHOLDERS AND DIRECTORS OF
ABC CORPORATION

We, the undersigned, being all of the stockholders and all of the directors of the ABC CORPORATION do hereby waive all notice of a joint special meeting of the stockholders and directors of said corporation, and do hereby agree and consent that the 10th day of August, 1974 at 10 o'clock in the forenoon, be and the same is hereby fixed as the time, and the office of Law & Law, Esqs., 50 Elm Street, in the City of New York, County of New York, State of New York as the place for holding the same; and that the purpose of said meeting be the adoption of a plan for the complete liquidation of the corporation, and for a distribution of all the assets of the corporation in complete liquidation less such assets to be retained as are required to meet corporate claims; and for the transaction of such other businss as may lawfully come before said meeting.

Dated, the 10th day of August, 1974.

Stockholders	*Directors*
A. Adams	A. Adams
B. Black	B. Black
C. Charles	C. Charles

MINUTES OF A JOINT SPECIAL MEETING
OF STOCKHOLDERS AND DIRECTORS OF
ABC CORPORATION

A joint special meeting of stockholders and directors of the ABC Corporation was held at the office of Law & Law, Esqs., 50 Elm Street, New York City, New York on the 10th day of August, 1974 at 10 o'clock in the forenoon.

The following being all of the stockholders and directors, were present:

STOCKHOLDERS	DIRECTORS
A. Adams	*A. Adams*
B. Black	*B. Black*
C. Charles	*C. Charles*

A. Adams, the President of the Corporation, acted as Chairman of the meeting and C. Charles, the Secretary of the Corporation, as Secretary thereof.

A written waiver of notice of this meeting, signed by all of the stockholders and directors, was then presented and read by the secretary and was ordered appended to these Minutes.

The Chairman then announced that the purpose of this meeting was to discuss and act upon a proposal to liquidate and dissolve the corporation. Counsel for the Corporation was asked for their opinion of the tax results to the Corporation, and the stockholders, caused by the complete liquidation and distribution of the corporate assets. The stockholders expressed their desire to liquidate and distribute the assets of the Corporation to the stockholders who would thereafter organize and form a general partnership to continue the operation of the business.

After hearing Counsel's explanation of the Tax Laws under the 1954 Internal Revenue Code, especially Section 331 thereof, and under the New York Franchise Tax Laws; after a full discussion by the stockholders and directors of the Corporation; after a report by the President of the Corporation as to the fair market value of the assets and the general financial condition, the following Resolution was unanimously adopted:

RESOLVED, that the following plan of liquidation, pursuant to Section 331 of the Internal Revenue Code of 1954, be and the same is hereby adopted:

I. Within thirty (30) days after the date of this meeting, Counsel for the Corporation shall file Form 966 with the Direction, Internal Revenue Service Center, attaching thereto a certified copy of this Resolution, indicating that the stockholders and directors have adopted a plan of complete liquidation pursuant to Section 331 of the Internal Revenue Code of 1954.

II. That the Corporation, by its duly authorized officers, proceed to liquidate the assets of the Corporation and distribute such assets, except those retained to meet certain liabilities, to the stockholders as an incident to the plan of complete liquidation adopted by the stockholders and directors pursuant to Section 331 of the Internal Revenue Code of 1954.

III. That as soon as practical thereafter, Counsel for the Corporation shall file a certificate for the dissolution of the Corporation pursuant to Section 1004 of the New York State Stock Corporation Law, and that the officers of the Corporation are hereby authorized to execute any and all documents necessary to effectuate such dissolution.

IV. That the officers and directors be and they are hereby empowered, authorized and directed to proceed in accordance with the resolution hereby adopted by the stockholders and directors, said officers and directors being authorized to adopt any subsequent resolutions to effectuate the intent of the stockholders and directors to liquidate the Corporation in accordance with the plan of liquidation adopted pursuant to Section 331 of the Internal Revenue Code of 1954.

There being no further business before the Meeting, the Meeting adjourned.
Dated: August 10th, 1974.

C. Charles
——————————————
                                                                    Secretary

ATTEST:___*A. Adams*___
                President

Form **966**
(Rev. Nov. 1973)
Department of the Treasury
Internal Revenue Service

Corporate Dissolution or Liquidation

(Required under Section 6043(a) of the Internal Revenue Code)

Please type or print

Name of corporation ABC CORPORATION	Employer identification number 13-1774568
Address (Number and street) 6 DRUE STREET	Check type of return
City or town, State and ZIP code NEW YORK, N.Y. 10010	☒ 1120 ☐ 1120DISC ☐ 1120L ☐ 1120M ☐ 1120S

1 Date incorporated 5/2/60	2 Place incorporated STATE OF NEW YORK	3 Type of liquidation ☒ Complete ☐ Partial

4 Internal Revenue Service Center where last income tax return was filed and taxable year covered thereby

Service Center ▶ HOLTSVILLE, N.Y.   Taxable year ▶ CALENDAR YEAR 1973

5 Date of adoption of resolution or plan of dissolution, or complete or partial liquidation 8/10/74	6 Taxable year of final return SHORT YEAR ENDING 8/31/74	7 Total number of shares outstanding at time of adoption of plan or liquidation
		Common 300 | Preferred ---

8 Dates of any amendments to plan of dissolution ---	9 Section of the Code under which the corporation is to be dissolved or liquidated 331	10 If this return is in respect of an amendment of or supplement to a resolution or plan previously adopted and return has previously been filed in respect of such resolution or plan, give the date such return was filed ---

11. Liquidation Within One Calendar Month.—If the corporation is a domestic corporation, and the plan of liquidation provides for a distribution in complete cancellation or redemption of all the capital stock of the corporation and for the transfer of all the property of the corporation under the liquidation entirely within one calendar month pursuant to section 333, and any shareholder claims the benefit of such section, then the corporation must also submit:

(a) A description of the voting power of each class of stock;

(b) A list of all the shareholders owning stock at the time of the adoption of the plan of liquidation, together with the number of shares of each class of stock owned by each shareholder, the certificate numbers thereof, and the total number of votes to which entitled on the adoption of the plan of liquidation;

(c) A list of all corporate shareholders as of January 1, 1954, together with the number of shares of each class of stock owned by each such shareholder, the certificate numbers thereof, the total number of votes to which entitled on the adoption of the plan of liquidation, and a statement of all changes in ownership of stock by corporate shareholders between January 1, 1954, and the date of the adoption of the plan of liquidation, both dates inclusive; and

(d) A computation as described in section 1.6043-2(b) (following the format in Revenue Procedure 65-10, C.B. 1965-1,738 and Revenue Procedure 67-12, C.B. 1967, 589) of accumulated earnings and profits including all items of income and expense accrued up to the date on which the transfer of all property is completed.

Attach a certified copy of the resolution or plan, together with all amendments or supplements not previously filed.

Under penalties of perjury, I declare that I have examined this return, including accompanying schedules and statements, and to the best of my knowledge and belief it is true, correct, and complete.

The Internal Revenue Service does not require a seal on this form, but if one is used, please place it here.	8/15/74 Date	A. Adams Signature of officer	President Title

Instructions

1. Who must file.—This form must be filed by every corporation that is to be dissolved or whose stock is to be liquidated in whole or in part.

Shareholders electing to be covered under section 333 of the Code must also file Form 964 within 30 days after the date of adoption of the plan of liquidation.

2. When to file.—This form must be filed within 30 days after the adoption of the resolution or plan for or in respect of the dissolution of a corporation or the liquidation in whole or in part of its capital stock. If after the filing of a Form 966 there is an amendment or supplement to the resolution or plan, an additional Form 966 based on the resolution or plan as amended or supplemented must be filed within 30 days after the adoption of such amendment or supplement. A return in respect of an amendment or supplement will be deemed sufficient if it gives the date the prior return was filed and contains a certified copy of such amendment or supplement and all other information required by this form which was not given in such prior return.

3. Where to file.—This form must be filed with the Internal Revenue Service Center with which the corporation is required to file its income tax return.

4. Signature.—The return must be signed either by the president, vice president, treasurer, assistant treasurer or chief accounting officer, or by any other corporate officer (such as tax officer) who is authorized to sign. A receiver, trustee, or assignee must sign any return which he is required to file on behalf of a corporation.

☆ U.S. GOVERNMENT PRINTING OFFICE : 1973-O-523-298

Form **966** (Rev. 11-73)

CERTIFIED COPY OF RESOLUTION
ABC CORPORATION

I hereby certify that the following Resolution was unanimously adopted at a Special Joint Meeting of the Stockholders and Directors held on the 10th day of August, 1974.

RESOLVED, that the following plan of liquidation, pursuant to Section 331 of the Internal Revenue Code of 1954, be and the same is hereby adopted:

I. Within thirty (30) days after the date of this meeting, Counsel for the Corporation shall file Form 966 with the Director, Internal Revenue Service Center, attaching thereto a certified copy of this Resolution, indicating that the stockholders and directors have adopted a plan of complete liquidation pursuant to Section 331 of the Internal Revenue Code of 1954.

II. That the Corporation, by its duly authorized officers, proceed to liquidate the assets of the Corporation and distribute such assets, except those retained to meet certain liabilities, to the stockholders, as an incident to the plan of complete liquidation adopted by the stockholders and directors pursuant to Section 331 of the Internal Revenue Code of 1954.

III. That as soon as practical thereafter, Counsel for the Corporation shall file a certificate for the dissolution of the Corporation under the provisions of the New York State Stock Corporation Law, and that the officers of the Corporation are hereby authorized to execute any and all documents necessary to effectuate such dissolution.

IV. That the officers and directors be and they are hereby empowered, authorized and directed to proceed in accordance with the resolution hereby adopted by the stockholders and directors, said officers and directors being authorized to adopt any subsequent resolutions to effectuate the intent of the stockholders and directors to liquidate the Corporation in accordance with the plan of liquidation adopted pursuant to Section 331 of the Internal Revenue Code of 1954.

Dated: August 10, 1974

C. Charles
_____
Secretary

FORM 1120 (FINAL RETURN)
CORPORATION INCOME TAX RETURN

A final return for the ABC Corporation showing a net profit of $6,000 (See Balance Sheet) must be filed for the period January 1, 1974 to August 31, 1974. This return will show the net profit of $6,000 with all the details and schedules completely filled in. The balance sheet, however, will only show the assets and liabilities and capital at January 1, 1974. No assets or liabilities will be shown at September 30, 1974 (End of Taxable Year). However, in the column of the balance sheet "End of the Taxable Year" a statement such as "Assets and Liabilities Distributed in Complete Liquidation under Section 331 (a) (1) IRC 1954 as of 8/31/74" should be inserted. A schedule should be inserted in the return (Form 1120) showing the assets and liabilities distributed to the stockholders.

As indicated in the text in prior chapters, the net income for the short final income tax return is not annualized for purposes of computing the Federal income tax liability.

COMPUTATION OF RECOGNIZED
GAIN ON LIQUIDATION

Fair market value of assets		$428,000
Less: Liabilities—		
Accounts Payable	$ 60,000	
Mortgage Payable	100,000	
Loan Payable—Stockholder	30,000	190,000
Net fair market value of assets		$238,000
Less: Capital stock & capital surplus . .		69,000
Recognized gain (capital) on liquidation		$169,000

COMPUTATION OF RECOGNIZED GAIN
TO EACH STOCKHOLDER

Stockholder	Net Fair Market Value of Assets	Capital Stock plus Capital Surplus	Recognized Capital Gain*
A. Adams	$ 79,333.33	$23,000.00	$ 56,333.33
B. Black	$ 79,333.33	23,000.00	56,333.33
C. Charles	79,333.34	23,000.00	56,333.34
Total	$238,000.00	$69,000.00	$169,000.00

JOURNAL ENTRY AT COMPLETE LIQUIDATION
ABC CORPORATION

Accounts Payable	$ 60,000
Mortgage Payable	100,000
Loan Payable—A. Adams	30,000
Reserve for Bad Debts	3,000
Reserve for Depreciation—Building	30,000
Reserve for Depreciation—Machinery	36,000
Capital Stock	60,000
Capital Surplus—Paid-in	9,000
Earned Surplus	41,000

---

*Long-term capital gain—holding period 5/2/60 to 8/31/74.

	Credit
Cash	$ 5,000
Accounts Receivable	60,000
Notes Receivable	12,000
Inventory	36,000
Land	25,000
Building	150,000
Machinery	80,000
Deferred Assets	1,000

To close out the assets and liabilities and capital in complete liquidation of the corporation under Sec. 331 (a) (1), IRC 1954 as of August 31, 1974.

JOURNAL ENTRY—TO OPEN BOOKS OF ACCOUNT OF SUCCESSOR PARTNERSHIP—THE ABC COMPANY

Cash	$ 5,000.00	
Accounts Receivable	55,000.00	
Notes Receivable	12,000.00	
Inventory	36,000.00	
Land	40,000.00	
Factory Building	195,000.00	
Machinery . . . . ,	84,000.00	
Deferred Assets	1,000.00	
Accounts Payable		$ 60,000.00
Mortgage Payable		100,000.00
Loan Payable—A. Adams		30,000.00
Partners' Capital:		
A. Adams		79,333.33
B. Black		79,333.33
C. Charles		79,333.34

To record the assets and liabilities and capital accounts at fair market value following the receipt of the liquidating dividend from the ABC Corporation as of August 31, 1974 in complete liquidation of the corporation.

Note: As explained in earlier chapters, the basis for tax purposes of the assets is the fair market value at date of liquidation. Thus, for example, the tax basis for depreciation of the factory building in the hands of the partnership would be $195,000. The life would be the estimated life from the date of the liquidating dividend, i.e., August 31, 1974.

Form **1096**	**Annual Summary and Transmittal of U.S. Information Returns**	1974

Department of the Treasury
Internal Revenue Service

(Magnetic tape filers: See the applicable Revenue Procedures
regarding transmittal of returns on magnetic tape.)

Enter number of documents	Place an "X" in the proper box to identify type of document being transmitted				All documents are: Place an "X" in the proper boxes. (See instructions.)			
3	1099–DIV	1099–INT	1099–MED	1099–MISC	Original	Corrected	With taxpayer identifying no.	Without taxpayer identifying no.
	1099–OID	1099–L **3**	1099–PATR	1087–DIV	**X**		**X**	
	1087–INT	1087–MED	1087–MISC	1087–OID				

PAYER'S identifying number ▶ **13-1774568**

ABC CORPORATION
6 DRUE STREET
NEW YORK, N.Y. 10010

Type or print PAYER'S name, address and ZIP code above.

Under penalties of perjury, I declare that I have examined this return, including accompanying documents and to the best of my knowledge and belief, it is true, correct, and complete. In the case of documents without recipients' identifying numbers I have complied with the requirements of the law by requesting such numbers from the recipients, but did not receive them.

Signature *A. Adams*   Title **PRESIDENT**   Date **2/15/75**

☆ U.S. GOVERNMENT PRINTING OFFICE:1973—O—458-087   E.I. 25-1118272

Form 1099L

Department of the Treasury
Internal Revenue Service

U.S. Information Return For

Distributions in Liquidation During Calendar Year

Shares owned		Distributions in liquidation		
Class	Number	Cash	Property	
			Description	Fair market value at date of distribution
COMMON	100	$ 1,666.66	Receivables, Inventory, Land, Factory Building, Machinery, and Sundry Assets	$ 141,000.00

Shareholder's tax identifying number ▶ 100-01-1000

13-1774568

A. ADAMS
10 FIRST STREET
SCARSDALE, N.Y. 11501

ABC CORPORATION
6 DRUE STREET
NEW YORK, N.Y. 10010

Shareholder.—Name, address, and ZIP code. If account is for multiple payees place an asterisk (*) by the name of the person or entity to whom the identifying number belongs.

Corporation.—Name, address, ZIP code, and employer identification number of corporation in liquidation. **(OVER)**

Form 1099L

Department of the Treasury
Internal Revenue Service

U.S. Information Return For

Distributions in Liquidation During Calendar Year

Shares owned		Distributions in liquidation		
Class	Number	Cash	Property	
			Description	Fair market value at date of distribution
COMMON	100	$ 1,666.66	Receivables, Inventory, Land, Factory Building, Machinery, and Sundry Assets	$ 141,000.00

Shareholder's tax identifying number ▶ 100-02-2000

13-1774568

B. BLACK
HOTEL ROYAL
NEW YORK, N.Y. 10018

ABC CORPORATION
6 DRUE STREET
NEW YORK, N.Y. 10010

Shareholder.—Name, address, and ZIP code. If account is for multiple payees place an asterisk (*) by the name of the person or entity to whom the identifying number belongs.

Corporation.—Name, address, ZIP code, and employer identification number of corporation in liquidation. **(OVER)**

Form 1099L

Department of the Treasury
Internal Revenue Service

U.S. Information Return For

Distributions in Liquidation During Calendar Year

Shares owned		Distributions in liquidation		
Class	Number	Cash	Property	
			Description	Fair market value at date of distribution
COMMON	100	$ 1,666.67	Receivables, Inventory, Land, Factory Building, Machinery, and Sundry Assets	$ 141,000.00

Shareholder's tax identifying number ▶ 100-03-3000

13-1774568

C. CHARLES
HARBOUR LAND
HICKSVILLE, N.Y. 11530

ABC CORPORATION
6 DRUE STREET
NEW YORK, N.Y. 10010

Shareholder.—Name, address, and ZIP code. If account is for multiple payees place an asterisk (*) by the name of the person or entity to whom the identifying number belongs.

Corporation.—Name, address, ZIP code, and employer identification number of corporation in liquidation. **(OVER)**

EIGHT

Calendar Month Liquidation – Section 333, IRC 1954

HISTORY OF THE SECTION.

Prior to the enactment of the Internal Revenue Code of 1954, the predecessor sections of Section 333 were temporary sections for relief of corporations in liquidation under certain conditions. For example, Section 112 (b) (7) of the Internal Revenue Code of 1939 applied first to a liquidation of a corporation within the month of December, 1938. Thereafter, the section was made applicable to calendar month liquidation in 1944. The section was not re-enacted again until 1951 and, thereafter, it was extended for the years 1952 and 1953 on a yearly basis. The Internal Revenue Code of 1954 made this section, now known as Section 333, a permanent section of the Code.

A RELIEF SECTION—STRICT INTERPRETATION—A WARNING.

Section 333, IRC 1954 is a relief section as to the non-recognition of gain under certain conditions. The basic rule adopted by the Internal Revenue Service and supported by the courts is that where a taxpayer adopts a relief section it shall be strictly construed; any deviation shall be interpreted to the disadvantage of the taxpayer.[1] Thus, as explained later, unless the provisions of the Code and the Regulations are strictly followed, the relief will be denied and the provisions of Section 331 will be applied, normally at a considerable tax cost to the taxpayer stockholders.

Example: X Company, Inc. owned several parcels of real estate which had an adjusted book basis of $100,000 and a current fair market value of $297,000. X, the sole stockholder, had a cost basis for his capital stock of $25,000. At the date of liquidation, the corporation had no other assets. The only liability was a mortgage on one of the properties amounting to $72,000. The earned surplus was $3,000. X, single, had other income in 1969 consisting of commissions of $20,000. X elected to liquidate the X Company, Inc. during the month of June, 1969. X's return for 1969 was as follows:

Commissions	$ 20,000
Earned Surplus of X Company, Inc., taxable under Sec. 333, as ordinary dividend . .	3,000
Adjusted Gross Income	$ 23,000
Less: Standard Deduction and Personal Deduction	1,600
Taxable Income	$ 21,400
Tax on $21,400	$ 6,742

Upon audit, the Internal Revenue Service found that the election had been improperly made and, therefore, recomputed the tax under Section 331 (a), IRC 1954 as follows:

Commissions		$ 20,000
Liquidating Dividend under Sec. 331 (a):		
Net fair market value of assets . . .	$225,000	
	25,000	
X 50%		100,000
		$120,000
Less: Standard Deduction and Personal Deduction		1,600
Taxable Income		$118,400
Tax on $118,400 under alternate method		$ 55,350
Increase resulting from disallowance of election under Sec. 333		$ 48,608

LIMITED NONRECOGNITION OF GAIN.

Under certain conditions, the stockholders of a corporation may receive, in complete liquidation of the corporation, the property that has appreciated in value without the recognition of gain. Section 333 does not apply to losses.[2] However, if the liquidating corporation has an earned surplus, the surplus is taxed to the stockholders as an ordinary dividend. The cash which is distributed in liquidation to the extent that it exceeds the earned surplus (if any) is taxed as a capital gain. The basis of the property distributed in complete liquidation is based upon the basis of the stock in the hands of the stockholders (with adjustments described later).[3]

CONDITIONS FOR ELECTION.

In order to elect Section 333, IRC 1954, all of the following conditions must be met:

(a) Complete Liquidation: The corporation must be a domestic corporation and must be completely liquidated. A status of liquidation exists for the purposes of Section 333 when the corporation ceases to be a going concern and its activities are merely for the purpose of winding up the corporate affairs, paying its debts and distributing the balance to the stockholders.[4]

The retention of the corporate charter is not fatal.[5] However, the reactivation of the corporation in the same or a different type of business could result in the disqualification of the calendar month liquidation and result in a partial liquidation or a reorganization to the disadvantage of the shareholders.[6]

(b) Adoption of Plan: The liquidation must be made in pursuance of a plan of liquidation adopted on or after June 22, 1954. The plan must be adopted before any distribution of the corporate assets is made in the liquidation of the corporation.[7] The adoption of the plan occurs when the required number of qualified stockholders elect to liquidate under this section.[8]

(c) Redemption of Corporate Stock: The liquidation and distribution of the assets must be in complete cancellation or redemption of all of the outstanding capital stock of the corporation.[9]

(d) One Calendar Month: The transfer of all of the assets in complete redemption or cancellation of the capital stock must be completed in one calendar month; not within 30 days.[10] Thus, if such a liquidation is contemplated, the liquidation (transfer of assets) should begin as close to the first of the calendar month selected as possible so as to insure a complete transfer of the assets within the calendar month.

For example, if the assets consist of real property, the deed must be redrawn in the names of the liquidating stockholders and recorded (if required under state or local law) within the calendar month of liquidation. Mortgages and other claims against the property should be transferred or assigned as well as insurance policies, deposits receivable or payable and other similar items.

Exceptions: There are two exceptions to the complete transfer of all assets within the calendar month:

(1) Sufficient cash may be retained under arrangements for the payment, after the close of the liquidating month, of unascertained or contingent liabilities and expenses.

Such retention must be made in good faith and the amount set aside is reasonable relative to the estimated payment which will be required.[11]

(2) Many corporations electing Section 333 have substantial investments in stocks and securities. The Internal Revenue Service has recognized that the transfer agents in connection with the transfer of the securities held by the corporation may take more than a calendar month to complete the transfer from the liquidating corporation to the electing stockholders. As a result, the date of transfer is the date on which the stock or securities are mailed to the transfer agent for the purposes of Section 333.[12] Since all of the provisions of Section 333 are strictly enforced, extreme care should be taken to keep the necessary records to establish the date of mailing.

Certificates for fractional shares may be issued to a nominee with irrevocable instructions to sell the certificates and distribute the proceeds among the stockholders. For liquidation purposes, the proceeds will be considered "cash" as discussed later. Any dividends on stock payable after the end of the calendar month of liquidation may be assigned to the stockholders directly. Such dividends are taxable to the stockholders, not to the corporation.

(e) Proper Timely Election: Too much stress cannot be placed upon this condition of election. Based upon the fact that Section 333 is a relief section, the time element for filing the required forms of election by the stockholders is strictly enforced. The election, as explained in more detail later and in Chapter 6, is made by each of the qualified electing stockholders on Form 964. Each stockholder must file an original and a duplicate of Form 964 within 30 days after the adoption of the plan of liquidation with the Director, Internal Revenue Service Center in the center in which the corporation will file its final return.

The Regulation provides that "Under no circumstances shall Section 333 be applicable to any shareholders who fail to file their election within the 30-day period prescribed."[13] Where the election Form 964 was mailed one day after the prescribed 30-day period, the election was held untimely and Section 333 was not allowed to be used in the liquidation of the corporation.[14]

In another case, two equal stockholders elected to liquidate their corporation under Section 333 at a timely held special meeting of the stockholders and directors. Stockholder Number 1 filed Form 964 (Stockholder's election form) within the 30-day period provided by the Regulations whereas Stockholder Number 2 did not file Form 964 in time. The Court held that the benefits of Section 333, at least 80 per cent of the voting stock must elect this method of liquidation. Stockholder Number 2 failed to make a timely election and, therefore, was automatically precluded from the benefits of Section 333.[15] Where the corporation filed Form 966 but the stockholders failed to file Form 964, the election under Section 333 was invalid and the liquidation was computed under Section 331 (a) (1)—the general method.[16]

QUALIFIED ELECTING SHAREHOLDERS.

For purposes of electing and using the benefits of Section 333, stockholders are divided into two classes (a) shareholders other than corporations, i.e., individuals, and

(b) corporate shareholders.[17] However, no corporate stockholder may be a qualified electing shareholder if at any time between January 1, 1954 and the date of the plan, inclusive, the corporation owned stock of the liquidating corporation possessing 50 per cent or more of the total combined voting power of all classes of stock entitled to vote upon adoption of the liquidation plan.

Any shareholder of either group, (a) or (b), (whether or not the stock he owns is entitled to vote), is a qualified electing shareholder if: (1) his written election has been properly filed; and (2) like elections have been made and filed by owners of stock possessing at least 80% of the total combined voting power of all classes of stock owned by shareholders of the same group.

The ownership must exist at the time of the adoption of the plan. The shareholder may be an electing shareholder whether or not the shareholder making the election under Section 333 actually realizes gain upon the cancellation or redemption of his stock. Whether the stock is of par value or no par value is immaterial. Only the capital stock with voting power for purposes of adopting a plan of liquidation is counted in measuring the 80% requirement.

Example 1: Corporation A's capital stock consisted of 100 shares voting common no par value stock, all of which was issued and outstanding. Each share was entitled to one vote upon the adoption of a plan of liquidation. The MO Corporation owned 81 shares and an individual owned the balance of 19 shares. The individual stockholder may elect Section 333 since he owns 100% of the qualifying shares. Corporation A by owning 81% (more than 50%) is an excluded corporation.[18]

Example 2: Corporation B's capital stock consisted of 100 shares voting common no par value stock and 100 shares of nonvoting preferred $100 par value stock. The common stock was owned 50% each by P and S. P owned all of the preferred stock. In order to elect Section 333, P and S must both file elections as owners together of more than 80% of the total combined voting power of all classes (common stock). If only P or S filed an election, Section 333 could not be used to liquidate the corporation.

Example 3: Corporation C's capital stock consisted of 100 shares voting common no par value stock. Three individuals own all of the capital stock as follows: E 40 shares; F 40 shares; and G 20 shares. If E and F file the proper elections, Section 333 may be used (at least 80%).

EFFECT OF ELECTION.

The Regulations provide that the election once made is binding and cannot be withdrawn or revoked.[19] The Tax Court has held that a stockholder's election cannot be revoked in the absence of proof of the lack of full knowledge of the facts. In this case, the stockholder's contention that he did not intend to make the election was rejected. The corporation involved had no assets that had appreciated in value but did have an earned surplus.[20]

MISTAKE OF FACTS.

The courts have also ruled on the election based upon a mistake of fact as against a mistake of law. The Fifth Circuit Court permitted the stockholders to withdraw their election where the stockholders were motivated by a mistake of fact. In this case, at the time of liquidation the stockholders relied upon the fact that the book earned surplus was approximately $80,000. The Commissioner, upon audit, increased the earned surplus to over $1,000,000, based upon a 15-year-old transaction.[21] In another decision, the bookkeeper advised the stockholders that the surplus was $28,000 but due to certain transactions involving dividends, the actual amount of surplus for liquidation purposes was $56,000. The District Court found that the election was under a mistake of fact.[22]

MISTAKE OF LAW.

The election may not be withdrawn or revoked if the stockholders have made a mistake of law. The corporation's counsel advised the corporation to amortize goodwill. As a result, the corporation deducted the amortization for tax purposes. This improper treatment reduced the surplus account so that, at date of liquidation, the stockholders were under a mistaken impression as to the amount of the corporation's earned surplus. The Court held that this was a mistake of law and, therefore, no revocation of election was permitted.[23]

WATCH STATE LAW.

The Court held that the taxpayer stockholders may rescind the election made on Form 964 if, prior to such election, the corporation was already dissolved under State Law. In other words, the plan of liquidation must be adopted not later than the date of dissolution of the corporation under state law. In this case, the corporation received a certificate of dissolution on March 27th. The stockholders on March 31 adopted a plan of liquidation under Section 333, IRC 1954 and the stockholder filed Form 964 on April 29th. Elecion may be rescinded.[24]

GENERAL RULES OF RECOGNITION OF GAIN ON LIQUIDATION.

As in the case of complete liquidation under Section 331 (a), discussed in previous chapters, the amount received by a qualified electing shareholder is treated as in full payment in exchange for the capital stock. However, unlike Section 331 (a), Section 333, the calendar month liquidation section, the gain may be in part ordinary gain, in part capital gain and in part no gain or loss is recognized depending upon the corporation's assets and liabilities, surplus or deficit and capital.

Gain or loss must be computed separately on each share of stock owned. The nonrecognition rules apply only to the gain on the stock of an electing stockholder on which gain is realized. It does not apply to the net gain by offsetting of losses on certain shares against the gains on other shares.[25]

The provisions of Section 333 apply only to the recognition of gain. Losses realized on the liquidation will be allowed only in the year of liquidation. This rule applies to all electing shareholders even though one or more of such stockholders will realize only losses on such liquidation.[26] As illustrated later, the basis of the capital stock in the hands of each stockholder, as against the receipts in liquidation, determines the recognition or nonrecognition of gain or loss upon the liquidation.

THREE ELEMENTS TO DETERMINE GAIN.

For the purposes of determining the gain, there must be computed in respect to the corporation:

(a) the accumulated earnings and profits (earned surplus) as of the last day of the calendar month in which the liquidation is to take place. The earned surplus as of the close of the calendar month of liquidation shall be computed without a deduction for any distributions to the stockholders during that month. However, the computation of the earned surplus should take into account all amounts of income and expenses accrued to the date of the liquidation.[27]

In addition to the usual accruals, there are two important groups, one resulting from the enactment of the recapture of depreciation provisions of several Revenue Acts[28] and the other resulting from expenses of liquidation.

(1) As discussed more fully later, if the corporation distributes in liquidation depreciable personal property and/or depreciable real property after the effective dates as provided in the Internal Revenue Code, the income (or loss) must be adjusted by the recaptured depreciation since the amount of the recaptured depreciation is taxable to the corporation in its final corporate tax return for the year of liquidation.[29]

(2) Legal, accounting and other expenses involved in the transfers and the liquidation of the corporation should be set up if unpaid at the end of the calendar month with sufficient money retained to meet these expenses. In addition, the corporation should set up sufficient money to cover the unpaid Federal corporate income tax including the dissolution tax, if any.[30]

(b) the amount of money as of the close of the calendar month selected for the liquidation.[31]

(c) the fair market value of all stocks and securities acquired by the liquidating corporation after 12/31/53. The replacement of lost certificates or the change of certificates into smaller or larger denomination after 12/31/53 of stock and securities acquired prior to 12/31/53 does not consitute an acquisition after 12/31/53. The receipt of stock certificates after 12/31/53 based upon a subscription to the securities made by the corporation and accepted on or before 12/31/53 does not represent an acquisition after 12/31/53 for this purpose. [32]

Thus, *in summary,* as the rule applies to individual stockholders: the appreciation in the value of the assets is recognized for tax purposes only to the extent of the earned surplus (adjusted by the amount of the recaptured depreciation in the year of liquidation and the other accruals as described above) and the cash and securities acquired after 12/31/53 by the corporation (capital gain). For corporate stockholders, the gain resulting from the earned surplus and the cash and the securities is capital gain.

In the year of liquidation, the corporation must report as ordinary income the income (or loss) from operations and, where applicable, the depreciation recaptured under Sections 1245 and 1250, Internal Revenue Code of 1954.

FAIR MARKET VALUE.

The fair market value of the assets of the liquidating corporation is not a factor in determining the reportable capital gain of the stockholders since the assets, in effect, are transferred out of the corporation at book value. However, as the result of the enactment of the depreciation recapture provisions applicable to depreciable personal and real property, the fair market value must be determined where such assets are distributed to the stockholders in order to compute the amount of the ordinary income taxable to the corporation resulting from the depreciation claimed. The general rule as to the taxability of the distributions received by the stockholders is illustrated in the following example.

Example: Corporation M's balance sheet included cash $10,000, securities acquired after 12/31/53 $0 and other assets (land and buildings) $75,000. The other assets had a fair market value of $100,000 at liquidation. The earned surplus was $6,000. The sole stockholder's basis for his capital stock was $40,000.

Assets distributed to stockholder:
(a) Cash	$ 10,000
(b) Securities acquired after 12/31/53	0
	10,000
(c) Other property (fair market value)	100,000
Total Distribution	110,000
Adjusted basis of shareholder's stock....................	40,000
Actual (not taxable) gain to stockholder	$ 70,000
Earned Surplus	6,000
Taxable to stockholder under Section 333:	
(a) Earned surplus (ordinary dividend)	$ 6,000
(b) Excess of cash and securities acquired after 12/31/53 over earned surplus (capital gain)	4,000
(c) Not recognized as gain at liquidation	60,000

ORDINARY DIVIDEND—SECTIONS 34 AND 116, IRC 1954.

The earned surplus is taxed as an ordinary dividend. As such it is subject to the basic $50 exclusion applicable to taxable years ending prior to January 1, 1964 and to the basic $100 exclusion applicable to taxable years beginning after December 31, 1963 as provided in Section 116, IRC 1954. Where a joint stock ownership exists between a husband and wife and where both qualify for the basic exclusion, the exclusion is $100 ($50 each) for taxable years ending prior to January 1, 1964 and $200 ($100 each) for taxable years beginning after December 31, 1963.

The dividend is also subject to a 4% dividends-received credit under Section 34, IRC 1954 for such dividends received before January 1, 1964 and to a 2% credit for such dividends received after December 31, 1963 and before January 1, 1965. No credit is allowed for dividends received after December 31, 1964.

CAPITAL GAIN.

The gain in respect to the cash and securities acquired after 12/31/53 is short-term or long-term capital gain depending upon the period of time the capital stock was held by the stockholder. Thus, the period of time is measured from the date of acquisition of the stock by the shareholder to the date of the liquidating dividend. [33]

OTHER ASSETS RECEIVED—HOLDING PERIOD.

The other assets received in liquidation result in no recognition of gain to the stockholders upon receipt of the liquidating dividend. Hence, for tax purposes, the receipt of such property is a continuing transaction as against a closed transaction. In such case, the holding period does not stop at the date of liquidating dividend but includes the period of time during which the stockholder held the capital stock. [34]

Example: The Corporation was organized on May 1, 1968 by X, an individual, and at the same time it acquired real property. During the calendar month of October 1969, the Corporation liquidated under Section 333. The stockholder received the real property on which no gain was recognized under the election Section 333. In December, 1969, the stockholder sold the real property at a gain. The gain is a long-term capital gain since the holding period runs from May 1, 1968 to the date of sale in December, 1969 (more than 6 months), (more than 12 months after 1969).

EXCEPTION TO GENERAL RULE—HOLDING PERIOD.

Under certain conditions, the general rule for the holding period does not apply. For example, a corporation owned a 99 year lease on land plus an option to purchase the land. After the corporation was in existence for seven years, the corporation and the stockholder adopted a plan to liquidate under Section 333. The assets distributed included the lease and the option to buy. The stockholder immediately following the liquidation exercised the option to buy the land. Four days later, the stockholder sold the land at a gain. The recognized gain on the sale of the land is short-term. The holding period of the stock cannot be "tacked" on. The stockholder in liquidation received the option to buy. He did not receive the land.[35]

WHERE TO START.

The basic starting point for a Section 333 liquidation is the balance sheet.

(a) "True" Earned Surplus. Since the earned surplus is taxed as an ordinary dividend, the accumulated earnings and profits (earned surplus) should be examined carefully to ascertain the "true" earned surplus. The surplus shown on the balance sheet is only a dollar amount. What is its composition? It is common for corporations, particularly closely held corporations, to declare non-taxable stock dividends which

merely transfer surplus to the capital account. In order to compute the "true" earned surplus for purposes of Section 333, these stock dividends should be added back to the earned surplus account. In other words, reverse the entry. All debits to the surplus account should be reviewed to determine if the transactions were merely bookkeeping entries or tax entries. [36]

A deficit (true) for purposes of Section 333 is considered zero and has in itself no effect on the gain or loss.

(b) Effect of Depreciation Recapture. As already indicated, if the fair market value of depreciable personal and real property is in excess of the adjusted (book) basis of the assets at the date of liquidation of the corporation under Section 333, IRC 1954, the corporation realizes ordinary income on the amount of depreciation subject to recapture. The recapture applies, in the case of depreciable personal property, only to liquidations which occur after December 31, 1962 and, in the case of depreciable real property, to liquidations occurring after December 31, 1963. The rules of computation are set forth in Chapters 3 and 4.

Warning. The recapture provisions may increase the accumulated earned surplus to a point where the calendar month method of liquidating may not be the most favorable method taxwise under which to liquidate the corporation. In fact, the adjustment for depreciation recapture may convert an accumulated deficit into an earned surplus. In such cases, an individual stockholder would be required to report a taxable ordinary dividend equal to his pro rata share of the *created* earned surplus based upon the recaptured depreciation.

Example 1: The balance sheet of the Y Corporation showed an accumulated deficit of $3,500 as of June 30, 1969. The corporation and its stockholders had elected to liquidate under Section 333 in the month of July 1969. Operating net income to the date of liquidation amounted to $2,000. The Federal corporate income tax on such income was $440 ($2,000 × 22%). There were no other surplus adjustments. Assume that the depreciation recapture provisions did not apply to the assets distributed. The accumulated deficit in July 1969 at liquidation was $1,940 ($3,500 − $2,000 + $440). The individual stockholders would have no ordinary dividend income to report as taxable income.

Example 2: Assume the same facts as in Example 1 above except that the depreciation subject to recapture and taxable as ordinary income to the corporation in its corporate income tax return for the period ending July 31, 1969 amounts to $10,000. The net income subject to corporate income tax would be $12,000 ($2,000 + $10,000), and the Federal income tax $2,640. The surplus at the date of distribution in July 1969 would be $5,860. Under the tax rules of Section 333, each stockholder of the corporation would be required to report as an ordinary dividend the pro rata share of the earned surplus at the date of liquidation, i.e. $5,860.

(c) Money. The amount of the money as compared with the earned surplus is another tax factor, i.e., capital gain, as described in other paragraphs of this chapter.

However, the possibility of paying off corporate debts and liabilities should be examined so as to reduce the amount of money. It is possible by this means to eliminate the capital gain feature of Section 333. However, the cancellation of a stockholder's debt has been held the equivalent of "cash." [37]

(d) Note Receivable from Stockholder. A note receivable from a stockholder held by the corporation constitutes money for purposes of determining the excess of cash over the earned surplus which is taxable as a capital gain. [38]

(e) Securities. The securities acquired by the corporation after December 31, 1953 are treated, in effect, the same as money to the extent of the fair market value as of the calendar month of liquidation. In other words, to measure the capital gain recognized, the money and the securities acquired after December 31, 1953 are totaled to determine the excess over the earned surplus. Securities acquired prior to January 1, 1954 are treated as "other assets" on which the gain is not recognized under this type of liquidation.

(f) "Other Assets." The gain on all "other assets" is deferred until such time as the assets are sold or otherwise disposed of by the shareholders following the liquidation.

Recapture of Investment Credit. The Revenue Act of 1962 provided for an investment tax credit on the purchase, or other acquisition, and, in some cases, the leasing of assets known as Section 38 Assets. [39] The provision became effective for tax years ending after December 31, 1961 but only as to qualified investments acquired, constructed, or reconstructed after December 31, 1961. As a result of later Revenue Acts (explained in Chapter 5), the investment credit was repealed and subsequently re-enacted. The estimated life established for the asset determined the amount of the investment credit. [40] If the asset was disposed of by the taxpayer prior to the established life, the law requires a recomputation of the allowed credit and, in some cases, the credit in whole or in part must be repaid as a tax in the year of disposition of the asset. [41] In other words, the credit previously allowed is recaptured in whole or in part.

The recapture provision applies to all sales, exchanges, transfers, distributions and involuntary conversions. The question is whether the investment credit is subject to recapture where there is a corporate liquidation under the calendar month method—Section 333. The statute provides that there is no recapture where there is a mere change in the form of conducting the business and where such property is retained in the trade or business and the taxpayer-stockholders retain a substantial interest in such trade or business. [42] Thus, if a corporation liquidates and the stockholder or stockholders continue to operate the business as a proprietorship or partnership with substantially the same interest, the liquidating corporation is not subject to recapture. However, in other cases, the liquidating corporation with its final return must repay the investment credit as recomputed based upon the early disposition.

However, in a subsequent sale or other disposition, the recapture provisions will apply to such disposition by the new entity.

BASIS OF PROPERTY RECEIVED IN LIQUIDATION.

The basis of the assets received (other than money) by the shareholders in liquidation under Section 333 is computed as follows:

Basis of capital stock redeemed or cancelled in liquidation	$xxxxxxxxxx
Minus: Money received in liquidation	xxxxxx
Plus: Total of amount of gain (ordinary and capital) recognized; the amount unsecured and specific liability	xxxxxxxxxx
Basis of "other property" received	$xxxxxxxxxx

If the stockholders received in liquidation more than one parcel or type of property, the basis arrived at in the formula above should be allocated to the various assets received on the basis of their fair market values. The net fair market value for this purpose is the fair market value less any specific mortgage or pledge to which it is subject.

The basis of the capital stock must be allocated over all types of assets including such assets as accounts receivable and other receivables. [43]

After determining the portion of the basis for each asset, the amount of the lien against such property is added back. Where a lien is applicable to more than one piece of property, the amount of the lien must be divided among the properties based upon fair market value of each parcel to the total. Whether the mortgage indebtedness is assumed by the shareholders or the property is taken subject to the mortgage is immaterial. [44]

Example: X Corporation was liquidated under Section 333. A, an individual stockholder, owned 100 shares of the capital stock for which he received in full cancellation $1,000 cash; $4,000 fair market value of securities acquired after 12/31/53, and $22,000 fair market value of other property subject to a lien of $1,000. A also assumed a corporate liability of $2,000. The basis of the stock to A was $12,000. At liquidation, A's share of the corporation's earned surplus was $2,500.

Assets received in liquidation:	
Cash	$ 1,000
Securities acquired after 12/31/53	4,000
	$ 5,000
Other assets (less liabilities)	19,000
Total	$24,000
Less: Basis of stock	12,000
Actual Gain	$12,000
Earned Surplus	$ 2,500

Recognized Gain to Stockholder:

Earned surplus (ordinary dividend)	$ 2,500
Money and securities (capital gain)	2,500

The basis of the securities and other assets is $19,000, computed as follows:

Adjusted basis of stock cancelled	$12,000
Less: Money received	1,000
	$11,000
Add: Liability assumed	2,000
Specific lien against property	1,000
Gain recognized (ordinary and capital)	5,000
Basis of assets	$19,000

The basis ($19,000) less the specific lien ($1,000) or $18,000 must be apportioned among the classes of property received (other than money) as follows:

$$21,000/25,000 \times 18,000 = 15,120 \quad \text{plus} \quad \$1,000 = \$16,120 \text{ (Basis of}$$
$$\text{other property)}$$
$$4,000/25,000 \times 18,000 = \$2,880 \text{ (Basis of securities)}$$

Example: Corporation X elected to liquidate under Section 333 during the month of May, 1969. Smith, the sole stockholder, paid $10,000 for the capital stock at the time the corporation was formed. At the date of liquidation, the balance sheet was as follows:

	Per Books	F.M.V.
Cash	$ 7,000	$ 7,000
Accounts Receivable	50,000	45,000
Land & Building (Net)	80,000	200,000
	$137,000	$252,000
(balance forward)	$137,000	$252,000
Accounts Payable	$ 23,000	
Mortgage on Land & Building	100,000	
Capital Stock	10,000	
Earned Surplus	4,000	
	$137,000	

COMPUTATION OF BASIS OF
"OTHER PROPERTY"

Adjusted Basis of Stock Cancelled		$ 10,000
Less: Money Received		7,000
		$ 3,000
Add: Liabilities Assumed	$ 23,000	
Specific Liens	$100,000	
Gain Recognized (ordinary		
& Capital Gain)	7,000	$130,000
Basis of Assets Subject to Apportionment		$133,000
Minus: Specific Liens		100,000
Basis to be Apportioned		$ 33,000
Accounts Receivable		$ 45,000
Land & Building	$200,000	
Less: Specific Liens	100,000	100,000
		$145,000

$$\frac{45,000}{145,000} \times \$33,000 = \$10,241 \quad \cdots \cdots \cdots \cdots \quad \$ 10,241$$

$$\frac{100,000}{145,000} \times \$33,000 = \$22,759 + \$100,000 = \quad \$122,759$$

$$\$133,000$$

The basis of the accounts receivable is $10,241 while the basis of the land and building is $122,759 which must be again apportioned between the land and the building based upon the proportionate fair market value.

Specific Summary Examples—Individual Stockholders: The following examples illustrate the various problems which usually arise in Section 333 liquidations. The problems are not related to each other.

	1	2	3	4	5	6
Distribution to stockholder:						
Money	$ 0	$ 0	$ 5,000	$ 5,000	$ 5,000	$ 5,000
Securities	0	0	0	0	0	10,000
	$ 0	$ 0	$ 5,000	$ 5,000	$ 5,000	$15,000
Other Assets	80,000	80,000	80,000	80,000	80,000	80,000
Total	$80,000	$80,000	$85,000	$85,000	$85,000	$95,000

Basis of stock-holders' stock	1	2	3	4	5	6
	20,000	20,000	20,000	20,000	20,000	20,000
Actual Gain	$60,000	$60,000	$65,000	$65,000	$65,000	$75,000
Earned Surplus (or deficit)	$ 0	$(5,000)	$ 0	$ 8,000	$ 2,000	$ 8,000
Application of Section 333 Ordinary dividend:	$ 0	$ 0	$ 0	$ 8,000	$ 2,000	$ 8,000
Capital gain:	0	0	5,000	0	3,000	7,000
Non-recognized gain:	60,000	60,000	60,000	57,000	60,000	60,000

Specific Summary Examples—Corporate Stockholders: Assume the same facts as above, except that one of the stockholders is a corporation whose basis for the capital stock is $20,000.

Application of Section 333 Capital gain	$ 0	$ 0	$ 5,000	$ 8,000	$ 5,000	$15,000
Non-recognized gain	60,000	60,000	60,000	57,000	60,000	60,000

The Other 20%: Under Section 333, IRC 1954, stockholders possessing at least 80% of the voting stock must elect. Suppose, however, that there are two stockholders. A owns stock possessing 85% of the voting power and B 15%. A and B disagree as to the method of liquidating their corporation. As a result, A elects to liquidate under Section 333; B does not.

A will compute his recognized gain under Section 333, provided he executes the proper forms and files them timely. B, on the other hand, will be required to use Section 331 (a), IRC 1954, the complete general method of liquidation. (See Chapter 3.)

Procedure—Form 964: Form 964, in duplicate, must be filed by each qualified electing shareholder within 30 days after the adoption of the plan of liquidation. The plan of liquidation is normally adopted by a resolution of the directors and stockholders in joint or separate meetings. The election is considered as timely filed if Form 964 is placed in the mail on or before midnight of the 30th day after the adoption of the plan as evidenced by the postmark on the envelope or other available evidence. Due to the strict interpretation of the 30-day period, it is suggested that the forms should be mailed by certified or registered mail to the Director, Internal Revenue Service Center. If delivered to the office of the District Director personally, it is an excellent idea to have a third copy stamped by the Internal Revenue Service with their official date stamp.

The electing stockholder must be the actual owner of the stock and not a mere record holder such as a nominee. Moreover, the stockholder must be the owner of the stock at the time of the adoption of the plan of liquidation. Form 964 in the case of an individual stockholder may be signed by the shareholder's attorney or agent, provided such action is specifically authorized by a power of attorney, which if not previously filed, should be attached to Form 964. If the election is made by the executor, administrator or trustee or similar fiduciary on behalf of an estate or trust, such person may execute Form 964 provided it is accompanied by letters testamentary or other instruments authorizing the right to sign.

The election by a corporate stockholder should be signed in the name of the corporation by an officer empowered under the law to sign for the corporation.

Form 964 (in duplicate) must be filed with the District Director of Internal Revenue for the district in which the final return of the corporation will be filed.

A third copy of Form 964 must be attached to and be made a part of the stockholder's income tax return for the taxable year in which the transfer of all of the property under the liquidation occurs. [45]

Where a corporation timely filed Form 966 as discussed below but the stockholders failed to file Form 964, Section 333 was held not applicable. Thus, the filing of Form 964 by each stockholder is a "must." [46]

Form 966: Each corporation to be liquidated under Section 333 must file Form 966 within 30 days after the adoption of the plan of liquidation. The form must be filed with the District Director of Internal Revenue in the district in which the corporation will file its final return. There must be attached to such Form 966 a certified copy of the resolution adopting the plan of liquidation. Any amendment to the original plan requires the filing of an additional Form 966, together with a certified copy of the amendment. [47]

Form 966 must be filed regardless of whether the shareholders of the liquidating corporation will show a recognized gain or not.

In addition to the specific information on Form 966, there must be attached to the form when filed a statement showing the following information: (1) the number of shares of each class of stock outstanding at the time of the adoption of the plan and a description of the voting power of each class of stock; (2) a list of all the stockholders owning stock at the time of the adoption of the plan of liquidation and the number of shares of each class of stock owned by each shareholder, the certificate number and the total number of votes to which each is entitled; (3) a list of all corporate shareholders as of January 1, 1954, the number of shares owned and the number of votes to which each is entitled, and a statement of all changes in ownership from January 1, 1954 to date of adoption of the plan of liquidation. [48]

Form 966 must be signed in the corporate name, followed by the signature and title of a corporate officer empowered under the laws of the state or country where incorporated to sign for the corporation. The corporate seal must be affixed to Form

966. In the event that the corporation has lost the seal or has no seal, the form (966) must be filed, accompanied by a certified copy of a corporate resolution passed by the Board of Directors which empowers the officer with the authority to sign for the corporation.

Records by Shareholders: The electing shareholders are required to keep permanent records in substantial form concerning the distribution received in liquidation. Thus, for example, a list and a description of each asset received must be retained as a basis to establish gain or loss on any subsequent sale or exchange of such assets.

Form 1040—Electing Shareholder: The shareholder must attach to his individual income tax returns for the year in which the liquidation occurs the following: (1) a statement of his ownership in the liquidating corporation as of the date of distribution, showing the number of shares of each class owned on such date and the cost or other basis of each such share; (2) a list of all the property, including money, received upon the distribution, showing the fair market value of each item of such property other than money on the date of distribution and stating what items, if any, consist of stock or securities acquired by liquidating corporation after December 31, 1953; (3) a statement of his rateable share of the earnings and profits of the liquidating corporation accumulated after February 28, 1961, computed without diminution by reason of distributions made during the month of liquidation; and (4) a copy of such shareholder's written election—Form 964. [49]

Form 1096: Form 1096 must be filed as the letter of transmittal to accompany Form 1099 L. It is filed in duplicate.

Form 1099 L for each shareholder receiving a liquidating dividend or distribution of $600 or more must be attached to the duplicate copy of the form, Form 1096, the letter of transmittal.

Form 1099 L: Every corporation making any distribution of $600 or more during a calendar year to any shareholder in liquidation of the whole or any part of its capital stock must file a return of information on Form 1096 and 1099 L.[50] A separate Form 1099 L must be prepared for each shareholder. Form 1099 L must be filed on or before February 28 of the year following the calendar year in which the distribution in liquidation occurred. The forms are attached to Form 1096 and filed in the Internal Revenue Information Centers. (See Footnote 36 following Chapter 6.)

DISSOLUTION FOLLOWING LIQUIDATION?

Neither the Code nor the Regulations provide for the legal dissolution of the corporation. Based upon a current trend of decisions and the strict interpretation of Section 333, it would be advisable to legally dissolve within a reasonable time after the liquidation has been completed as already stated earlier in the chapter.

PERSONAL HOLDING COMPANIES—RELIEF.

The Revenue Act of 1964 amended the provisions relating to personal holding companies so that many corporations which were not personal holding companies in 1963 and prior years are classed as personal holding companies for 1964 and subsequent years. [51] Under special rules, a personal holding company as the result of the 1964 tests may elect to liquidate under certain favorable provisions.

The rules and their application may be simply stated as follows: [52]

(a) A corporation was not a personal holding company for one of its two most recent years ending before 2/26/64 but would have been if the 1964 tests had applied to its income.

(b) If such a corporation liquidates before 1966, the tax liability for 1964 and 1965 is computed based on the pre-1964 personal holding company tests. In other words, the personal holding company tests are those which were applicable for 1963 and prior years.

(c) If such a corporation liquidates before 1/1/67, the rateable share of the earned surplus is taxable to individual and corporate stockholders as long-term capital gain (not as an ordinary dividend) and no capital gain will be imposed upon the distribution of stock and securities acquired by the corporation prior to 1963.

(d) If such a corporation liquidates after 12/31/66, the rules in (c) above apply except that the stockholders are taxed on post-1966 earned surplus as if it were an ordinary dividend.

The election to liquidate may be revoked if the election is made in error as to the results as provided for in the Code.

CITATIONS

[1] N.H. Kelley, et al., Memo TC 1951–43.

[2] Slater v Comm., 356 F 2d 668, aff. Memo TC 1964–169.

[3] Sec. 333, IRC 1954.

[4] Reg. Sec. 1.333–1 (b) (1).

[5] Rev. Rul. 54–518.

[6] Rev. Rul. 60–50; Rev. Rul. 61–156.

[7] Sec. 333 (a) (1), IRC 1954.

[8] Chapter 8–Minutes.

[9] Sec. 333 (a) (2), IRC 1954.

[10] *Ibid.*

[11] Reg. Sec. 1.333 (b) (1).

[12] Rev. Rul. 56–286, CB 1956–1, pg. 172.

[13] Reg. Sec. 1.333–3; Posey v U.S. 449 F 2d 228.

[14] N.H. Kelley, et al., Memo TC 1951; Lambert, 338 F 2d 4, aff. TC Memo 1963–296.

[15] Virginia E. Ragen, 33 TC 706.

[16] Lambert, Memo TC 1963–296, aff. 338 F 2d 4; Posey v U.S. 449 F 2d 228.

[17] Sec. 333 (c), IRC 1954; Reg. Sec. 1.333–2.

[18] Rev. Rul. 56–212, CB 1956–1, pg. 170.

[19] Reg. Sec. 1.333–2 (b) (1).

[20] Sam Goldman, Memo TC 1950.

[21] Est. of Robert B. Meyer, et al., v Comm., 200 F 2d 592, rev. 15 TC 850.

[22] Cockrell v U.S., DC, Texas, Dallas Div., 1 AFTR 2d 394.

[23] Raymond v U.S., 269 F 2d 181, aff. DC, Mich., 1 AFTR 2d 1275.

[24] Frank T. Shull, 271 F 2d 447, rev. 34 TC 533 (Virginia); Estate of Lena B. Knox, TC Memo 1961–129 (Georgia).

[25] Reg. Sec. 1.333–4 (a).

[26] *Ibid.*

[27] Sec. 333 (e) (1), IRC 1954; Reg. Sec. 1.333–4 (b) (1).

[28] Sec. 1245; 1250, IRC 1954; Chapters 3 & 4.

[29] Sec. 1245 (d); 1250 (h), IRC 1954.

[30] Rev. Rul. 56–286, CB 1956–1, pg. 172.

[31] Reg. Sec. 1.333–4 (b) (2).

[32]Reg. Sec. 1.333–4 (b) (2).

[33]Sec. 1223, IRC 1954.

[34]Letter Ruling dated 1/1/45, signed Norman D. Cann, Deputy Commissioner, by R.S. Gayton, Head of Division.

[35]Molbreak, 61 TC No. 43.

[36]Sec. 312, IRC, 1954.

[37]Walker, DC, Fla., 11/27/62.

[38]Rev. Rul. 70–409.

[39]Sec. 48, IRC 1954.

[40]Sec. 46 (c), IRC 1954.

[41]Sec. 47, IRC 1954.

[42]Sec. 47 (b), IRC 1954, Committee Report, Rev. Act of 1962.

[43]Garrow, 43 TC 890.

[44]Sec. 334 (c), IRC 1954; Reg. Sec. 1.334–2.

[45]Reg. Sec. 1.333–3; Instruction to Form 964.

[46]Posey v U.S., 449 F 2d 228.

[47]Sec. 6043, IRC 1954; Reg. Sec. 1.6043–1.

[48]Reg. Sec. 1.6043–1 (b) (2).

[49]Reg. Sec. 1.333–5 (a).

[50]Reg. Sec. 1.6043–2 (a).

[51]Sec. 541–545, IRC 1954.

[52]Sec. 333 (g), IRC as added by the Rev. Act of 1964.

NINE

Calendar Month Liquidation:
Specimen Problem

THE XYZ CORPORATION

of 8 Moore Street, New York, N.Y. 10006 was organized on June 16, 1951 by E. Davis (Second Avenue, Plainfield, New York) and F. Factor (Hines Road, Fairview, New Jersey). At organization, E. Davis subscribed for 250 shares (Certificate No. 1) and F. Factor for 750 shares (Certificate No. 2) of the 1,000 shares common no par value capital stock. Each share is entitled to one vote. The two stockholders paid in $2,500 and $7,500, respectively. The stockholders and their accountant, Jay Count, were the directors of the corporation. The corporation adopted the calendar year and accrual basis for reporting its corporate net income for Federal income tax purposes, filing on Form 1120. The corporation filed its return in the Internal Revenue Center at Holtsville, New York. Identification #11-1234567. Social Security #E Davis 100-30-1000; F. Factor 104-04-4000.

At 10 A.M. on July 28, 1974, the directors and the stockholders held a joint special meeting at the office of the corporation's attorney, Smith and Law of 1 Wall Street, New York, N.Y. At this special meeting, the directors and the stockholders adopted a resolution to liquidate the Corporation under Section 333 during the month of August, 1974. (*Note:* In some states, separate special meetings must be held by the directors and the stockholders; the directors adopting the resolution to liquidate and the stockholders thereafter approving the directors' action.)

The assets and liabilities of the corporation were distributed in complete liquidation to the stockholders during the month of August, 1974 and legally dissolved on September 12, 1974 under the laws of the State of New York.

The balance sheet as of the date of liquidation in August, 1974 was as follows:

XYZ CORPORATION

ASSETS		Per Books
Cash		$ 7,000
Land No. 1 ·		15,000
Apartment building No. 1	$120,000	
Less: Reserve for depreciation	30,000	90,000
Land No. 2		5,000
Apartment building No. 2	$ 65,000	
Less: Reserve for depreciation	15,000	50,000
Rent Receivable		1,000
Total		$168,000

LIABILITIES & CAPITAL		
Bills payable		$ 13,400
Mortgage payable No. 1		100,000
Mortgage payable No. 2		40,000
Capital stock		10,000
Earned Surplus as of 12/31/73	$ 3,000	
Net Income 1/1/74–8/31/74 including $1,200 recaptured depreciation	1,600	4,600
Total		$168,000

Based upon expert appraisals, the assets of the corporation for purposes of liquidation were valued as follows:

XYZ CORPORATION

ASSETS	Fair Market Value August 1974
Cash	$ 7,000
Land No. 1	30,000
Apartment building No. 1	170,000
Land No. 2	10,000
Apartment building No. 2	100,000
Rent Receivable	1,000
Total	$318,000

WAIVER OF NOTICE OF JOINT SPECIAL MEETING
OF STOCKHOLDERS AND DIRECTORS OF
XYZ CORPORATION

We, the undersigned, being all of the stockholders and all of the directors of the XYZ Corporation do hereby waive all notice of a Joint Special Meeting of Stockholders and Directors of said corporation, and do hereby agree and consent that the 28th day of July, 1974 at 10 A.M. in the forenoon, be and same is hereby fixed as the time, and the office of Smith and Law, Esqs., 1 Wall Street, in the City of New York, County of New York, State of New York, as the place for holding the same; and that the purpose of said meeting be the adoption of a plan for the complete liquidation of the corporation, and for a distribution of all of the assets of such corporation in complete liquidation during the month of August, 1974; and for the transaction of such other business as may lawfully come before said meeting.

Dated, the 28th day of July, 1974.

Stockholders	Directors
E. Davis	*E. Davis*
F. Factor	*F. Factor*
	Jay Count

MINUTES OF A JOINT SPECIAL MEETING
OF STOCKHOLDERS AND DIRECTORS OF
XYZ CORPORATION

A Joint Special Meeting of Stockholders and Directors of the XYZ Corporation was held at the office of Smith and Law, Esqs., 1 Wall Street, New York City, New York on the 28th day of July 1974 at 10 A.M. in the forenoon.

The following, being all of the stockholders and the directors, were present:

STOCKHOLDERS	DIRECTORS
E. Davis	*E. Davis*
F. Factor	*F. Factor*
	Jay Count

E. Davis, President of the Corporation, acted as Chairman of the meeting and F. Factor, the Secretary, as Secretary thereof.

A written waiver of notice of this Meeting, signed by all of the stockholders and directors, was then presented and read by the Secretary and was ordered appended to these Minutes.

The Chairman announced that the purpose of this meeting was to discuss and act upon a proposal to liquidate and dissolve the corporation. Counsel for the Corporation were asked for their opinion of the tax results to the corporation and to the stockholders, caused by the liquidation and distribution of the corporate assets. The stockholders expressed a desire to liquidate and distribute the assets of the corporation since the assets had sharply appreciated in value since acquisition. After hearing Counsel's explanation of the Tax Laws under the 1954 Internal Revenue Code, especially Section 333 thereof, and under the New York Franchise Tax Laws; after a full discussion by the Stockholders and Directors of the Corporation; after a report by the President of the Corporation as to the financial position, the following Resolution was unanimously adopted:

RESOLVED, that the following plan of liquidation, pursuant to Section 333 of the 1954 Internal Revenue Code, be and the same is hereby adopted:

I. Within thirty (30) days after the date of this meeting, Counsel for the Corporation shall file Form 966 with the District Director of Internal Revenue, Manhattan, New York, attaching thereto a certified copy of this Resolution, indicating that the Stockholders and the Directors have adopted a plan of liquidation pursuant to Section 333, Internal Revenue Code of 1954.

II. The Counsel for the Corporation shall see that the stockholders prepare and file within thirty (30) days of this meeting, Form 964 in duplicate with the District Director of Internal Revenue, Manhattan, New York, thereby electing the benefits of Section 333, Internal Revenue Code of 1954.

III. That the Corporation, by its duly authorized officers, proceed to liquidate and transfer the assets and liabilities to the stockholders in cancellation and redemption of the capital stock within the calendar month of August 1974.

IV. That as soon as practical after the distribution and transfer of the assets and liabilities to the stockholders in exchange for their capital stock, Counsel for the Corporation shall file a certificate for the dissolution of the Corporation pursuant to the provisions of the New York State Stock Corporation Law, and that the officers of the Corporation are hereby authorized to execute any and all documents necessary to effectuate such dissolution.

V. That the officers and directors be and they are hereby empowered, authorized and directed to proceed in accordance with the resolution hereby adopted by the stockholders and directors, said officers and directors being authorized to adopt any subsequent resolutions to effectuate the intent of the Stockholders and Directors to liquidate the Corporation in accordance with a plan of liquidation adopted pursuant to Section 333, Internal Revenue Code of 1954.

There being no further business before the Meeting, the Meeting adjourned.

Dated: July 28, 1974.

F. Factor
_____
Secretary

ATTEST:

E. Davis
_____
President

Form 964 (Rev. July 1972) Department of the Treasury Internal Revenue Service	**Election of Shareholder under Section 333 Liquidation** (To be filed in duplicate within 30 days after the adoption of the plan of liquidation. See Instructions on page 4.)

Name of shareholder E. DAVIS	Identifying Number (See instruction F.) 100–03–3000

Address of shareholder (Number, street, city, State, and ZIP code)
SECOND AVENUE, PLAINFIELD, NEW YORK 11751

Name of corporation XYZ CORPORATION	Employer Identification Number 12-1234567

Address of corporation (Number, street, city, State, and ZIP code)
8 MOORE STREET, NEW YORK, N.Y. 10006

Time and date of adoption of plan of liquidation 10:00 A.M. JULY 28, 1974	Calendar month of transfer of all property AUGUST 1974

The above named shareholder hereby elects to have recognized and taxed in accordance with section 333 of the Internal Revenue Code the gain on each and every share of the capital stock of the above named corporation owned by him at the time of the adoption of the plan of complete liquidation providing for a distribution in complete cancellation or redemption of all corporate stock and for the transfer of all corporate property under the liquidation entirely within the above stated calendar month of transfer of all property.

SCHEDULE A
Statement of Shares of Stock Owned at the Time and Date of Adoption of Plan of Liquidation

Class of stock	Certificate numbers	Number of shares	Total number of votes to which entitled on adoption of plan of liquidation
COMMON – NO PAR VALUE	1	250	250

SCHEDULE B
Statement of Shares of Stock Owned on Date of Execution of Election

Class of stock	Certificate numbers	Number of shares	Total number of votes to which entitled on adoption of plan of liquidation
COMMON — NO PAR VALUE	1	250	250

SCHEDULE C
Statement of Shares of Stock Owned on January 1, 1954
(To be filled in only by corporate shareholders)

Class of stock	Certificate numbers	Number of shares	Total number of votes to which entitled on adoption of plan of liquidation

Attach a statement showing all shares acquired or disposed of between January 1, 1954, and the time and date of adoption of plan of liquidation, both dates inclusive, giving date on which any share was acquired or disposed of, class of stock, the certificate numbers thereof, the number of shares involved in each transaction, the total number of votes to which entitled on adoption of plan of liquidation, and the name of the person from whom acquired or to whom transferred.   **NONE**

SCHEDULE D

If any of thé shares listed in any of the above schedules are not registered in the name of the person by whom this election is made, list below the name of the person in whose name such stock is registered giving the class of stock, the certificate numbers thereof, the number of shares, the total number of votes to which entitled on adoption of plan of liquidation, and all facts pertinent to the claim of ownership.

(Use additional sheets if necessary)

Under penalties of perjury, I declare that I have examined this return, including accompanying schedules and statements, and to the best of my knowledge and belief it is true, correct, and complete.

AUGUST 8, 1974   E. DAVIS

    (Date)   (Electing shareholder)

If a corporation

> The Internal Revenue Service does not require a seal on this form, but if one is used, please place it here.

    (Date)   (Signature of officer)   (Title)

Form 964
(Rev. July 1972)
Department of the Treasury
Internal Revenue Service

Election of Shareholder under Section 333 Liquidation

(To be filed in duplicate within 30 days after the adoption of the plan of liquidation. See Instructions on page 4.)

Name of shareholder	Identifying Number (See instruction F.)
F. FACTOR	104-04-4000

Address of shareholder (Number, street, city, State, and ZIP code)
HINES ROAD, FAIRVIEW, NEW JERSEY 17001

Name of corporation	Employer Identification Number
XYZ CORPORATION	12-1234567

Address of corporation (Number, street, city, State, and ZIP code)
8 MOORE STREET, NEW YORK, N.Y. 10006

Time and date of adoption of plan of liquidation	Calendar month of transfer of all property
10:00 A.M. JULY 28, 1974	AUGUST 1974

The above named shareholder hereby elects to have recognized and taxed in accordance with section 333 of the Internal Revenue Code the gain on each and every share of the capital stock of the above named corporation owned by him at the time of the adoption of the plan of complete liquidation providing for a distribution in complete cancellation or redemption of all corporate stock and for the transfer of all corporate property under the liquidation entirely within the above stated calendar month of transfer of all property.

SCHEDULE A
Statement of Shares of Stock Owned at the Time and Date of Adoption of Plan of Liquidation

Class of stock	Certificate numbers	Number of shares	Total number of votes to which entitled on adoption of plan of liquidation
COMMON – NO PAR VALUE	2	750	750

Form **964** (Rev. 7-72)

SCHEDULE B
Statement of Shares of Stock Owned on Date of Execution of Election

Class of stock	Certificate numbers	Number of shares	Total number of votes to which entitled on adoption of plan of liquidation
COMMON – NO PAR VALUE	2	750	750

SCHEDULE C
Statement of Shares of Stock Owned on January 1, 1954
(To be filled in only by corporate shareholders)

Class of stock	Certificate numbers	Number of shares	Total number of votes to which entitled on adoption of plan of liquidation

Attach a statement showing all shares acquired or disposed of between January 1, 1954, and the time and date of adoption of plan of liquidation, both dates inclusive, giving date on which any share was acquired or disposed of, class of stock, the certificate numbers thereof, the number of shares involved in each transaction, the total number of votes to which entitled on adoption of plan of liquidation, and the name of the person from whom acquired or to whom transferred.　　**NONE**

SCHEDULE D

If any of the shares listed in any of the above schedules are not registered in the name of the person by whom this election is made, list below the name of the person in whose name such stock is registered giving the class of stock, the certificate numbers thereof, the number of shares, the total number of votes to which entitled on adoption of plan of liquidation, and all facts pertinent to the claim of ownership.

(Use additional sheets if necessary)

Under penalties of perjury, I declare that I have examined this return, including accompanying schedules and statements, and to the best of my knowledge and belief it is true, correct, and complete.

AUGUST 8, 1974   F. FACTOR

--------------------------   --------------------------

(Date)   (Electing shareholder)

If a corporation

The Internal Revenue Service does not require a seal on this form, but if one is used, please place it here.

--------------------------   --------------------------   --------------------------

(Date)   (Signature of officer)   (Title)

Form **966** (Rev. Nov. 1973) Department of the Treasury Internal Revenue Service	**Corporate Dissolution or Liquidation** (Required under Section 6043(a) of the Internal Revenue Code)	

Please type or print

Name of corporation XYZ CORPORATION	Employer identification number 11-1234567
Address (Number and street) 8 MOORE STREET	Check type of return
City or town, State and ZIP code NEW YORK, NEW YORK 10006	☒ 1120 ☐ 1120DISC ☐ 1120L ☐ 1120M ☐ 1120S

1 Date incorporated JUNE 16, 1951	2 Place incorporated STATE OF NEW YORK	3 Type of liquidation ☒ Complete ☐ Partial

4 Internal Revenue Service Center where last income tax return was filed and taxable year covered thereby Service Center ▶ HOLTSVILLE, NEW YORK   Taxable year ▶ 1973

5 Date of adoption of resolution or plan of dissolution, or complete or partial liquidation JULY 28, 1974	6 Taxable year of final return PERIOD ENDING AUGUST 1974	7 Total number of shares outstanding at time of adoption of plan or liquidation
		Common 1,000	Preferred ---

8 Dates of any amendments to plan of dissolution --	9 Section of the Code under which the corporation is to be dissolved or liquidated 333	10 If this return is in respect of an amendment of or supplement to a resolution or plan previously adopted and return has previously been filed in respect of such resolution or plan, give the date such return was filed ---

11. Liquidation Within One Calendar Month.—If the corporation is a domestic corporation, and the plan of liquidation provides for a distribution in complete cancellation or redemption of all the capital stock of the corporation and for the transfer of all the property of the corporation under the liquidation entirely within one calendar month pursuant to section 333, and any shareholder claims the benefit of such section, then the corporation must also submit:

(a) A description of the voting power of each class of stock;

(b) A list of all the shareholders owning stock at the time of the adoption of the plan of liquidation, together with the number of shares of each class of stock owned by each shareholder, the certificate numbers thereof, and the total number of votes to which entitled on the adoption of the plan of liquidation;

(c) A list of all corporate shareholders as of January 1, 1954, together with the number of shares of each class of stock owned by each such shareholder, the certificate numbers thereof, the total number of votes to which entitled on the adoption of the plan of liquidation, and a statement of all changes in ownership of stock by corporate shareholders between January 1, 1954, and the date of the adoption of the plan of liquidation, both dates inclusive; and

(d) A computation as described in section 1.6043-2(b) (following the format in Revenue Procedure 65-10, C.B. 1965-1,738 and Revenue Procedure 67-12, C.B. 1967, 589) of accumulated earnings and profits including all items of income and expense accrued up to the date on which the transfer of all property is completed.

Attach a certified copy of the resolution or plan, together with all amendments or supplements not previously filed.

Under penalties of perjury, I declare that I have examined this return, including accompanying schedules and statements, and to the best of my knowledge and belief it is true, correct, and complete.

The Internal Revenue Service does not require a seal on this form, but if one is used, please place it here.	8/8/74 Date	E. DAVIS Signature of officer	PRESIDENT Title

Instructions

1. Who must file.—This form must be filed by every corporation that is to be dissolved or whose stock is to be liquidated in whole or in part.

Shareholders electing to be covered under section 333 of the Code must also file Form 964 within 30 days after the date of adoption of the plan of liquidation.

2. When to file.—This form must be filed within 30 days after the adoption of the resolution or plan for or in respect of the dissolution of a corporation or the liquidation in whole or in part of its capital stock. If after the filing of a Form 966 there is an amendment or supplement to the resolution or plan, an additional Form 966 based on the resolution or plan as amended or supplemented must be filed within 30 days after the adoption of such amendment or supplement. A return in respect of an amendment or supplement will be deemed sufficient if it gives the date the prior return was filed and contains a certified copy of such amendment or supplement and all other information required by this form which was not given in such prior return.

3. Where to file.—This form must be filed with the Internal Revenue Service Center with which the corporation is required to file its income tax return.

4. Signature.—The return must be signed either by the president, vice president, treasurer, assistant treasurer or chief accounting officer, or by any other corporate officer (such as tax officer) who is authorized to sign. A receiver, trustee, or assignee must sign any return which he is required to file on behalf of a corporation.

CERTIFIED COPY OF RESOLUTION
XYZ CORPORATION

I hereby certify that the following Resolution was unanimously adopted at a Special Joint Meeting of the Stockholders and Directors held on the 28th day of July, 1974.

RESOLVED, that the following plan of liquidation, pursuant to Section 333 of the 1954 Internal Revenue Code, be and the same is hereby adopted:

I. Within thirty (30) days after the date of this meeting, Counsel for the Corporation shall file Form 966 with the District Director of Internal Revenue, Manhattan, New York, attaching thereto a certified copy of this Resolution, indicating that the Stockholders and the Directors have adopted a plan of liquidation pursuant to Section 333, Internal Revenue Code of 1954.

II. The Counsel for the Corporation shall see that the stockholders prepare and file within thirty (30) days of this meeting, Form 964 in duplicate with the District Director of Internal Revenue, Manhattan, New York, thereby electing the benefits of Section 333, Internal Revenue Code of 1954.

III. That the Corporation, by its duly authorized officers proceed to liquidate and transfer the assets and liabilities to the stockholders in cancellation and redemption of the capital stock within the calendar month of August, 1974.

IV. That as soon as practical after the distribution and transfer of the assets and liabilities to the stockholders in exchange for their capital stock, Counsel for the Corporation shall file a certificate for the dissolution of the Corporation pursuant to the provisions of the New York State Stock Corporation Law, and that the officers of the Corporation are hereby authorized to execute any and all documents necessary to effectuate such dissolution.

V. That the officers and directors be and they are hereby empowered, authorized and directed to proceed in accordance with the resolution hereby adopted by the stockholders and directors, said officers and directors being authorized to adopt any subsequent resolutions to effectuate the intent of the Stockholders and Directors to liquidate the Corporation in accordance with a plan of liquidation adopted pursuant to Section 333, Internal Revenue Code of 1954.

There being no further business before the Meeting, the Meeting adjourned.

Dated: July 28, 1974.

F. Factor
_____
Secretary

SCHEDULE TO BE ATTACHED TO FORM 966

1. Number of shares outstanding at adoption of plan	1,000
Number of votes per share	1
Total number of votes	1,000

2. *Stockholders at date of adoption of plan*	*Number of shares*	*Certificate number*	*Number of votes*
E. Davis	250	No. 1	250
F. Factor	750	No. 2	750

3. No corporate stockholders as of 1/1/54

4. Changes in ownership–January 1, 1954 to July 28, 1974, date of adoption of plan: No corporate stockholders between 1/1/54 and date of liquidation.

NOTE: Information in 3 and 4 applies only to corporate stockholders.

FORM 1120 (FINAL RETURN)
CORPORATION INCOME TAX RETURN

A final return for the XYZ Corporation showing a Taxable Income of $1,600, including recapture of depreciation (see Balance Sheet) must be filed for the period January 1, 1974 to August 31, 1974. This return will show the Taxable Income of $1,600 with all of the details and the schedules completely filled in. The balance sheet, however, will only show the assets and liabilities and capital at January 1, 1974. No assets and liabilities will be shown at August 31, 1974 (End of Taxable Year). However, in this column of the balance sheet "End of Taxable Year" a statement such as "Assets and Liabilities Distributed in Liquidation under Section 333, IRC 1954 during the month of August, 1974" should be inserted.

The final return should be filed within two and a half months after the date of dissolution with the District Director in the district in which the corporation usually files its return.

COMPUTATION OF RECOGNIZED GAIN ON LIQUIDATION

Distribution to Stockholders:	*E. Davis*	*F. Factor*	*Total*
Money	$ 1,750	$ 5,250	$ 7,000
Securities acquired after 12/31/53	0	0	0
	$ 1,750	$ 5,250	$ 7,000
Rent Receivable	250	750	1,000
Other Assets (which have appreciated in value but unrealized at liquidation under Section 333)	77,500	232,500	310,000
Total Distribution	$79,500	$238,500	$318,000

Basis of Stockholder's Stock:	2,500	7,500	10,000
Actual Gain:	$77,000	$231,000	$308,000
Earned Surplus:	$ 1,150	$ 3,450	$ 4,600

Application of Section 333:

Ordinary Dividend	$ 1,150	$ 3,450	$ 4,600
Capital Gain (Long-term)	600	1,800	2,400
Non-recognized Gain	75,250	225,750	301,000

COMPUTATION OF BASIS OF OTHER ASSETS

Adjusted Basis of Stock Cancelled		$ 10,000
Less: Money Received		7,000
		$ 3,000
Add: Liabilities assumed (Bills Payable) . . .	$ 13,400	
Specific liens against property (Mortgages)	140,000	
Gain recognized (ordinary and capital gain)	7,000	
		160,400
Basis of Assets (subject to apportionment) . .		$ 163,400
Basis of Assets subject to apportionment . . .		$ 163,400
Minus: Specific liens against property		140,000
Basis to be apportioned		$ 23,400
Rent		$ 1,000
Land and Building No. 1	$200,000	
Less: Specific lien	100,000	100,000
Land and Building No. 2	$110,000	
Less: Specific lien	40,000	70,000
Total		171,000

1,000/171,000 × 23,400	=	$ 136.84
100,000/171,000 × 23,400 = 13,684.21 plus 100,000	=	113,684.21
70,000/171,000 × 23,400 = 9,578.95 plus 40,000	=	49,578.95
		$163,400.00

SCHEDULE TO BE ATTACHED TO FORM 1040
OF E. DAVIS FOR CALENDAR YEAR 1974

E. Davis was stockholder in the XYZ Corporation of 8 Moore Street, New York, N.Y. 10006 which was liquidated under Section 333, Internal Revenue Code of 1954 during the month of August 1974. At the date of liquidation, E. Davis owned 250 shares common no par value capital stock. The basis at the time of incorporation—June 16, 1951—and which has not changed since that date was $2,500.

In liquidation, E. Davis received $1,750 in money and an undivided one quarter interest in the following assets:

Assets	Fair Market Value
Land and Building No. 1	$200,000
Land and Building No. 2	110,000
Rent Receivable	1,000

E. Davis's rateable share of the earnings and profits at liquidation was $1,150.

SCHEDULE TO BE ATTACHED TO FORM 1040
OF F. FACTOR FOR CALENDAR YEAR 1974

F. Factor was a stockholder in the XYZ Corporation of 8 Moore Street, New York, N.Y. 10006 which was liquidated under Section 333, Internal Revenue Code of 1954 during the month of August 1974. At the date of liquidation, F. Factor owned 750 shares common no par value capital stock. The basis at the time of incorporation—June 16, 1951—and which has not changed since that date was $7,500.

In liquidation, F. Factor received $5,250 in money and an undivided three quarter interest in the following assets:

Assets	Fair Market Value
Land and Building No. 1	$200,000
Land and Building No. 2	110,000
Rent Receivable	1,000

F. Factor's rateable share of the earnings and profits at liquidation was $3,450.

JOURNAL ENTRY TO CLOSE (LIQUIDATE) THE
BOOKS OF THE XYZ CORPORATION

Bills Payable	$ 13,400	
Mortgage Payable No. 1	100,000	
Mortgage Payable No. 2	40,000	
Capital Stock	10,000	
Reserve for Deprec. No. 1	30,000	
Reserve for Deprec. No. 2	15,000	
Earned Surplus	4,600	
Cash		$ 7,000
Land No. 1		15,000
Apartment Building No. 1		120,000
Land No. 2		5,000
Apartment Building No. 2		65,000
Rent Receivable		1,000

| Form **1096** | **Annual Summary and Transmittal of U.S. Information Returns** | | | **197** |

Department of the Treasury
Internal Revenue Service

(Magnetic tape filers: See the applicable Revenue Procedures regarding transmittal of returns on magnetic tape.)

Enter number of documents	Place an "X" in the proper box to identify type of document being transmitted				All documents are: Place an "X" in the proper boxes. (See instructions.)			
					Original	Corrected	With taxpayer identifying no.	Without taxpayer identifying no.
2	1099–DIV	1099–INT	1099–MED	1099–MISC	X		X	
	1099–OID	1099–L **2**	1099–PATR	1087–DIV				
	1087–INT	1087–MED	1087–MISC	1087–OID				

PAYER'S identifying number ▶   12-1234567

XYZ   CORPORATION

8 MOORE STREET

NEW YORK, NEW YORK 10006

Type or print PAYER'S name, address and ZIP code above.

Under penalties of perjury, I declare that I have examined this return, including accompanying documents and to the best of my knowledge and belief, it is true, correct, and complete. In the case of documents without recipients' identifying numbers I have complied with the requirements of the law by requesting such numbers from the recipients, but did not receive them.

Signature   **E. DAVIS**   Title   **PRESIDENT**   Date   **2/2/75**

☆ U.S. GOVERNMENT PRINTING OFFICE:1973—O–458-087   E.I. 25-1118272

To record closing entry following distribution in liquidation under Section 333, IRC 1954.

JOURNAL ENTRY TO OPEN BOOKS OF
DAVIS AND FACTOR, JOINT VENTURE

Cash	$ 7,000.00	
Land No. 1	17,052.63	
Building No. 1	96,631.58	
Land No. 2	4,507.18	
Building No. 2	45,071.77	
Rent Receivable	1,000.00	
Bills Payable		$ 13,400
Mortgage Payable No. 1		100,000
Mortgage Payable No. 2		40,000
Capital Account—Davis		4,250
Factor		12,750

To open books of account of joint venture of Davis and Factor, following liquidation of XYZ Corporation under Section 333, IRC 1954.

Notes: 1. The partners' capital accounts are computed as follows:

Form **1099L** Department of the Treasury Internal Revenue Service	U.S. Information Return For **Distributions in Liquidation During Calendar Year**		19⃣7⃣

Shares owned		Distributions in liquidation		
Class	Number	Cash	Property	
			Description	Fair market value at date of distribution
COMMON	250	$ 1,750.00	LAND & APARTMENT BLDGS. RENT RECEIVABLE	$ 77,500.00 250.00

Shareholder's tax identifying number ▶ 100-03-3000	12-1234567
E. DAVIS SECOND AVENUE PLAINFIELD, N.Y. 11751	XYZ CORPORATION 8 MOORE STREET NEW YORK, N.Y. 10006

Shareholder.—Name, address, and ZIP code. If account is for multiple payees place an asterisk (°) by the name of the person or entity to whom the identifying number belongs.

Corporation.—Name, address, ZIP code, and employer identification number of corporation in liquidation. **(OVER)**

Form **1099L** Department of the Treasury Internal Revenue Service	U.S. Information Return For **Distributions in Liquidation During Calendar Year**		19⃣7⃣

Shares owned		Distributions in liquidation		
Class	Number	Cash	Property	
			Description	Fair market value at date of distribution
COMMON	750	$ 5,250.00	LAND & APARTMENT BLDGS. RENT RECEIVABLE	$ 233,500.00 750.00

Shareholder's tax identifying number ▶ 104-04-40000	12-1234567
F. FACTOR HINES ROAD FAIRVIEW, NEW JERSEY 17,001	XYZ CORPORATION 8 MOORE STREET NEW YORK, N.Y. 10006

Shareholder.—Name, address, and ZIP code. If account is for multiple payees place an asterisk (°) by the name of the person or entity to whom the identifying number belongs.

Corporation.—Name, address, ZIP code, and employer identification number of corporation in liquidation. **(OVER)**

	Davis	*Factor*	*Total*
Original investment— XYZ Corporation	$2,500	$ 7,500	$10,000
Ordinary dividend and capital gain taxable in liquidation	1,750	5,250	7,000
Total	$4,250	$12,750	$17,000

2. The basis of the rent receivable is $136.84. At the time the rent is received ($1,000), the difference of $863.16 will be taxed as ordinary income.

3. The land and building in each case will be apportioned based upon the appraisal value in order to establish the proper basis for depreciation.

Land No. 1 $113,684.21 × 30,000/200,000 = $17,052.63 (basis of land)
Apartment Building No. 1 $113,684.21 × 170,000/200,000 = $96,631.58 (basis of building)
Land No. 2 $49,578.95 × 10,000/110,000 = $4,507.18 (basis of land)
Apartment Building No. 2 $49,578.95 × 100,000/110,000 = $45,071.77 (basis of building)

Since the assets have been partially depreciated by the corporation, the double declining balance and the sum-of-the-year-digits methods may not be adopted. However, the 150 per cent declining balance method may be elected.

4. *Proof:* The total assets shown in the balance sheet on page 116 total $168,000. The opening journal entry of the joint venture totals $170,400, an increase of $2,400. The increase ($2,400) should equal the recognized gain reported by the stockholders ($7,000) less the earned surplus at date of liquidation ($4,600).

TEN

Liquidation Under
Section 337

INTRODUCTION.

Prior to the enactment of the Internal Revenue Code of 1954, if a corporation sold its assets at a gain and then distributed the proceeds in complete liquidation of the corporation, the sale and liquidation would result in a double tax. The corporation would first pay a tax on the recognized gain on the sale and then the stockholders, upon receipt of the proceeds in the liquidation of the corporation, would be liable for a tax on the difference between the amount received in liquidation and the basis of the capital stock investment.

Example: A calendar year corporation had the following assets and liabilities:

Assets:		Liabilities & Capital:	
Cash	$ 5,000	Mortgage Payable	$ 80,000
Land*	20,000	Earned Surplus	15,000
Building (after de-		Capital Stock	30,000
preciation)	100,000		
Total	$125,000	Total	$125,000

The corporation sold the land and building for $180,000 ($100,000 above the mortgage payable).

The recognized gain on the sale of the land and building to the corporation was $60,000 ($180,000 selling price less basis of land and building $120,000).

Assuming that the land and building was not an asset held for resale in the ordinary course of the corporation's business and that the corporation was not a collapsible corporation, the recognized gain of $60,000 would be a long-term capital gain and the tax payable by the corporation would be $15,000 (25% of $60,000).[1]

The balance sheet after the sale and payment of the Federal income tax but prior to the liquidating dividend to the stockholders would be as follows:

Assets:		Liabilities & Capital:	
Cash	$90,000	Earned Surplus	$60,000*
		Capital Stock	30,000
Total	$90,000	Total	$90,000

In the distribution of the liquidating dividend, the stockholder would have a recognized long-term capital gain of $60,000 (cash $90,000 minus basis of capital stock $30,000). The maximum tax on the long-term capital gain of $60,000 would be $15,000 (50% of $60,000 × 50%).

Thus, a combined tax of $30,000 would be payable by the corporation and the individual stockholder whereas if Section 337 had been elected, the corporate tax of $15,000 would have been saved.

ISSUES PRIOR TO 1954.

As illustrated in the example above, the sale of the asset by the corporation resulted in a double tax, first at the corporate level and then at the stockholders' level. In order to avoid the double tax, several methods were developed, (a) a distribution of the assets to the stockholders as a liquidating dividend, followed by a sale of the assets thereafter by the stockholders or (b) the capital stock was sold by the stockholders. In respect to the first method there arose a factual issue: Who made the sale?—the corporation or the stockholders?

In many cases, the Internal Revenue Service and the courts held that, despite the liquidation of the assets to the stockholders, the sale was really negotiated and consummated by the corporation through its stockholders acting for the corporation.[2] Despite the development of the "as, if and when" type of contract involving the sale of the assets by the stockholder as, if and when the assets were liquidated out to the stockholder, factual issues continued to harass the stockholder in respect to the always present possibility that the Internal Revenue Service would levy a double tax.[3]

The second method above also resulted in two additional serious tax problems. There was a question as to the tax basis of the assets and did the corporation in substance, sell the assets in a form of a sale of stock by the shareholders?[4]

AREA OF DANGER.

Section 337 was enacted as a part of the Internal Revenue Code of 1954 to provide a definitive rule to remove the uncertainties of liquidation under conditions which could lead to the imposition of a double tax, the question of form vs. substance and the establishment of the basis of the assets received in liquidation. However, unless the rules provided for in Section 337 are strictly followed, there is still a possible area of vulnerability to both the stockholders and the corporation.[5]

FORMAL PLAN OF LIQUIDATION.

The strict interpretation of the Internal Revenue Service with respect to all optional tax relief sections would seem to dictate the extreme importance of adopting a formal plan of liquidation. In several cases where no formal plan was adopted by the stockholders, the Court, in affirming the Internal Revenue Service, held that, without such a formal plan, there was no intention in the minds of the stockholders to liquidate under Section 337 and the gain in the sale was taxable to the corporation.[6] However, in a closely held corporation, informal discussions were held to be in substantial compliance.[7]

BASIC RULES OF SECTION 337:

The basic rules of Section 337 may be summarized as follows:

    (a) if a corporation adopts a plan of complete liquidation; and

    (b) within the 12-month period beginning on the date of adoption of the plan of liquidation, all of the assets of the corporation are distributed in complete liquidation (less assets retained to meet claims); then—

    (c) no gain or loss will be recognized to such corporation from the sale or exchange by the corporation of its property within the 12-month period. However, under the depreciation recapture provisions of Section 1245 and Section 1250 of the Internal Revenue Code of 1954 as amended by the Revenue Acts of 1962 and 1964, if these sections are applicable to the sale and liquidation under Section 337 they will result in ordinary income taxable to the corporation equal to the depreciation recaptured. The recapture provisions apply not only to the Section 1245 or Section 1250 property sold under the Section 337 election but also to such other assets required to be distributed within the 12-month period as more fully explained later.

Comment: Where a business subject to a regulatory license, i.e. freight transport, is sold and the proceeds of the sale are distributed within 12-months, the fact that the Regulatory body did not give its consent until after the 12-month period is immaterial.[8]

SALE OF ASSETS TO A STOCKHOLDER.

A sale of corporate assets to a stockholder of the corporation qualifies under Section 337, provided all of the prerequisites of Section 337 are met. In addition, the selling price must be established at arms length.[9]

DISTRIBUTION OF PROCEEDS TO A TRUST, ETC.

Under the general rule, a distribution by the corporation within 12 months to trustees for the stockholders qualifies as the distribution requirement of Section 337.[10]

A corporation sold all its assets except land which was subject to a lease to a tenant-farmer. Due to the lease, the land was not readily marketable. The corporation within the 12 month period distributed sufficient cash to meet claims and debts and the land to an independent trustee for the stockholders. The distribution to the trust qualifies under Section 337. The stockholders will report a capital gain on the excess (if any) of the cash transferred after the payment of the claims and debts. The rent received by the trust from the tenant-farmer is taxable as ordinary income pro-rata for each stockholder of the liquidated corporation.[11]

Where a corporation within the 12 month period placed in escrow with an independent party sufficient cash to pay the dissenting stockholders when the value of the stock was finally determined, the distribution qualifies under Section 337.[12]

But where the proceeds of the sale were deposited within the 12 month period in a bank account which was in the corporate name and actually distributed to the stockholders after the 12 month period, Section 337 does not apply with respect to the sale. [13]

HOLDING PERIOD.

Where a corporation liquidates under Section 337, IRC 1954, in installments during the 12-month period, gain is not recognized until the investment in the capital is received, i.e., the capital recovery theory. The holding period of the capital stock exchanged in such liquidation ends with the receipt of the total amount on which the capital gain is recognized—the final liquidating distribution rather than the earlier date or dates of receipt in liquidation following the decision to liquidate as set forth in the minutes.[14]

The computation of the period is explained fully in Chapter 3.

PROCEDURE UNDER SECTION 337.

Briefly, the normal procedure to execute a complete liquidation under Section 337 involving the sale of the assets of the corporation would take the following steps:

(a) Corporation and prospective purchaser execute a contract of sale of the assets owned by the corporation;

(b) Corporation adopts a plan of complete liquidation under Section 337;

(c) Within 30 days after the adoption of the plan, the corporation files Form 966 and a certified copy of the Resolution to liquidate with the District Director in the district where the corporation normally files its corporate income tax return;

(d) Corporation and purchaser execute the closing of title;

(e) Within 12 months after the adoption of the plan of liquidation the corporation distributes in complete liquidation all of the remaining assets, including the proceeds of sale. Corporation may retain sufficient cash to meet claims and unascertained payables;

(f) File final Form 1120 for the calendar, fiscal or short year to date of dissolution. In some cases where the 12-month liquidation period overruns the regular tax year-end closing, a second return may be necessary. In such cases, this is the final return. The final return should be marked "Final Return" and a schedule of pertinent information as described later attached thereto;

(g) A Form 1099 L for each stockholder receiving a liquidating dividend of $600 or more in any calendar year must be filed showing the details of the liquidating dividend. Where the 12-month period overruns the close of a calendar year and if the corporation has distributed the assets and proceeds in two calendar years, a second Form 1099 L will be required for the second distribution. Form 1096, the letter of transmittal, must be filed with Form 1099 L.

(h) Legally dissolve the corporation under the laws of the state of incorporation.

12-Month Period: The 12-month period begins with the date of the adoption of the plan of complete liquidation under Section 337.[15]

Example: Corporation held a joint special meeting of its directors and stockholders on December 4, 1973, adopting a Resolution for the complete liquidation of the corporation under Section 337. The corporation must distribute its assets (less assets retained to meet claims) on or before December 3, 1974.

No extension of the 12-month period will be granted by the Internal Revenue Service.[16]

PLAN ADOPTED ON OR AFTER JUNE 22, 1954.

The Internal Revenue Code of 1954 was enacted effective August 16, 1954. Section 337, however, applies to the adoption of a plan of complete liquidation adopted on or after June 22, 1954. As discussed later, the Code included certain special rules for plans adopted prior to June 22, 1954. The courts have also upheld the principles of Section 337 if the procedure was followed step-by-step as indicated above even though the plan was adopted previous to the June 22nd date.

In a recent decision,[17] the directors and the stockholders adopted a liquidation on May 9, 1954 which conformed to the provisions of Section 337 and which followed the procedure for liquidation. The Court held that the corporation had in effect used Section 337, and that the gain on the sale of the assets was taxable to the stockholders.

SALES OR EXCHANGES.

For the purposes of Section 337, the sale may be made on or after the day on which the plan is adopted.[18] When does a sale occur? The date on which a sale occurs depends primarily upon the intent of the parties based upon the terms of the contract and the surrounding circumstances. In determining whether the sale occurred on or after the date of adoption of the plan of complete liquidation, the fact that negotiations for sale may have been commenced either by the corporation or its stockholders or both is immaterial.

Furthermore, an executory contract to sell is to be distinguished from a contract of sale.[19] Ordinarily, a sale has not occurred when a contract to sell has been entered into, but title and possession of the property have not been transferred and the obligation of the seller or the buyer to buy is conditional. In the case of real estate, the sale occurs when a deed passes or when possession and the burdens and benefits of ownership are transferred to the buyer, whichever occurs first. [20]

The date of the sale is extremely important in many instances. For example, a corporation sold two pieces of property at a loss before electing Section 337. After the adoption of the plan under Section 337, the corporation sold the balance of its assets at a gain. The losses were held deductible by the corporation. The gains were taxable to the stockholders as a liquidating dividend under Section 337.[21]

CONDEMNATION.

A condemnation is a "sale" for the purposes of Section 337, IRC 1954. In a New York case, the condemnation sale took place when the condemnation order was issued by the New York Supreme Court which vested title in the City of New York. The corporation had adopted a plan of complete liquidation at a special meeting of the directors and stockholders several days before the Court Order. The actual award was received by the corporation more than twelve months after the adoption of the plan. At the expiration of the 12-month period allowed for the liquidating dividend, the corporation, since it had not received the award, distributed an estimated award receivable on which the stockholders computed the recognized gain.[22]

The condemnation statutes in other states may vary from that of New York and, therefore, the attorney for the corporation should check the local law as to when title (the sale for this purpose) passes upon a condemnation.

FIRE-CASUALTY LOSS.

The Internal Revenue Service has now ruled that the receipt of the insurance proceeds in respect to the destruction of a building by fire constitutes a "sale" for the purposes of a Section 337 liquidation,[23] agreeing with the major Court decisions.[24]

However, under the provisions of Section 337, only sales made after the date of the adoption of the resolution to liquidate are subject to the nonrecognition of gain rules. The U.S. Supreme Court has issued a decision that the date of a fire is the date of the involuntary sale for the purposes of Section 337. In this case, the corporation adopted a resolution to liquidate under Section 337 eight months after the fire occurred. The insurance proceeds received were in excess of the adjusted basis of the property destroyed in the fire. Therefore, the gain is taxable to the corporation due to the post-fire adoption of the resolution and the filing of Form 966. The fact that the corporation could not reasonably estimate the amount of the insurance proceeds is immaterial.[25]

Comment: The above decision was a five to four decision by the U.S. Supreme Court. It should be noted that the dissenting opinion pointed out that the Internal Revenue Service accepts a resolution to liquidate under Section 337 if adopted on the *same* day as the conversion by fire took place.

ASSETS RETAINED TO MEET CLAIMS.

Any assets retained after the expiration of the 12-month period for the payment of claims must be specifically set apart for that purpose and must be reasonable in amount in relation to the items involved. Claims include unascertained or contingent liabilities or expenses.[26] A schedule of such liabilities and expenses must be attached to the corporate income tax return when it is filed.[27]

PROPERTY DEFINED.

The Statute specifically defines what property of the corporation may not be sold under the double tax relief provisions. Property, for purposes of Section 337, does not include:

(a) Stock in trade of the corporation or other property of a kind which would properly be included in the inventory of the corporation if on hand at the close of the taxable year, and property held by the corporation primarily for sale to customers in the ordinary course of its trade or business. Thus, under the general rule, and despite a proper election under Section 337, the gain or loss on the inventory if sold by the corporation will be taxed to the corporation; not to the stockholders. However, the Code provides an exception.

Exception to General Rule on Inventory: If the other prerequisites of Section 337 are satisfied, and a sale of the inventory is made to one person in one transaction, the gain on such sale is taxable to the shareholders in liquidation as a capital gain. The distinction is clear. The corporation is not selling its inventory as it would in the ordinary course of business but rather in a bulk sale in the winding-up of the affairs of the business of the corporation as a step in the Section 337 liquidation. "Person" as used above includes an individual, a trust, estate, partnership, corporation, company or an association.[28]

The gain on the bulk sale of the inventory results in a capital gain to the stockholders which is either long-term or short-term depending upon the length of time that the capital stock was held by the stockholder.

Where a corporation is engaged in two or more distinct businesses or trades, the inventory rule applies to each business or trade separately if sold in a bulk sale.[29]

Note: In computing the corporate gross profit for the tax year of liquidation, the inventory must be taken into account as the closing inventory. The capital gain or loss on the sale of the inventory which is eliminated by reason of Section 337 is only that portion of the selling price which represents the difference between the inventory at which it is valued for gross profit purposes and the selling price.

Example 1: A corporation operates two department stores and a warehouse in which it maintains the inventory for both stores. The corporation adopts a Section 337 plan of liquidation under which department store No. 1, including the inventory in such store (but not including any portion of the inventory in the warehouse ear-marked for Store No. 1) is sold to one person. The sale of the store and the inventory is taxable to the stockholders (capital gain).

Example 2: A corporation operates a grocery store in the Apex Shopping Center and a hardware store in the Rally Shopping Center. Pursuant to a plan of liquidation under Section 337, the grocery store, including its inventory, is sold to the Reves Grocery Chain, Inc. The sale of the inventory of the grocery store is a bulk sale under Section 337, regardless of the disposition of the other store.

If the inventory is sold as a bulk sale on the installment or deferred payment plan, the installment obligations are not treated as "property" for the purposes of recognition of gain to the stockholders, but when distributed will be taxed as capital gain to the shareholders based upon the fair market value of the obligations receivable. The deferred profit is not taxable to the corporation.[30]

Warning: The benefits of Section 337 do not apply if the inventory is sold in a bulk sale to one person and, within the 12-month period permitted for liquidation, the inventory is replaced or there is an acquisition of a new kind of inventory which is sold in the normal course of trade or business during the remainder of the 12-month period.[31]

(b) Installment Obligations—Property Sold under Section 337: Property does not include installment obligations received in connection with the sale of property of the corporation within the 12-month period. Therefore, if the corporation has elected Section 337, the additional benefits of the installment method of paying the tax as the installments are received by the seller are not permitted.[32] Thus, the stockholders will be required to pick up the obligations on the basis of their fair market value.

Example: A plan of liquidation under Section 337 was timely adopted. On July 1, 1960, the calendar-year corporation sold its real estate on the basis of 30 per cent down as the initial payment and the balance on a purchase money mortgage payable over a ten-year amortization period, beginning July 1, 1961. The other assets of the corporation and the mortgage receivable were distributed to the shareholders within the 12-month period. The collections on the mortgage when received by the shareholders are not included in their individual returns as payment on the installment sale. Instead, the mortgage receivable will be distributed to the shareholders on the basis of its fair market value at the date of the liquidating dividend since the provisions of Section 331 (a) (1), IRC 1954 apply to such distributions.[33] Thus, in the above example, the shareholders' gain will be based on the fair market value and as the collections are received, the stockholder will recover his capital (the fair market value reported as a liquidating dividend).

As indicated, the stockholder is required to report such obligations based upon their fair market value. Under such conditions, the depreciation recapture provision applies to the sale and the corporation will be required to report the recaptured depreciation as ordinary income and the stockholder a capital gain

The deferred profit on an installment sale, made in conjunction with a liquidation under Section 337, is not taxable to the corporation upon distribution to the stockholders.[34] However, if the corporation is on the accrual basis, the accrued interest on the mortgage to the date of liquidation is taxable to the corporation as ordinary income.

Example: Assume in the above example, that the real estate was sold for $100,000. The corporation received $30,000 as an initial payment and a purchase money mortgage of $70,000. The adjusted basis of the real estate at the date of sale was $60,000. The gross profit percentage on the sale is 40% ($40,000 profit divided by

$100,000 contract price). The gross profit of $12,000 on the initial payment of $30,000 ($30,000 × 40%) will be taxed to the stockholders upon liquidation. The deferred profit of $28,000 ($70,000 × 40%) will not be taxed to the corporation but, as explained above, the mortgage to the extent of its fair market value will be an asset distributed to the stockholder in the Section 337 liquidation.

(c) Installment Obligations—Sales Prior to Section 337 Adoption: Suppose a corporation had sold one or more of its assets on the installment basis in years prior to the adoption of the plan to liquidate under Section 337. At the date of the liquidation under Section 337, the corporation's balance sheet showed a deferred profit on the prior sale. Under Section 453 (d), in the year of liquidation, the corporation will be required to include the deferred profit in its entirety in its corporate income tax return for the year of liquidation (contrary to (a) and (b) above). In other words, the liquidation of the mortgage or notes receivable to the stockholders is a "disposition" as defined in Section 453 (d), IRC 1954 and the gain is taxable to the corporation; not to the stockholders. Thus, the installment obligation cannot be "passed on" to the shareholder.

Example: In 1968, a corporation sold real estate for $100,000 which at that time had a basis of $60,000. The terms of sale were $30,000 down in 1968 and a mortgage of $70,000, payable $10,000 a year beginning in 1969. The corporation adopted a plan of liquidation under Section 337 in July, 1970 in respect to its remaining assets. The corporation distributed all of its assets by December 31, 1970 and filed a return for the calendar year 1970 as its final return.

The total recognized gain on the sale in 1968 was $40,000 of which the corporation reported a taxable gain of $12,000 ($30,000 × 40%). In 1969, the corporation received $10,000 and reported a taxable gain of $4,000. In 1970, the corporation completely liquidated under Section 337. In this return, the corporation will be required to include the balance of the gain in taxable income, i.e., $24,000 (balance of mortgage $60,000 × 40%).

In addition, the accrued interest for the taxable year 1970 will be included as ordinary interest income.

(d) Interest—Property sold under Section 337: Interest on mortgages, notes and other indebtedness received as a result of a sale of property under Section 337 is not "property" as defined in Section 337. The sale includes only the gain on the sale of the property. It does not include any interest paid or payable by the purchaser. The interest element of the sale is taxable as ordinary income to the shareholders when distributed within the 12 month period as provided in Section 337.[35]

Example: A corporation sold a shopping center for (1) cash; (2) the assumption of an existing mortgage and (3) a promissory note for the balance. In addition, the purchaser paid 5 years prepaid interest on the note at the date of the closing. The corporation within the 12 month period distributed all of the proceeds of the sale, including the prepaid interest.

The prepaid interest is not a Section 337 property. Therefore, it is taxable as ordinary income to the liquidating stockholders.

(e) Non-compete Agreement: A non-compete agreement is not Section 337 property. Therefore, the amount received is taxable as ordinary income. It is not a part of the Section 337 property subject to the recognition of capital gain involved in the Section 337 election to liquidate.[36]

Example: A corporation entered into an agreement for the sale of its assets, electing to liquidate under Section 337. The sale involved (1) the sale of the assets for 90 X dollars and (2) a non-compete agreement for 10 X dollars. Total consideration 100 X dollars. The non-compete agreement was separately negotiated. Under its terms, the corporation could not compete with the purchaser for a stated period of time and within a specific geographical area.

The 10 X dollars received in connection with the non-compete agreement is ordinary income to the corporation. The gain on the sale of the assets under Section 337 is a capital gain to the stockholders upon distribution within the 12 month period.

Comment: The amount received in consideration for a covenant not to compete which is *separately* bargained for is clearly *severable* from goodwill (as in the above example). In general, goodwill, if sold, is treated as a capital asset.[37]

MORTGAGES, CLAIMS AND RECEIVABLES–NO ASCERTAINABLE VALUE AT LIQUIDATION.

If a corporation distributes in complete liquidation under Section 337, IRC 1954, claims which at the date of liquidation had no ascertainable value, the stockholder will, upon receipt of any payment on such claims, have a recognized capital gain; not ordinary income.[38] For example, prior to liquidation, a corporation had claims on file to recover certain customs duties. The claims for refund, at the date of liquidation, had no ascertainable value. After the corporation was liquidated, the former stockholders received the refunds. These refunds are to be treated as capital gains in the hands of the stockholders.[39] The length of time that the stock was owned will determine whether the capital gain is long-term or short-term.

On the other hand, if claims and receivables have a value at the date of liquidation, the distribution of such claims or receivables is a closed transaction and gain or loss must be computed as part of the liquidating dividend. Thus, where a corporation distributed in complete liquidation insurance renewal commissions which had ascertainable value, the stockholder had a liquidating dividend equal to the fair market value. To the extent that the former stockholders received payments in excess of the basis, i.e., fair market value at liquidation, the stockholders received ordinary income; not capital gain.[40] The gain at the time of the liquidating dividend, to the extent that the fair market value exceeded the cost basis of the stock, was capital gain.[41]

Royalties received by former stockholders under a patent licensing agreement distributed in complete liquidation of a corporation and which had ascertainable value at that time were held to be ordinary income to the former stockholders receiving the royalties after the liquidation; not capital gain.[42]

UNREALIZED RECEIVABLES—CASH BASIS.

Unrealized receivables of a cash basis taxpayer are not considered "property" under Section 337, IRC 1954. In one case, for example, the unrealized receivables were three construction contracts which were sold following the adoption of the plan of liquidation under Section 337.[43] The profit on such contracts was held taxable to the corporation as ordinary income.[44] Where a cash basis taxpayer sold its product on the basis of a down payment and monthly installments, the installment obligations were held not "Section 337 property," and the gain was taxable to the corporation; not to the stockholders under the plan of liquidation elected under Section 337, IRC 1954.[45]

ANTICIPATORY ASSIGNMENT OF GAIN.

Following the decision to liquidate under Section 337, a substantial stockholder donated over 50 per cent of his stockholdings in the corporation to a university. Thereafter, the assets were distributed. The gain on liquidation to the extent of the shares donated to the university is not taxable to the university but to the donating stockholder. A stockholder by donating stock cannot make an anticipatory assignment of gain and thus avoid the tax on the distribution of the assets or the proceeds.[46]

PROPERTY SOLD UNDER PLAN OF LIQUIDATION—SECTION 337.

Due to the enactment of the depreciation recapture provisions which are effective for Section 337 liquidations with respect to depreciable personal property (on or after 1/1/63) and with respect to depreciable real property (on or after 1/1/64), the explanation by necessity must be separated into two parts for complete clarity.

(a) Depreciation Recapture Provisions Not Applicable. The gain or loss on the sale of the corporate property is recognized and taxed to the stockholders as a distribution in liquidation under Section 337. The following simple examples will illustrate the application of the Code to such sales.

Example 1: A calendar year corporation which was organized in 1965 adopted a plan of liquidation under Section 337 in April, 1970. The real property was sold on May 1, 1970 for $100,000. The purchaser assumed the existing mortgage. To date of sale, the corporation's only income was rent of $2,500 and expenses of $1,500, including depreciation. The balance sheet as of various dates during 1970 was as follows:

Assets:	*Prior to Sale*	*After Sale*	*At Liquidation*
Cash	$ 3,000	$68,000	$67,700
Land & Building			
(After depreciation)	60,000	—	—
Total	$63,000	$68,000	$67,700

Liab. & Capital:

Mortgage Payable	$35,000	$ ___	$ ___
Capital Stock	20,000	20,000	20,000
Earned Surplus	8,000	8,000	7,700
Special 337 Surplus	___	40,000	40,000
Total	$63,000	$68,000	$67,600

To make the example as simple as possible, the corporation's income tax was deducted from the cash and the earned surplus as of the date of liquidation. In practice, unpaid Federal income taxes (and state franchise on dissolution where applicable) reduces the recognized gain on liquidation.[47]

The recognized gain on the liquidation is $47,700 ($67,700 liquidating dividend minus $20,000 basis of capital stock). The gain would be a long-term capital gain (1965 to 1970).

Example 2: Assume the same facts as in Example 1, except that the balance sheet was as follows:

Assets:	Prior to Sale	After Sale	At Liquidation
Cash	$ 3,000	$55,000	$54,700
Land & Building (Net after depreciation)	60,000	___	___
Total	$63,000	$55,000	$54,700

Liab. & Capital:			
Mortgage Payable	$48,000	$ ___	$ ___
Capital Stock	20,000	20,000	20,000
Deficit	(5,000)	(5,000)	(5,300)
Special 337 Surplus	___	40,000	40,000
Total	$63,000	$55,000	$54,700

The recognized gain on the liquidation is $34,700 ($54,700 liquidating dividend minus $20,000 basis of capital stock). The gain would be a long-term capital gain (1965 to 12/31/70).

(b) Depreciation Recapture Provisions Applicable. If the selling price of the depreciable personal property and/or depreciable real property is in excess of the adjusted (book) basis of the assets at the date of sale under Section 337, the corporation realizes ordinary income on the amount of depreciation subject to recapture. The recapture applies, in the case of depreciable personal property, only to a Section 337 sale and liquidation which occur on or after January 1, 1963 and, in the case of depreciable real property, only to a Section 337 sale and liquidation which

occur on or after January 1, 1964. The rules of computation are set forth in Chapter 3 and 4.

The recapture provisions also apply to depreciable personal and real property which remain unsold at the date of liquidation. In such cases, since Section 331 (a) (1) applies, the basis of the recapture computation is the fair market value of such assets at the date of actual distribution to the stockholders.

Example 3: A calendar year corporation organized in 1960 adopted a plan of liquidation under Section 337 in April 1965. The real property was sold on May 1, 1965 for $100,000 (land $30,000; building $70,000). The purchaser assumed the existing mortgage. In 1965, to date of sale, the corporation's only income was rent of $2,500, and its expenses were $1,500, including depreciation. Total depreciation allowed or allowable since acquisition was $20,000, of which $3,000 is Section 1250 depreciation. The balance sheet as of various dates during 1965 was as follows:

Assets:	*Prior to Sale*	*After Sale*	*At Liquidation*
Cash	$ 3,000	$68,000	$67,120
Land	20,000	—	—
Building (after depreciation	40,000	—	—
Total	$63,000	$68,000	$67,120
Liab. & Capital:			
Mortgage Payable	$35,000	$ —	$ —
Capital Stock	20,000	20,000	20,000
Earned Surplus	8,000	11,000	10,120
Special 337 Surplus	—	37,000	37,000
Total	$63,000	$68,000	$67,120

The gain on the sale of the land and building must be computed separately since the depreciation recapture applies only to the gain on the building. In other words, the selling price must be allocated (or stated in the contract) between the land and the building. The gain taxable to the stockholder and the ordinary income taxable to the corporation is as follows:

Selling Price–Land		$30,000
Basis of Land		20,000
		$10,000
Selling Price–Building	$70,000	
Adjusted Basis of Building	40,000	
Total Gain on Building	$30,000	

Depreciation Subject to Recapture 3,000
_____

Balance of Gain 27,000
_____

Gain Taxable to Stockholders (Special 337
Surplus) $37,000

The corporate tax return for 1965 will show the following:

Income from Rents	$2,500
Less: Expenses	1,500
Net Income	$1,000
Plus: Recaptured Depreciation	3,000
Taxable Income	$4,000
Corporate Income Tax (22%)	$ 880

The stockholders will report a long-term capital gain on liquidation under Section 337 of $47,120 (net assets received of $67,120 less basis of capital stock of $20,000).

Example 4: Assume the same facts as in Example 3, except that the balance sheet was as follows:

Assets:	Prior to Sale	After Sale	At Liquidation
Cash	$ 3,000	$55,000	$54,120
Land	20,000	—	—
Building (after depreciation)	40,000	—	—
Total	$63,000	$55,000	$54,120
Liab. & Capital:			
Mortgage Payable	$48,000	$ —	$ —
Capital Stock	20,000	20,000	20,000
Deficit	(5,000)	(2,000)	(2,880)
Special 337 Surplus	—	37,000	37,000
Total	$63,000	$55,000	$54,120

The recognized long-term gain on the liquidation is $34,120 (net worth of $54,120 less basis of capital stock of $20,000). As in Example 3, the corporation will increase its operating income of $1,000 by the $3,000 recaptured depreciation.

However, where a corporation sold an office building, which included a stockpile of coal, plumbing supplies, and small tools, that part of the proceeds attributable to the coal, etc., which had been deducted in a prior year as expense, is ordinary income.[48]

SECTION 331 APPLIES TO PROPERTY UNSOLD AT END OF 12 MONTHS.

Assume a corporation has owned two pieces of improved real property since organization in 1956. In July, 1960, the corporation adopts a plan of liquidation under Section 337 since it has entered into a contract to sell one of the pieces of real estate in August, 1960. The sale is consummated. At the expiration of the 12-month period (July 1961), the corporation in order to fulfill the prerequisites of Section 337 must distribute all of the assets in complete liquidation.

The second piece of real estate unsold at the expiration of the 12-month period must be distributed in liquidation at its fair market value under Section 331 (a) (1), IRC 1954. (See Chapter 6.)

Example: Assume the same facts as above as to the adoption of the plan and the sale of the real property and that the balance sheet was as follows:

Assets:	Per Books	Fair Market Value	Liab. & Capital:	Per Books
Cash	$ 2,000	$ 2,000	Mortgage Pay. No. 2	$ 72,000
Land & Bldg.*	60,000	100,000	Capital Stock	50,000
Land & Bldg.*	80,000	130,000	Earned Surplus	20,000
Total	$142,000	$232,000	Total	$142,000

The land and building No. 1 is sold in August, 1960 for $100,000 cash. In July, 1961, the corporation liquidated its assets to the sole stockholder. The balance sheet at liquidation was as follows:

Assets:	Per Books	Fair Market Value	Liab. & Capital:	Per Books
Cash	$102,000	$102,000	Mortgage Pay. No. 2	$ 72,000
Land & Bldg.*	80,000	130,000	Capital Stock	50,000
			Earned Surplus	20,000
			Special 337 Surplus	40,000
Total	$182,000	$232,000	Total	$182,000

---

*Acquired 5 years prior.
*Earned surplus at beginning $15,000 plus recognized gain $60,000 minus the Federal tax payable $15,000.

Computation of recognized capital gain:

Land and Building No. 2–FMV	$130,000
Cash	102,000
Fair Market Value of Assets	$232,000
Less: Mortgage Payable No. 2	72,000
Net Fair Market Value of Assets	$160,000
Less: Capital Stock (cost or adjusted basis to shareholder)	50,000
Recognized Gain on Liquidation	$110,000
Proof: Earned Surplus	$ 20,000
Special 337 Surplus	40,000
Increase in Value of Land and Building No. 2 over book basis	50,000
Recognized Gain	$110,000

*Net of depreciation.

The basis for a future sale or exchange in the hands of the liquidating stockholder of the land and building No. 2 is $130,000, the fair market value. This basis must be allocated between land and building based upon the fair market value ratio. The period of time for purposes of capital gain or loss upon the subsequent sale of the property received is the date of receipt of the liquidating dividend by the shareholder to the date of the subsequent sale.

As already indicated, the recapture of depreciation provisions apply to the assets being liquidated even though not sold by the corporation under a Section 337 election. Thus, in the above example, the corporation will be required to include in its taxable income the recaptured depreciation with respect to building No. 2 since the fair market value is in excess of the adjusted (book) basis of the building. Despite the recognition of ordinary income by the corporation, the capital gain taxable to the stockholders is still based upon the fair market value of the assets as received by the stockholders. The method of computation is illustrated in Chapter 6.

Recapture of the 7% Investment Credit. The Revenue Act of 1962 provided for an investment credit on the purchase or other acquisition of a Section 38 asset. If, however, the asset is disposed of by sale or otherwise before the estimated life established at the time the credit was computed, the corporation is required to recompute the credit and repay a part or all of the credit.[49] Where an asset is sold under a Section 337 election, the asset is "disposed of" for the purposes of recapture and requires a recomputation of the 7% credit. In such cases the corporation will be required to repay the credit as recomputed in the year of the Section 337 sale.[50]

Where a corporation had other assets which qualify under Section 38 and which were not sold under the Section 337 election, the recapture depends upon the following rule. Where such property is retained in the trade or business as a Section 38 asset and the taxpayers (former stockholders) retain a substantial interest in such trade or business, apparently there would be no recapture at the date of liquidation. However, a subsequent sale (disposition) by the new entity would invoke the recapture provisions.

DISTRIBUTION OF CLAIMS, ETC.

Where a corporation distributes nonliquid assets such as a claim for refund, the asset must be distributed or placed in the hands of an independent trustee for the benefit of the stockholders.[51] The ruling of the Commissioner is a strict interpretation of procedure. Normally, such assets are distributed to a stockholder for the benefit of the stockholders as a group, the proceeds to be distributed when collected.

SECTION 337 ELECTION—BINDING?

The election under Section 337 may be revoked prior to the actual liquidation. It is necessary for the directors and the stockholders to rescind the Resolution which adopted the plan within the 12-month period. However, the Internal Revenue Service Center with whom the Form 966 was filed will not return the form to the corporation. The corporation may rescind the first election by filing the proper minutes and resolution with Form 966. Thereafter, the corporation may elect to liquidate under Section 337 by again filing the proper minutes and resolutions with Form 966. [52]

Warning: Extreme care must be exercised that a valid election is in effect at the date of the sale, otherwise the gain will be taxable to the corporation.

Example: A corporation had two pieces of property. The corporation became aware that the state was going to condemn the properties. It adopted a resolution to liquidate under Section 337 for both parcels. One was condemned and the proceeds received. Thereafter, the corporation revoked its Section 337 resolution with respect to the second parcel. However, the state also condemned the second parcel and the proceeds were received by the corporation at a time when no valid election was in effect. Result: The gain on the second piece is taxable to the corporation.[53]

REINCORPORATION OF ASSETS OR BUSINESS.

The Internal Revenue Service has announced that it will not issue advance rulings on the tax effect of a corporation which has adopted a plan of liquidation under Section 337 where a part or all of the business or assets are sold to a new corporation and the stockholders of the liquidating corporation own more than a nominal amount of the capital stock of the new corporation. The Internal Revenue Service refers to such transactions as the "reincorporation of the previous business or assets."[54] The current announcement broadens the position of the Internal Revenue Service since under a previous ruling the request for a ruling was denied only where the stockholders of the liquidating corporation own at least 50 per cent of the voting stock of the acquiring corporation.[55] The current position is based upon a Supreme Court decision which held that it is necessary only that the stockholders continue to have a definite and substantial equity in the assets of the acquiring corporation.[56]

However, the Tax Court ruled that, if in order to avoid personal liability in a new type of business in the corporation, the business was transferred to a new corporation, a bona fide liquidation took place; not a reincorporation.[57]

Warning: While the Internal Revenue Service will not, upon request, issue a ruling to a taxpayer on this subject, it has already clearly stated its position.[58] For example, the X Corporation adopted a plan of liquidation under Section 337, IRC 1954. The corporation had an excellent income record and high value assets. The stockholders of the X Corporation organized the Y Corporation. X Corporation sold its assets to the Y Corporation for cash and part of the Y's capital stock (45 per cent). The cash was acquired by selling the balance of the Y Corporation's capital (55 per cent) to persons who were not previously stockholders or interested in the X Corporation. The stockholders of X Corporation under the plan of liquidation received cash and the stock of the Y Corporation (45 per cent interest). The distribution was held to be an ordinary dividend in connection with a Section 368 (a) (1) (E) or (F) statutory reorganization. Furthermore, the transaction did not constitute a sale and the acquiring corporation received the assets at the same basis as that in the hands of the X Corporation (no stepped-up basis allowed).

COLLAPSIBLE CORPORATIONS.

Section 337 does not apply to any sale or exchange made by a collapsible corporation.[59] A corporation was denied the right to use Section 337 on the basis that it was a collapsible corporation. As a result of this finding, the corporation reported ordinary gain on the sale of the property and paid a tax thereon. The Internal Revenue Service has held that the stockholders received capital gain on the liquidating dividend thereafter since the corporation had realized all of the taxable income on the property as provided in Section 341, IRC 1954.[60]

LIQUIDATION TO WHICH SECTION 333 APPLIES.

Section 337 does not apply to sales by a corporation if Section 333 applies to the liquidation of such corporation.[61] Thus, stockholders of a corporation may not elect Section 333 and also use the benefits of Section 337 in respect to the sale of the property.

LIQUIDATION TO WHICH SECTION 332 APPLIES.

Section 332, IRC 1954, covers the tax-free liquidation of a subsidiary by its parent corporation. (See Chapter 13.) Section 337 does not apply if the basis of the property on the books of the parent is determined by reference to the basis of the property in the hands of the subsidiary.[62] In such cases, the amount of the gain not recognized may not be greater than the excess of (a) that portion of the adjusted basis (adjusted as provided in Section 334 (b) (2), IRC 1954)[63] of the stock of the liquidating corporation in the hands of the parent corporation allocable to the property sold or exchanged over (b) the adjusted basis of such property in the hands of the liquidating corporation.

The depreciation recapture provisions do not apply if the basis of the property in the hands of the parent corporation is determined under Section 334 (b) (1), IRC 1954.[64] See also Chapter 14.

Example: Corporation A owns more than 80% of the stock of Corporation B which it had purchased for $10,000. Corporation B adopts a plan of liquidation under Section 337. All of the assets of Corporation B, having a total basis of $4,000, are sold for $12,000. The portion of the realized gain of $8,000 which is not recognized is $6,000, computed as follows:

Basis of stock allocable to property sold	$10,000
Basis of property sold	4,000
Excess (not recognized)	$ 6,000
Gain recognized to liquidating corporation (B)	$ 2,000

Where a liquidating distribution is made by a subsidiary to its parent corporation, which is also undergoing liquidation, the gain of the parent on the surrender of the subsidiary's capital stock is a gain from a sale or exchange which is not recognized under Section 337, IRC 1954.[65]

PARENT—SUBSIDIARY v MINORITY STOCKHOLDER.

Under Section 337, as enacted in the Internal Revenue Code of 1954, if a corporation owned at least 80% of the stock of another corporation and the balance of the stock was owned by an individual shareholder, the election to liquidate under Section 337 would cause a hardship to the individual stockholder. The reason for this hardship is that a liquidation of a parent-subsidiary is tax-free[66] whereas the liquidating dividend is taxable to the individual stockholders. In order to eliminate this hardship and give relief to the minority stockholder, the Technical Amendments Act of 1958 added subsection (d) to Section 337, IRC 1954, effective for corporation's adopting a plan of liquidation on or after 1/1/58.

The new rule is applicable only (a) where the corporation is owned 80% or more by another corporation and (b) there is a complete liquidation which is taxfree to the majority stockholder (the parent corporation) under Section 332 with the corporate shareholder taking as its basis for the property received by it the basis of such property in the hands of the liquidating (subsidiary) corporation.[67]

Example: Corporation S is owned 90% by Corporation P and 10% by A, an individual. A's basis for his stock is $10,000. Corporation S owns two pieces of property, each having a fair market value of $100,000 and an adjusted basis of $50,000.

On August 1, 1960, Corporation S adopts a plan of liquidation. On September 1, 1960, Corporation S sells one of the properties for $100,000 and distributes in complete liquidation during the following month the other building and the proceeds of sale (less $12,500 retained to pay the taxes on such sale). Under Section 337 (d), the amount realized by A on the distribution is increased by $1,250 (A's proportionate share of the amount by which the tax imposed upon Corporation S on such sale would have been reduced—using a 25% tax rate—if Section 337 had been applicable). The tax imposed upon A with respect to the complete liquidation is computed as follows:

Amount realized by A:

1/10 of $100,000 (building not sold)	$10,000
1/10 of $ 87,500 ($100,000–12,500)	8,750
	$18,750
Plus: A's proportionate share of tax	1,250
	$20,000
Less: A's basis for capital stock	10,000
Recognized capital gain	10,000
Tax (assuming 25% rate)	$ 2,500

A will be deemed to have paid $1,250 in tax. Accordingly, after the credit, A will have a balance of $17,500 in property and money.

DISTRIBUTION—STOCKHOLDER NOT AVAILABLE.

The distribution under Section 337 must be made within 12 months after the adoption of the plan. If a stockholder cannot be located so that the distribution can be made within the time limit, the liquidating distribution may be made to a State official, trustee or other person authorized by law to receive such distribution for the benefit of the stockholder.[68]

DISSOLUTION AFTER LIQUIDATION—WARNING.

The Regulations are silent as to whether or not after the liquidation within the 12-month period the corporation must be legally dissolved under the state law. However, it is advisable to legally dissolve the corporation based upon the trend of current rulings and the other sections of the Code applicable to liquidations.

In one ruling, a corporation adopted a plan of liquidation under Section 337 and made a timely distribution in complete liquidation (within the 12-month period). Thereafter, the corporation was reactivated by its former stockholders in a line of business different from that prior to the Section 337 liquidation. The Internal Revenue Service held that the liquidation was a partial liquidation under Section 331 (a) (2), IRC 1954. (See Chapter 10.)[69] A corporation adopted a Section 337 liquidation. The assets were sold to a new corporation. The stockholders of the liquidating corporation owned 45 per cent of the stock of the new corporation. The liquidation was held invalid. The transaction was in fact a reorganization.[70]

12-MONTH LIQUIDATION PRIOR TO 6/22/54.

Section 337, as enacted by the Internal Revenue Code of 1954, applied only to a plan adopted on or after 6/22/54. However, the Code provided special rules for such liquidations occurring prior to 6/22/54.[71]

INCOME, DEDUCTIONS AND GAINS AFTER ADOPTION OF PLAN.

Despite the election under Section 337, the corporation is required to compute its income and deduction for the taxable year, or years or portion thereof included in the 12-month liquidation period. A net operating loss is not affected by a Section 337 election and the loss may be carried back.[72]

A cash basis corporation sold all of its assets under a Section 337 liquidation. Interest on discounted notes earned but not actually received at date of sale is taxable to the corporation as ordinary income.[73]

When the assets, including receivables, are sold by the corporation, the balance in the reserve account is income to the corporation in the year of liquidation.[74]

No gain is recognized by the corporation on the sale of emergency facilities under Section 168, IRC 1954.[75]

After the adoption of a Section 337 plan of liquidation, the corporation sold not only the assets for which it had adopted the plan but other assets owned by the corporation. The gain on the other assets passes through to the stockholder. The gain is not taxable to the corporation.[76] This rule also applies to the gain on temporary assets purchased and sold after the adoption of the plan.[77] However, if the sale occurred prior to the adoption of the plan, the gain is taxable to the corporation.[78]

Legal fees, commissions and similar expenses in connection with the sale of the assets are not currently deductible in the year of liquidation but are an offset against the selling price of the assets.[79] But if such expenses are associated with the liquidation, the expenses are deductible.[80]

SECTION 337 NOT APPLICABLE.

Where all of the assets are distributed to the creditor and none to the stockholders, Section 337 does not apply.[81]

PROCEDURE—ADOPTION OF PLAN.

The first step under Section 337 is to elect to liquidate by adopting a plan in resolution form in a joint (or separate) meeting of the directors and stockholders.

Form 966: Within 30 days after the adoption of the plan, the corporation must file Form 966 together with a certified copy of the Resolution. Form 966 is filed in the office of the Internal Revenue Service Center in which the corporation files its corporate income tax return Form 1120.[82]

Form 1096-1099 L: Every corporation making any distribution of $600 or more during a calendar year to any stockholder in liquidation must file a Form 1099 L for each such stockholder. Form 1099 L must be filed on or before February 28 of the year following the calendar year during which the stockholders received the liquidating dividend. Form 1096 is the letter of transmittal accompanying Form 1099 L. The forms are filed with the proper service center.[83]

Form 1120: There must be attached to the corporate income tax return of the liquidating corporation, the following information:

(a) A copy of the minutes of the stockholders' meeting at which the plan of liquidation was formally adopted, including a copy of the plan of liquidation;

(b) A statement of the assets sold *after* the adoption of the plan of liquidation, including the dates of such sales. If Section 337 (c) (2) (B), relating to limited recognition of gain on sales of subsidiaries, is applicable, the statement must include a computation of the total gain and of the gain not recognized under this section;

(c) Information as to the date of the final liquidating distribution;

(d) A statement of the assets, if any, retained to pay liabilities and the nature of the liabilities.[84]

STATE INCOME TAX—DEDUCTIBLE.

A corporation properly elected a plan of liquidation under Section 337, IRC 1954. The gain on the sale of the assets is taxable to the stockholders for federal purposes. If the state franchise tax provisions recognize Section 337, the gain under this federal section is also taxable to the stockholders for state income tax purposes. The Internal Revenue Service held such state franchise tax *not deductible* for federal purposes since the income (gain) was "wholly exempt" from tax. The courts hold that the state franchise tax *is deductible,* distinguishing between "wholly exempt income" and non-recognized gains.[85]

CITATIONS

[1] Sec. 1231, IRC 1954.

[2] Comm. v Court Holding Co., 324 U.S. 331; Gregory v Helvering, 293 U.S. 465; Dobson v Comm., 320 U.S. 489; Comm. v Heininger, 320 U.S. 467.

[3] "Whereas, vendors (stockholders) except to acquire all of such electric transmission and distribution lines and facilities of Cumberland (corporation), and in the event of such acquisition, desire to sell to the purchaser the * * *." U.S. Cumberland Public Service Co., 338 U.S. 451.

[4] Dallas Downtown Development Co., 12 TC 114; Texas Bank & Trust Co. of Dallas, Memo TC 1953; Robert Campbell, et al., 15 TC 312.

[5] Rev. Rul. 56–387 CB 1956–2, pg. 189; Reg. Sec. 1.377–2 (b).

[6] Whitson v Rockwood, DC, N.D., 2/13/61, 7 AFTR 2d 677; Intercounty Development Corp., TC Memo 1961–217.

[7] Alameda Realty Corp., 42 TC 273 (acq.).

[8] Male, Memo TC 1971–301.

[9] Rev. Rul. 73–551.

[10] Rev. Rul. 63–245.

[11] Rev. Rul. 72–137.

[12] Rev. Rul. 65-257.

[13] Vern Realty, Inc., 58 TC 1005.

[14] Mattison v U.S., 163 F. Supp. 754; Alvina Ludorff, 40 BTA 32.

[15] Letter Ruling, dated 11/30/55, signed H.T. Swartz, Director, Tax Rulings Division, U.S. Treasury Dept.; Rev. Rul. 59–108 CB 1959–1, pg. 72; Reg. Sec. 1.337–1; Rev. Rul. 58–391 CB 1958–2, pg. 139; Virginia Ice & Freezing Corporation, et al., 30 TC 1251.

[16] Reg. Sec. 1.337–1; Maxine Development Co., Inc., Memo TC 1963–300.

[17] Powell's Pontiac-Cadillac, Inc. v Gross, DC, N.J., 5 AFTR 2d 977.

[18] Reg. Sec. 1.337–1.

[19] Reg. Sec. 1.337–2 (a); Comm. v Segall, 114 F 2d 706, rev. 38 BTA 43.

[20] Lucas v North Texas Lumber Co., 281 U.S. 11.

[21] Virginia Ice & Freezing Corporation, 30 TC 1251; Rev. Rul. 57–140 CB 1957–1, pg. 118; Rev. Rul. 58–391, CB 1958–2, pg. 139.

[22] Rev. Rul. 59–108 CB 1959–1, pg. 72; Driscoll Bros. & Co., 221 F. Supp. 603; Wood Herman Corp., 311 F 2d 918, aff. 206 F. Supp. 733; Wendell, 326 F 2d 600, aff. 39 TC 809; Dwight, 225 F. Supp. 933, aff. 328 F 2d 973; Gallina, 53 TC 130.

[23] Rev. Rul. 64–100, revoking Rev. Rul. 56–372, CB 1957–2, pg. 187.

[24] Kent Manufacturing Corporation, 288 F 2d 812, rev. 33 TC 930; Towanda Textiles, Inc. v U.S., 180 F Supp. 373, U.S. v Morton, 388 F 2d 441, aff. 258 F. Supp. 922.

[25] Central Tablet Mfg. Co. v U.S., U.S. Supreme Court 6/19/74, aff. CA-6, 32 AFTR 2d 5361.

[26] Reg. Sec. 1.337–1.

[27] Reg. Sec. 1.337–5.

[28] Sec. 7701 (a) (1), IRC 1954.

[29] Reg. Sec. 1.337–3 (c) (d).

[30] Reg. Sec. 1.337–3 (c).

[31] Senate Finance Committee Report, IRC 1954.

[32] Sec. 337 (b) (1) (B), IRC 1954; Sec. 453 (d) (4) (B), IRC 1954.

[33] Letter Ruling dated 8/3/55, signed E. Randolph Dale, Chief, Reorganization and Dividend Branch, U.S. Treasury Dept.

[34] Sec. 453 (d) (4) (B), IRC 1954; Reg. Sec. 1.453–9 (c).

[35] Mele, 61 TC No. 41.

[36] Rev. Rul. 74–29; Ullman v Comm., 264 F 2d 305; Harvey Radio Laboratories, Inc., Memo TC 1972–85, aff. 470 I 2d 118.

[37] Michaels, 12 TC 17.

[38] L.H. Burnett, TC Memo 1956–210; Westover v Smith, 173 F 2d 90; Susan J. Carter, 9 TC 364, aff. 170 F 2d 911; George J. Lentz, et al., 28 TC 1157; John H. Altorfer, et al., TC Memo 1961–48.

[39] H.D. McDonald v U.S., DC, WD Wash., 2/24/60.

[40] Anthony Campagna v U.S., CCA–2 (5/10/61), 7 AFTR 2d 1358, aff. 179 F. Supp. 140; Burnett v. Logan, 283 U.S. 404.

[41] Est. of Abraham Goldstein, et al., 33 TC No. 116.

[42] Est. of Sam Marsack, TC Memo 1960–75, aff. 228 F 2d 533.

[43] Sec. 453 (d) (4) (B), IRC 1954; Reg. Sec. 1.453–9 (c).

[44] Henry A. Kuckenberg, et al., 309 F 2d 202, rev. 35 TC 473.

[45] Family Record Plan, Incorporated, 36 TC No. 33; Sarah G. Wimp, et al., TC Memo 1961–342.

[46] Kinsey, 58 TC No. 25.

[47] Herman Levy, et al., TC Memo 1960–22.

[48] Rev. Rul. 61–214.

[49] Sec. 38 etc., IRC 1954.

[50] Sec. 47, IRC 1954.

[51] Rev. Rul. 63–245.

[52] Rev. Rul. 67–273, 1967–2 CB 137.

[53] West Street-Erie Boulevard Corporation v U.S., 411 F 2d 738. Drummond v V.S., DC, Calif. 9/10/68.

[54] Rev. Rul. 61–156, 1961–2 CB 62.

[55] Comm. v Berghash, 361 F 2d 257, aff. 43 TC 743.

[56] John A. Nelson Co. v Helvering, 296 U.S. 374; Rommer v U.S., 268 F. Supp. 740.

[57] Kind, 54 TC 600.

[58] Rev. Rul. 61–156, IRC 1961–34, pg. 10.

[59] Sec. 337 (c) (1) (A), IRC 1954; Reg. Sec. 1.337–1; Sec. 341, IRC 1954.

[60] Rev. Rul. 58–241, CB 1958–1, pg. 179.

[61] Sec. 337 (c) (1) (B), IRC 1954; Reg. Sec. 1.337–1.

[62] Sec. 337 (c) (2), IRC 1954; Reg. Sec. 1.337–4; Rev. Rul. 57–243.

[63] Reg. Sec. 1.344–1 (c).

[64] Committee Report, Rev. Act 1962 & 1964.

[65] Rev. Rul. 57–243, CB 1957–1, pg. 116.

[66] Sec. 332, IRC 1954. See also Chapter 12.

[67] Senate Finance Committee Report–Technical Amendments Act of 1958.

[68]Reg. Sec. 1.337–2 (b); Rev. Rul. 57–140, CB 1957–1, pg. 118.

[69]Rev. Rul. 60–50, CB 1960–1, pg. 150.

[70]Rev. Rul. 61–156, 1961–2 CB 62.

[71]Sec. 392 (b), IRC 1954; Reg. Sec. 1.392–1; See also Footnote 11.

[72]Rev. Rul. 56–448, CB 1956–2, pg. 130.

[73]Rev. Rul. 59–120, CB 1959–1, pg. 74.

[74]West Seattle National Bank of Seattle, 33 TC 341.

[75]Rev. Rul. 59–308, CB 1959–2, pg. 110.

[76]Reg. Sec. 1.337–1.

[77]Verito, 43 TC 429.

[78]The Covered Wagon, Inc. v Comm., 369 F 2d 629.

[79]Alphaco, Inc. v Nelson, 385 F 2d 244; Washington Trust Bank v U.S., 44 F 2d 1235; Of Course, Inc. v Comm., CA-4, 7/2/74, rev. 59 TC 146. Decision in Pridemark, Inc., 345 Fed. 35 overruled.

[80]U.S. v Mountain States Mixed Feed Co., 365 F 2d 244.

[81]Rev. Rul. 56–387, CB 1956–2, pg. 189.

[82]Sec. 6043, IRC 1954; Reg. Sec. 1.6043–1.

[83]Reg. Sec. 1.6043–2.

[84]Reg. Sec. 1.337–5.

[85]Bertha Gassie McDonald, Trans., et al., 36 TC 1108 (acq.), aff. 320 F 2d 109; Hawaiian Trust Co., Ltd., 291 F 2d 761; Cotton States Fertilizer Co., 28 TC 1169; James F. Curtis, 3 TC 648, George W.P. Heffelfinger, 5 TC 985, Royal Oaks Apartments, Inc., 43 TC No. 23; Rev. Rul. 60–236, 1960–2 CB 109.

ELEVEN

Section 337 –
Specimen Problem

THE MNO CORPORATION

of 10 Starr Street, New York, N.Y. 10004 was organized on March 20, 1952 under the laws of the State of New York by John Bell of Maple Drive, Bronxville, N.Y. and Frank Smith of 1081 Fifth Avenue, New York, N.Y. 10022. At organization, Bell subscribed for and paid in cash $20,000 for 100 shares no par value common capital stock (Certificate No. 1). On the same date, Smith subscribed for and paid in cash $40,000 for 200 shares no par value common capital stock (Certificate No. 2). No additional shares were issued. The corporation adopted a fiscal year ending February 28th. Its books of account were maintained on the accrual basis. The corporation was engaged in the manufacture of electronic equipment. The corporation filed on Form 1120. Identification # 10-5656565. The tax return was filed at the Internal Revenue Service Center at Holtsville, New York. Social Security numbers—Bell, 200-02-2002; Smith, 031-03-3003.

On March 5, 1974, the stockholders began negotiations for the sale of the corporation. The prospective purchaser refused to purchase the capital stock. He, however, offered to purchase all of the assets, except cash, subject to certain liabilities. The basis for the sale was the balance sheet as of the close of business May 31, 1974. On March 15, 1974, the parties signed the contract. The selling price was $262,000, subject to adjustment, if any, as of May 31, 1974. The contract broke down the selling price as follows:

Accounts Receivable		$ 48,000
Inventory		115,000
Land		50,000
Factory building		200,000
Prepaid insurance		2,000
		$415,000
Less: Accounts payable	$ 18,000	
Mortgage payable	135,000	153,000
Selling Price		$262,000

At 11 A.M. on March 18, 1974, the directors and stockholders held a special joint meeting at the office of the corporation's attorneys, Lawrence, Spruill and Lowe, Esqs., of 50 Broad Street, New York, N.Y. At this meeting, the Resolution to liquidate under Section 337, IRC 1954 was unanimously adopted. On March 21, 1974, the corporation filed Form 966 with the Internal Revenue Service Center, Holtsville, New York.

The balance sheet as of May 31, 1974, was as follows:

ASSETS:

Cash		$ 10,000
Accounts Receivable	$ 50,000	
Less: Reserve for Doubtful Accounts	2,000	48,000
Inventory		90,000
Land		30,000
Factory Building	$150,000	
Less: Reserve for Depreciation	25,000	125,000
Prepaid Insurance		2,000
Total		$305,000

LIABILITIES AND CAPITAL:

Accounts Payable	$ 18,000
Mortgage Payable	135,000
Taxes Payable	5,000
Capital Stock	60,000
Earned Surplus as at 2/29/74	75,000
Net Profit to 5/31/74 (includes $3,000 depreciation recapture)	12,000
Total	$305,000

The profit and loss statement for the period March 1, 1974 to May 31, 1974 was as follows:

Sales		$400,000
Less: Cost of Goods Sold		350,000
Gross Profit		$ 50,000
Salaries—officers	$12,000	
Salaries—other	3,000	
Other Deductible Expenses	23,000	38,000
Net Profit for Period		$ 12,000

The purchaser took title on June 6, 1974, effective May 31, 1974. On October 15, 1974, the corporation distributed the assets and the proceeds of the sale in complete liquidation under Section 337. Cash in the amount of $5,000 was retained to pay the estimated taxes—$3,600 Federal income tax and $1,400 state franchise tax. On November 30, 1974, the corporation was legally dissolved under the laws of the State of New York.

WAIVER OF NOTICE OF JOINT SPECIAL MEETING OF STOCKHOLDERS AND DIRECTORS OF MNO CORPORATION

We, the undersigned, being all of the stockholders and all of the directors of MNO CORPORATION do hereby waive all notice of a Joint Special Meeting of Stockholders and Directors of said corporation, and do hereby agree and consent that the 18th day of March at 11:00 o'clock in the forenoon, be and the same is hereby fixed as the time, and the office of Lawrence, Spruill and Lowe, Esqs., 50 Broad Street, in the City of New York, County of New York, State of New York, as the place for holding the same; and that the purpose of said meeting be the adoption of a plan for the complete liquidation of the corporation, and for a distribution of all of the assets of the corporation in complete liquidation less such assets to be retained as are required to meet corporate claims, within twelve (12) months beginning on the date of the adoption of such plan; and for the transaction of such other business as may lawfully come before said meeting.

Dated, the 18th day of March 1974.

Stockholders	Directors
John Bell	*John Bell*
Frank Smith	*Frank Smith*

MINUTES OF A JOINT SPECIAL MEETING OF STOCKHOLDERS AND DIRECTORS OF MNO CORPORATION

A Joint Special Meeting of Stockholders and Directors of MNO Corporation was held at the office of Lawrence, Spruill & Lowe, Esqs., 50 Broad Street, New York City, New York on the 18th day of March, 1974 at 11:00 o'clock in the forenoon.

The following, being all of the stockholders and directors were present:

STOCKHOLDERS	DIRECTORS
John Bell	John Bell
Frank Smith	Frank Smith

John Bell, the President of the Corporation acted as Chairman of the meeting and Frank Smith the secretary, as secretary thereof.

A written waiver of notice of this Meeting, signed by all of the stockholders and directors, was then presented and read by the Secretary and was ordered appended to these Minutes.

The Chairman then announced that the purpose of this meeting was to discuss and act upon a proposal to liquidate and dissolve the corporation. Counsel for the Corporation was asked for their opinion of the tax results to the Corporation, and the stockholders, caused by the liquidation and distribution of the corporate assets. The stockholders expressed a desire to liquidate and distribute the assets of the Corporation since the purposes for which it was formed no longer exist. After hearing Counsel's explanation of the Tax Laws under the 1954 Internal Revenue Code, especially Section 337 thereof, and under the New York Franchise Tax Laws; after a full discussion by the Stockholders and Directors of the Corporation; after a report by the President of the Corporation that a contract had been entered into for the sale of the Corporate assets, the following Resolution was unanimously adopted:

RESOLVED, that the following plan of liquidation, pursuant to Section 337 of the 1954 Internal Revenue Code, be and the same is hereby adopted:

I. Within thirty (30) days after the date of this meeting, Counsel for the Corporation shall file Form 966 with the Director of Internal Revenue, Upper Manhattan, New York, attaching to said form a certified copy of this Resolution, indicating that the Stockholders and Directors have adopted a plan of liquidating pursuant to Section 337 of the 1954 Internal Revenue Code.

II. That the Corporation, by its duly authorized officers proceed to complete the sale of its property as an incident to the plan of liquidation adopted by the stockholders and directors pursuant to Section 337 of the 1954 Internal Revenue Code.

III. That the Corporation, by its duly authorized officers, within twelve (12) months after the date of the adoption of the Plan distribute all of its assets, except those retained to meet corporate obligations, to all of the stockholders in ratio of each stockholder's holdings to the total outstanding and issued stock of the Corporation.

IV. That as soon as practical, but not later than twelve (12) months after the date of this meeting, Counsel for the Corporation shall file a certificate for the dissolution of the Corporation to the New York State Stock Corporation Law, and that the officers of this Corporation are hereby authorized to execute any and all documents necessary to effectuate such dissolution.

V. That the officers and directors be and they are hereby empowered, authorized and directed to proceed in accordance with the resolution hereby adopted by the stockholders and directors, said officers and directors being authorized to adopt any subsequent resolutions to effectuate the intent of the Stockholders and Directors to liquidate the Corporation in accordance with a plan of liquidation adopted pursuant to Section 337 of the Internal Revenue Code.

There being no further business before the Meeting, the Meeting adjourned.

Dated: March 18, 1974.

Frank Smith
Secretary

ATTEST

John Bell
President

CERTIFIED COPY OF RESOLUTION
MNO CORPORATION

I hereby certify that the following Resolution was unanimously adopted at a Special Joint Meeting of the Stockholders and Directors held on March 18, 1974 at 11 A.M. in the forenoon.

RESOLVED, that the following plan of liquidation pursuant to Section 337 of the 1954 Internal Revenue Code, be and the same is hereby adopted:

I. Within thirty (30) days after the date of this meeting, Counsel for the Corporation shall file Form 966 with the Director of Internal Revenue, Upper Manhattan, New York, attaching to said form a certified copy of this Resolution, indicating that the Stockholders and Directors have adopted a plan of liquidating pursuant to Section 337 of the 1954 Internal Revenue Code.

II. That the Corporation, by its duly authorized officers proceed to complete the sale of its property as an incident to the plan of liquidation adopted by the stockholders and directors pursuant to Section 337 of the 1954 Internal Revenue Code.

III. That the Corporation, by its duly authorized officers, within twelve (12) months after the date of the adoption of the Plan distribute all of its assets, except those retained to meet corporate obligations, to all of the stockholders in ratio of each stockholder's holdings to the total outstanding and issued stock of the Corporation.

IV. That as soon as practical, but not later than twelve (12) months after the date of this meeting, Counsel for the Corporation shall file a certificate for the dissolution of the Corporation to the New York State Stock Corporation Law, and that the officers of this Corporation are hereby authorized to execute any and all documents necessary to effectuate such dissolution.

V. That the officers and directors be and they are hereby empowered, authorized and directed to proceed in accordance with the resolution hereby adopted by the stockholders and directors, said officers and directors being authorized to adopt any subsequent resolutions to effectuate the intent of the Stockholders and Directors to

Form **966**		**Corporate Dissolution or Liquidation**		
(Rev. Nov. 1973) Department of the Treasury Internal Revenue Service		(Required under Section 6043(a) of the Internal Revenue Code)		

Name of corporation
    MNO   CORPORATION
	Employer identification number
	  10-5656565

Address (Number and street) 10 STARR STREET	Check type of return X☐ 1120 ☐ 1120DISC ☐ 1120L

City or town, State and ZIP code NEW YORK, N.Y. 10004	☐ 1120M ☐ 1120S

1 Date incorporated 3/20/52	**2** Place incorporated STATE OF NEW YORK	**3** Type of liquidation X Complete ☐ Partial

4 Internal Revenue Service Center where last income tax return was filed and taxable year covered thereby

Service Center ▶   HOLTSVILLE, NEW YORK   Taxable year ▶   FYE 2/28/74

5 Date of adoption of resolution or plan of dissolution, or complete or partial liquidation 3/18/74	**6** Taxable year of final return SHORT YEAR ENDING 11/30/74	**7** Total number of shares outstanding at time of adoption of plan or liquidation

		Common	Preferred
		300	---

8 Dates of any amendments to plan of dissolution ---	**9** Section of the Code under which the corporation is to be dissolved or liquidated 337	**10** If this return is in respect of an amendment of or supplement to a resolution or plan previously adopted and return has previously been filed in respect of such resolution or plan, give the date such return was filed ---

11. Liquidation Within One Calendar Month.—If the corporation is a domestic corporation, and the plan of liquidation provides for a distribution in complete cancellation or redemption of all the capital stock of the corporation and for the transfer of all the property of the corporation under the liquidation entirely within one calendar month pursuant to section 333, and any shareholder claims the benefit of such section, then the corporation must also submit:

(a) A description of the voting power of each class of stock;

(b) A list of all the shareholders owning stock at the time of the adoption of the plan of liquidation, together with the number of shares of each class of stock owned by each shareholder, the certificate numbers thereof, and the total number of votes to which entitled on the adoption of the plan of liquidation;

(c) A list of all corporate shareholders as of January 1, 1954, together with the number of shares of each class of stock owned by each such shareholder, the certificate numbers thereof, the total number of votes to which entitled on the adoption of the plan of liquidation, and a statement of all changes in ownership of stock by corporate shareholders between January 1, 1954, and the date of the adoption of the plan of liquidation, both dates inclusive; and

(d) A computation as described in section 1.6043-2(b) (following the format in Revenue Procedure 65-10, C.B. 1965-1,738 and Revenue Procedure 67-12, C.B. 1967, 589) of accumulated earnings and profits including all items of income and expense accrued up to the date on which the transfer of all property is completed.

Attach a certified copy of the resolution or plan, together with all amendments or supplements not previously filed.

Under penalties of perjury, I declare that I have examined this return, including accompanying schedules and statements, and to the best of my knowledge and belief it is true, correct, and complete.

The Internal Revenue Service does not require a seal on this form, but if one is used, please place it here.	3/21/74 Date	JOHN BELL Signature of officer	PRESIDENT Title

Instructions

1. Who must file.—This form must be filed by every corporation that is to be dissolved or whose stock is to be liquidated in whole or in part.

Shareholders electing to be covered under section 333 of the Code must also file Form 964 within 30 days after the date of adoption of the plan of liquidation.

2. When to file.—This form must be filed within 30 days after the adoption of the resolution or plan for or in respect of the dissolution of a corporation or the liquidation in whole or in part of its capital stock. If after the filing of a Form 966 there is an amendment or supplement to the resolution or plan, an additional Form 966 based on the resolution or plan as amended or supplemented must be filed within 30 days after the adoption of such amendment or supplement. A return in respect of an amendment or supplement will be deemed sufficient if it gives the date the prior return was filed and contains a certified copy of such amendment or supplement and all other information required by this form which was not given in such prior return.

3. Where to file.—This form must be filed with the Internal Revenue Service Center with which the corporation is required to file its income tax return.

4. Signature.—The return must be signed either by the president, vice president, treasurer, assistant treasurer or chief accounting officer, or by any other corporate officer (such as tax officer) who is authorized to sign. A receiver, trustee, or assignee must sign any return which he is required to file on behalf of a corporation.

liquidate the Corporation in accordance with a plan of liquidation adopted pursuant to Section 337 of the Internal Revenue Code.

There being no further business before the Meeting, the Meeting was adjourned.

Dated: March 18, 1974.

Frank Smith
_____
Secretary

JOURNAL ENTRY TO RECORD THE SALE
UNDER SECTION 337

Cash	$262,000
Mortgage Payable	135,000
Accounts Payable	18,000
Reserve for Doubtful Accounts	2,000
Reserve for Depreciation	25,000
Accounts Receivable	50,000
Inventory	90,000
Land	30,000
Factory Building	150,000
Prepaid Insurance	2,000
Special Section 337 Surplus	120,000

To record receipt of cash, assumption of liabilities by purchaser and to close out assets sold with their respective reserves as follows:

	Per Books	Selling Price	337 Gain
Accounts Receivable	$ 50,000		
Less: Reserve for Doubtful A/cs	2,000		
Net	48,000	$ 48,000	————
Inventory	90,000	115,000	$ 25,000
Land	30,000	50,000	20,000
Factory Building	150,000		
Less: Reserve	25,000		
Net	125,000	200,000	75,000
Prepaid Insurance	2,000	2,000	———
Accounts Payable	(18,000)	(18,000)	———
Mortgage Payable	(135,000)	(135,000)	———
Total Cost	$142,000		
Total Cash		$262,000	
Total Special 337 Surplus			$120,000

JOURNAL ENTRY TO DISTRIBUTE PROCEEDS OF SALE TO STOCKHOLDERS AND TO CLOSE THE BOOKS OF ACCOUNT

Taxes Payable	$ 5,000	
Capital Stock	60,000	
Earned Surplus	87,000	
Special 337 Surplus	120,000	
Cash in Bank		$272,000

To record assumption by shareholders of tax liability and record payments in liquidation by the corporation to the stockholders.

COMPUTATION OF RECOGNIZED CAPITAL TO STOCKHOLDER

Cash	$272,000.00
Less: Cash Retained	5,000.00
Balance to be Distributed	$267,000.00

Liquidating Dividend	*BELL*	*SMITH*	*TOTAL*
Cash	$89,000.00	$178,000.00	$267,000.00
Less: Capital Stock . . .	20,000.00	40,000.00	60,000.00
Recognized Gain . . .	$69,000.00	$138,000.00	$207,000.00

FORM 1120—FINAL RETURN—MNO CORPORATION.

The final return should be filed within two and a half months after the date of the legal dissolution, showing a net profit of $12,000. All of the schedules should be filled in as well as the balance sheet. However, the balance sheet should contain only the figures at the beginning of the taxable year. The column "End of Taxable Year" should show no figures if the assets and liabilities remaining after the sale have all been distributed to the stockholders. It should, however, contain a statement to the effect that the corporation was completely liquidated under Section 337, IRC 1954 and that the final liquidating dividend was distributed on October 15, 1974.

In addition, the following exhibits should be attached to Form 1120:

(a) An exact conformed copy of the Minutes, including the Resolution of the meeting at which the plan to liquidate was adopted:

(b) A schedule of the assets sold after the adoption of the plan, including the date or dates of sale of each asset.

(c) The following statement of retained assets—

Assets:	Cash	$5,000
Purpose of Retention:		
Federal corporate income tax		$3,600
State franchise tax		1,400
Total		$5,000

Note: If the $5,000 retained is insufficient to cover the taxes and the stockholders as transferees pay the balance, the amount paid reduces the recognized capital gain. If there is a balance unspent, the additional distribution to the stockholders increases the recognized capital gain.

Form **1096**	**Annual Summary and Transmittal of U.S. Information Returns**	**197**
Department of the Treasury Internal Revenue Service	(Magnetic tape filers: See the applicable Revenue Procedures regarding transmittal of returns on magnetic tape.)	

Enter number of documents	Place an "X" in the proper box to identify type of document being transmitted				All documents are: Place an "X" in the proper boxes. (See instructions.)			
					Original	Corrected	With taxpayer identifying no.	Without taxpayer identifying no.
2	1099–DIV	1099–INT	1099–MED	1099–MISC				
	1099–OID	1099–L	1099–PATR	1087–DIV	X		X	
	1087–INT	1087–MED X	1087–MISC	1087–OID				

PAYER'S identifying number ► 10-5656565

MNO CORPORATION

10 STARR STREE

NEW YORK, N.Y. 10004

Type or print PAYER'S name, address and ZIP code above.

Under penalties of perjury, I declare that I have examined this return, including accompanying documents and to the best of my knowledge and belief, it is true, correct, and complete. In the case of documents without recipients' identifying numbers I have complied with the requirements of the law by requesting such numbers from the recipients, but did not receive them.

Signature .... **JOHN BELL** .... Title .... **PRESIDENT** .... Date **2/28/75** ....

☆ U.S. GOVERNMENT PRINTING OFFICE:1973—O-458-087   E.I. 25-1118272

| Form **1099L**
Department of the Treasury
Internal Revenue Service | U.S. Information Return For
Distributions in Liquidation During Calendar Year | | | **197** |

Shares owned		Distributions in liquidation		
Class	Number	Cash	Property	
			Description	Fair market value at date of distribution
COMMON	100	$ 89,000.00	NONE	$ ---

| Shareholder's tax identifying number ▶ | 200-02-2002 | |
| JOHN BELL
MAPLE DRIVE
BRONXVILLE, N.Y. 11702 | 10-5656565

MNO CORPORATION
10 STARR STREET
NEW YORK, N.Y. 10004 |

Shareholder.—Name, address, and ZIP code. If account is for multiple payees place an asterisk (°) by the name of the person or entity to whom the identifying number belongs. | **Corporation.**—Name, address, ZIP code, and employer identification number of corporation in liquidation. **(OVER)**

| Form **1099L**
Department of the Treasury
Internal Revenue Service | U.S. Information Return For
Distributions in Liquidation During Calendar Year | | | **197** |

Shares owned		Distributions in liquidation		
Class	Number	Cash	Property	
			Description	Fair market value at date of distribution
COMMON	200	$ 178,000.00	NONE	$ ---

| Shareholder's tax identifying number ▶ | 031-03-3003 | |
| FRANK SMITH
1081 FIFTH AVENUE
NEW YORK, N.Y. 10022 | 10-5656565

MNO CORPORATION
10 STARR STREET
NEW YORK, N.Y. 10004 |

Shareholder.—Name, address, and ZIP code. If account is for multiple payees place an asterisk (°) by the name of the person or entity to whom the identifying number belongs. | **Corporation.**—Name, address, ZIP code, and employer identification number of corporation in liquidation. **(OVER)**

TWELVE

Partial Liquidations – Section 331 (a) (2)

PARTIAL LIQUIDATION v REDEMPTION OF STOCK.

If the distribution is a partial liquidation of the corporation under Section 331 (a) (2), IRC 1954, the difference between the adjusted basis of the capital stock and the amount received in liquidation (the partial liquidating dividend) is a capital gain or loss–short-term or long-term depending upon the length of time that the stock was held.

   If the distribution does not fall within the prerequisites of a partial liquidation of the corporation, it will be treated under the Internal Revenue Code of 1954 as a redemption of capital stock and will be taxed either as a capital gain at the capital gain rate or as an ordinary dividend at the ordinary income tax rates.[1] However, if the partial liquidation to a stockholder also qualifies under Section 302 as a redemption of the capital stock, then the capital gain provisions of the partial liquidation controls and the restrictions of Section 302 (c) (2) (A), IRC 1954 will not be imposed.

PARTIAL LIQUIDATION DEFINED.

A distribution to be taxable as a partial liquidation must satisfy either of the two following conditions: (a) it is one of a series of payments in redemption of all of the stock of a corporation pursuant to a plan, or (b) the distribution is not essentially equivalent to a dividend and is in redemption of a part of the stock of a corporation pursuant to a plan of partial liquidation and occurs within the taxable year in which the plan is adopted or within the succeeding year.[2]

The definition of a partial liquidation is based primarily on the concept of a corporate contraction. Thus, a genuine contraction of the business will always result in a partial liquidation, taxable as a capital gain.[3] The following examples illustrate partial liquidations.

Example 1: Part of the capital stock of a corporation was retired with fire insurance proceeds received when a fire destroyed the upper floors of the corporation's plant which curtailed the operations and the capital requirements were reduced.[4]

Example 2: The sole stockholder of a corporation sold a part of the capital stock back to the corporation in order that such stock could be sold to key employees as part of a plan to retain such employees.[5]

Example 3: A corporation owned by a husband and wife suffered a loss of part of its business as the result of the cancellation of a tractor distributorship franchise. Part of the shares owned by the husband were redeemed.[6]

Example 4: A corporation engaged in wholesaling and jobbing expanded into manufacturing and retailing. As the result of continued losses in the new fields, they were discontinued and a part of the capital no longer needed was redeemed.[7]

Example 5: A corporation operated two separate and distinct businesses. It sold all of the plant and assets relating to one of the businesses and distributed the proceeds in partial retirement of the capital stock.[8]

Example 6: A corporation owned and operated three buildings for rental investment purposes. It distributed one building to the stockholder under a plan of partial liquidation and retired a part of the capital stock.[9]

Example 7: A corporation's sale of a branch of the business qualifies as a partial liquidation.[10]

Example 8: Pursuant to a plan, X changed its operation from a full line department store to a small discount apparel store. Thirty-three of the 40 departments were eliminated. Most forms of credit were eliminated. Floor space was reduced by 85 per cent. Accounts receivable declined from 570 X dollars to 10 X dollars while sales dropped from 4000 X dollars to 600 X dollars. Employees were reduced from 275 to 20 persons. The reason for the change over was due to the building of two large shopping centers in the immediate area.[11]

Where property is distributed, the number of shares to be surrendered for redemption in the partial liquidation is based on the following ratio:

Number of Shares to be Surrendered	·	Total Number of Shares Outstanding	··	Fair Market Value of Property Distributed	·	Total F.M.V. of all Property

The following examples illustrate the transactions which were not partial liquidations falling under Section 331 (b) (2), IRC 1954.

Example 1: A corporation sold one of its buildings in 1952 and used the proceeds to pay off existing indebtedness. In 1957, under a plan of partial liquidation, the corporation distributed an amount equal to the proceeds of the 1952 sale. The distribution in 1957 was an ordinary dividend to the extent of the earned surplus.[12]

Example 2: A corporation owned mining land which it leased to others on a royalty basis (no mining operations) and also operated a business engaged in manufacturing paper products. The fee in the mining property was distributed in partial liquidation and retirement of the capital stock. The corporation was not engaged actively in the business of mining.[13]

Example 3: A corporation set up a reserve for an expansion program. Later, the expansion program was abandoned, and the fund was distributed to the stockholders in cancellation of part of the capital stock.[14]

Example 4: A taxpayer was in the business of raw skins—tanning and selling leather. The demand for products declined and the taxpayer changed over to another type of skins and sold to another segment of the leather trade. Losses continued and taxpayer sold the inventory and redeemed part of the capital stock. Taxable as an ordinary dividend—not a genuine contraction of business.[15]

However, in addition to the above partial liquidation based upon the contraction of business, a redemption and retirement of a part of the capital stock for more than par value;[16] a redemption of one class of stock;[17] and a redemption of a part of the preferred stock[18] were held to be partial liquidating dividends, taxable as capital gain.

At the end of the liquidating period as provided by the Code, i.e., year in which the plan is adopted or the succeeding year, the remaining assets were transferred to a new "liquidating" corporation. Thereafter, the liquidating corporation made a series of payments to the stockholders of the dissolved corporation in redemption of their stock. The Internal Revenue Service held that the amounts distributed were partial liquidating dividends. The basis of the stock for the purpose of computing the gain is the same as the basis of the stock of the dissolved corporation.[19]

CANCELLATION OF SHARES.

The partial liquidation applies only to the shares cancelled, not to all of the outstanding stock.[20] The Court held that there was no partial liquidating dividend if no stock was surrendered and the decision to liquidate was not reached until after the distribution had been declared.[21]

REDUCTION IN PAR OR STATED VALUE.

A reduction in the par or stated value of the capital stock followed by a distribution of this reduction to the stockholders is not a partial liquidating dividend in itself in the absence of evidence to show an intent to liquidate the corporation in whole or in part.[22] In such cases, the distribution is taxed as an ordinary dividend. However, where the corporation adopted a plan to liquidate, distributed the proceeds of the sale of part of its assets and stamped the amount of the distribution on the stock certificates, the distribution is a partial liquidating dividend.[23]

SURRENDER OF CAPITAL STOCK FOR FEWER SHARES AND CASH.

The question in such cases is decided upon the facts and intent. If it is merely a bookkeeping manipulation to create a loss (in this case), the distribution is not a partial liquidating dividend.

Example: The sole stockholder surrendered 1,500 shares and received a certificate for 1,000 shares. As a result of this transaction, the corporation had a surplus of assets over liabilities of $23,700, which was distributed to the shareholder. The taxpayer stockholder claimed a loss on the "partial liquidating dividend" based upon the difference between the cost of $50,000 for the 500 shares as against the amount received.[24]

However, a loss will be allowed on a bona-fide partial liquidating dividend as against a bookkeeping manipulation.[25]

LIQUIDATING DIVIDEND v SALE.

If the transaction is determined to be a sale instead of a partially liquidating dividend, the distinction is immaterial since both will result in capital gain.[26] However, as pointed out above, the question of whether the distribution is an ordinary dividend or a capital gain is the important problem tax-wise.

NOT ESSENTIALLY EQUIVALENT TO A DIVIDEND.

If the redemption of the stock falls under one of the allowable methods provided in Section 302, IRC 1954, the distribution is not essentially equivalent to a dividend and results in capital gain. However, if a partial liquidating dividend has been paid in redemption of part of the stock and is not covered specifically by Section 302, IRC 1954, a question arises as to whether it is a dividend taxable as ordinary income or capital gain.

The question of whether a redemption is essentially equivalent to dividend is predicated upon whether or not there was an element of tax avoidance in the plan of redemption. A transaction which is not essentially equivalent to a dividend is one which has a substantial business purpose. The business purpose motivated the redemption rather than tax avoidance.

Example: A and B each owned one-half of the capital stock of the X Corporation. C wished to purchase B's interest but did not have sufficient funds. A plan was set up whereby the corporation distributed the land and building (which it owned) to A and B in redemption of part of their stock. The reduced stock holding of B was then sold to C. The business purpose motive established the transaction as one not essentially equivalent to a dividend.[27]

As already discussed, the basic question is one of contraction of the corporate business. In addition, the following prerequisites must be met:

(a) the distribution is in redemption of a part of the stock of the corporation pursuant to a plan; and

(b) the distribution occurs within the taxable year or the succeeding year.

REQUIREMENTS FOR TERMINATION OF BUSINESS.

The Regulations provide the following requirements covering the termination of a business:

(a) the distribution is attributable to the corporation's ceasing to conduct business or consists of assets of a trade or business which has been actively conducted throughout the five-year period immediately before the distribution, which trade or business was not acquired by the corporation within such period in a transaction in which gain or loss was recognized in whole or in part (a tax-free exchange with or without boot),

(b) immediately after such distribution by the corporation it is actively engaged in the conduct of a trade or business, which trade or business was actively conducted throughout the five-year period ending on the date of such distribution and was not acquired by the corporation within such period in a transaction in which gain or loss was recognized in whole or in part (a tax-free exchange with or without boot).

A distribution is one in partial liquidation of the corporation if it consists of the proceeds of the sale of the assets of a trade or business actively conducted for the five-year period and has been terminated or if it is a distribution in kind of the assets of such business, or if it is a distribution in kind of some of the assets of such business and of the proceeds of the sale of the remainder of the assets of such business.

Such a distribution may include, but is not limited to, the following:

(a) assets, other than inventory, used in the trade or business throughout the five-year period immediately preceding the distribution. An asset which replaced another asset falls under the five-year rule;

(b) proceeds of the sale of the assets described in (a) above;

(c) the inventory of such trade or business held primarily for sale to customers in the ordinary course of trade or business, provided the items and the quantity included in the inventory are substantially similar to the inventory on hand in the regular conduct of the trade or business;

(d) proceeds from the sale of the inventory described in (c).[28]

ACTIVE CONDUCT OF A TRADE OR BUSINESS.

To qualify, a business must be actively conducted until the date of distribution or sale.[29] A trade or business consists of a specific existing group of activities being carried on for the purpose of earning income or profit from only such group activities, and the activities included in such group must include every operation which forms a part of, or a step in, the process of earning income or profit from such group. The activities, in other words, must include the collection of income and the payment of expenses.

Active business for this purpose does not include (a) the holding, for investment purposes, of stock, bonds, land and other property and commodities, including the casual sale thereof; (b) the ownership of land and building all or substantially all of which are used and occupied by the corporation owner; and (c) activities or group of activities which are incidental or insubstantial to the business of the corporation.[30]

Warning: To come within the confines of a partial liquidation, if the assets of the business are sold, they must be sold by the corporation and not by the stockholders.[31]

SALE OF ASSETS–RETENTION OF CHARTER.

Where a corporation sells its assets following the adoption of a plan of liquidation, retains its charter and, thereafter, the former stockholders reactivate the corporation in another line of business, the distribution in liquidation constitutes a partial liquidation. In such cases, the gain or loss in the sale of the corporate assets after the adoption of the plan of liquidation will be recognized to the corporation.[32]

PROCEDURE.

The corporation must, at a joint or separate special meeting of the stockholders and the directors, adopt a plan to partially redeem the capital stock of the corporation under Section 331 (a) (2) and Section 346, IRC 1954. The plan must cite the basis of the partial liquidation and the amount to be distributed in retirement or cancellation of the capital stock.

Form 966: Within 30 days of the date of adoption of the plan, Form 966, together with a certified copy of the resolution outlining the plan and the resolution, must be filed in the office of the Internal Revenue Service Center in the area in which the corporation files its return. If the original plan is amended or revised, a second copy of Form 966 must be filed with the certified copy of the amendments attached thereto.[33]

Form 1120: The corporation income tax return for the year in which the partial liquidating dividend was distributed must show, in schedule form, the full details of the assets or proceeds distributed, the name and address of the stockholder receiving a distribution, the number of shares owned, the certificate numbers, and the date or dates when the partial liquidating dividend was paid to the stockholders.

Form 1096–1099 L: The corporation is required to file a Form 1099 L for each stockholder to whom the corporation paid a dividend of $600 or more during a calendar year. Form 1096, the letter of transmittal, and the copy of Form 1099 L for each stockholder should be filed in the proper Service Director's office on or before February 28 of the year following the calendar year of the partial liquidating dividend.[34]

COMPUTATION OF PARTIAL LIQUIDATING DIVIDEND–CAPITAL GAIN.

A corporation was organized in 1951 for the purpose of operating an automobile and a farm implement business under two separate franchises. In 1960, the corporation lost the farm implement franchise. As a result, the corporation sold the remaining inventory. As of June 30, 1960, the corporation having liquidated the inventory, adopted a plan of partial liquidation. The earned surplus and the capital amounted to $190,000 (capital paid in $40,000; earned surplus $150,000).

The sole stockholder owned 200 shares of common no par capital stock for which he paid in $40,000. The stockholder turned in 50 shares under the plan. Based upon the normal volume of the two businesses, the stockholder decided that the corporation had an excess of working capital to the extent of $35,000 which was distributed to him. The recognized gain is $25,000 ($35,000 liquidating dividend minus $10,000 basis of 50 shares). The gain is a long-term capital gain (1951 to 1960).[35]

GAIN OR LOSS ON SALES OF ASSETS.

If the corporation sells the assets associated with the business to be discontinued, the ordinary gain or capital gain (or losses) is taxable to the corporation in the year of sale, i.e., sale of balance of inventory results in ordinary income or gain. The capital gain and loss rules apply to each asset.

If the assets are distributed in kind in the partial liquidation, the assets are distributed on the basis of the fair market value of the assets at the date of distribution as in the case of a complete liquidation. (See Chapter 6.)[36]

RECAPTURE OF DEPRECIATION.

A partial liquidation in which the assets are sold and the proceeds distributed to the stockholders in redemption of the stock results in ordinary income to the corporation based upon the recapture provisions of Section 1245 and Section 1250, IRC 1954. The same is true if an asset is distributed as part of the partial liquidating dividend since the asset will be distributed at its fair market value and is tantamount to a sale under the Code. In such cases, the corporation will report ordinary income on the recaptured depreciation and the stockholders a capital gain based upon the fair market value of the asset.

Recapture of the 7% Investment Credit. A partial liquidation is a "disposition" of a qualified Section 38 asset and, therefore, the corporation in the year of partial liquidation will be required to recompute the investment credit and repay the amount subject to recapture. This is based upon the estimated established life used in computing the credit as compared with the date of sale or distribution.[37]

CITATIONS

[1]Sec. 302; 317 (b), IRC 1954.

[2]Sec. 346, IRC 1954.

[3]Senate Finance Committee Report of IRC 1954; Reg. Sec. 1.346–1.

[4]Joseph Imler, 11 TC 836.

[5]Comm. v Snite, 177 F 2d 819, aff. 10 TC 523; H.F. Asmussen, 36 BTA 878; Rev. Rul. 54–408, CB 1954–2, pg. 165.

[6]Clarence R. O'Brion, Memo TC 1951; Rev. Rul. 55–373, CB 1955–1, pg. 363.

[7]Heber Scowcroft Investment Co., et al., Memo TC 1945.

[8]Rev. Rul. 56–513, CB 1956–2, pg. 191. See also Chapter 8.

[9]Rev. Rul. 57–334, CB 1957–2, pg. 240.

[10]Sam Rosania, Memo TC 1956–116.

[11]Rev. Rul. 74–296.

[12]Rev. Rul. 58–565, CB 1958–2, pg. 140; Sec 301 (a); Sec. 316, IRC 1954.

[13]Rev. Rul. 56–512, CB 1956–2, pg. 173.

[14]Reg. Sec. 1.346–1.

[15]Rev. Rul. 60–322, CB 1960–2, pg. 118.

[16]OD 479, CB June 1920, pg. 29.

[17]IT 2388, CB Dec. 1927, pg. 14.

[18]OD 488, CB June 1920, pg. 29.

[19]IT 2246, CB Dec. 1925, pg. 14.

[20]John B. Williams, 28 BTA 1279.

[21]Ronning v U.S., DC, Minn. 1956, 51 AFTR 1655.

[22]Avco Mfg. Co., 25 TC 975; Mabel I. Wilcox, et al., 43 BTA 931, aff. 137 F 2d 136.

[23]Bynum, et al. v Comm., 113 F 2d 1, rev. 40 BTA 336.

[24]Hellman v Helvering, 68 F 2d 763, aff. Memo BTA 1932.

[25]Kelly, et al. v Comm., 97 F 2d 915, rev. 36 BTA 507; Malone v Comm., 128 F 2d 967, rev. 45 BTA 305.

[26]Johnson-McReynolds Chevrolet Corp., 27 TC 300.

[27]U.S. v Carey, 289 F 2d 531. See also Est. of Arthur H. Squire, 35 TC 590, Acq.

[28]Reg. Sec. 1.346–1 (b).

[29]Reg. Sec. 1.346 (c).

[30]Reg. Sec. 1.355–1.

[31]Reg. Sec. 1.346–3; Standard Linen Service, Inc., et al., 33 TC 1, Acq.

[32]Rev. Rul. 60–50, CB 1960–1, pg. 150.

[33]Sec. 6043, IRC 1954; Reg. Sec. 1.6043–1.

[34]See Footnote 26, pg. 3.

[35]Rev. Rul. 60–232, CB 1960–2, pg. 115.

[36]Sec. 331 (a) (2), IRC 1954.

[37]Sec. 47 (a), IRC 1954.

THIRTEEN

Redemption of Stock — Section 302 IRC 1954

DEFINED.

A redemption occurs when a corporation acquires its stock from a stockholder or stockholders for money or property or both. It is immaterial whether or not the redeemed stock is cancelled, retired or held as treasury stock.[1]

Example: The XYZ Corporation was organized in 1950 by X, Y and Z. Each shareholder paid in $50,000 and received 100 shares of the common stock. In 1961, the corporation had an earned surplus of $275,000. Each of the three stockholders transferred 25 shares of the common stock back to the corporation in redemption thereof.

CAPITAL GAIN OR ORDINARY INCOME.

The vital question on the redemption described in the example above is whether the stockholders received capital gain on the redemption or ordinary income in the form of a dividend.

PRE-1954 CODE.

The Internal Revenue Service contended that sucn redemptions prior to January 1, 1954 were to be taxed as ordinary income. In other words, the distribution in redemption of the stock was tantamount to the payment of an ordinary dividend to the extent of the earned surplus[2] unless the distribution was "not essentially equivalent to a dividend." This was the sole test under the Internal Revenue Code of 1939. The pre-1954 decisions indicate the extreme danger to every stockholder in a redemption of stock. Unless there was a clear intent not to avoid a tax and a preponderance of evidence as to the business purpose, the distribution was taxed as an ordinary dividend, not a capital gain. Each case depended upon the facts and intent—there was no weighted formula.[3] A pro-rata redemption was invariably treated as a redemption.

THE 1954 CODE.

The enactment of Section 302 in the Internal Revenue Code of 1954 eliminates, in part, the danger of a distribution in redemption of the stock of a corporation being taxed as a dividend rather than as a capital gain. The 1954 Code provides three basic methods for the redemption of stock. Thus, the statute provides that where a redemption falls under any one of these three methods it shall be treated as an exchange and taxed as capital gain. The three methods are:

(a) if the redemption is not essentially equivalent to a dividend;

(b) if the redemption is substantially disproportionate with respect to the shareholder;

(c) if the redemption is in complete redemption of all of the stock of the corporation owned by the shareholder.[4]

Thus, the 1954 Code carried over from the 1939 Code the sole test provided in that Code. As a result, stockholders continue to be in *a danger zone* with respect to this type of redemption unless they can qualify under one of the other two methods. With regard to the other two methods of distribution in redemption of stock, the rules are specific and, if followed, assure the stockholder of capital gain treatment on the redemption of their stock.[5]

NOT ESSENTIALLY EQUIVALENT TO A DIVIDEND.

There is no exact definition of what distributions are or are not essentially equivalent to a dividend. The courts for almost thirty years have attempted to solve this question and have at best established only general rules based upon the facts in each case.[6]

From these many decisions, one may gather that *the basic criterion* established by the courts is "the net effect of the distribution rather than the motives and plans of the taxpayer or his corporations."

For example, a corporation made an extraordinarily large profit on a particular transaction. Thereafter, the corporation made a distribution, redeeming 60 per cent of its stock. There was no intent to liquidate the corporation or of accomplishing any business need or purpose by such redemption. The distribution was held essentially equivalent to a dividend since the principal purpose of the distribution was to enable the stockholders to avoid income taxes.[7]

In addition, the court scrutinizes the redemption and distribution with respect to the time and manner when it occurs and the circumstances surrounding it at that time.

Thus, if a corporation redeems its preferred stock or a part of its common stock at a time when it had a substantial earned surplus available for distribution (assuming no business purpose or intent to liquidate), the *prima facie* conclusion would be that the distribution was essentially equivalent to a dividend.[8] The dividend paying history of the corporation is an important consideration.

The conclusion reached in the prior decision was extended in a subsequent decision which held that "a taxpayer may well act with the utmost good purpose and without evil intent and yet his transactions may in effect be the equivalent of the distribution of a taxable dividend."[9] The motive behind the distribution in redemption, while important, is not controlling.[10]

Under the 1939 Code, a redemption due to a contraction of the corporation's business was generally held to be a distribution which was not essentially equivalent to a taxable dividend.[11] Under the 1954 Code, a genuine contraction of the business results in a partial liquidation; taxable as a capital gain; not an ordinary dividend.[12]

A pro-rata redemption was, except in rare instances, considered a distribution which was essentially equivalent to an ordinary dividend.[13] But where two classes of stock were outstanding and the same interests did not own each class, a pro-rata redemption was held not a dividend.[14]

In addition to a contraction of business, the decisions rendered under the 1939 Code which held that the distribution was not essentially equivalent to a dividend may be grouped under three general headings (a) good business purpose;[15] (b) corporation in process of liquidating;[16] and (c) the total redemption of a stockholder's interest in the corporation.[17] It should be noted that the latter decisions formed the basis for one of the three methods provided for in the 1954 Code.[18]

The redemption by a corporation of the stock interest of one stockholder does not constitute a dividend to the other stockholders merely because the redemption increased the percentage interest of these stockholders.[19]

Example: A corporation's stock was owned 50 per cent by A and 50 per cent by B. The corporation purchased (redeemed) B's 50 per cent interest and, thereafter, A owned 100 per cent of the corporation. A does not have a dividend as the result of his increased percentage ownership. There was no increase in his economic interest.

However, if the stock of B was in reality acquired by A and paid for by the corporation out of earned surplus, the acquisition would be taxed as an ordinary dividend to the remaining stockholder (or stockholders).[20]

Where the redemption was actually a sale of the stock, the redemption rules do not apply and an ordinary dividend results.

Example: A corporation was owned by a husband, wife and a son. The father entered into a contract to sell his stock interest to an unrelated party over a period of time. As shares were sold, the money was used to redeem the stock of the mother and son.[21]

SUBSTANTIAL DISPROPORTIONATE REDEMPTION.

The rule applies to each stockholder separately, not to the stockholders as a group.

Thus, in the case of a particular stockholder, the redemption of his stock is treated as an exchange resulting in a capital gain or loss if:

(a) the redemption is substantially disproportionate with respect to the stockholder, and

(b) immediately after the redemption, the stockholder owns less than 50 per cent of all classes of stock entitled to vote.[22]

Since the disproportionate rule is applied to each stockholder separately, if more than one stockholder redeems part of his stock, some stockholders may have a capital gain while others have an ordinary dividend.[23] In applying the substantially disproportionate test, the stockholder must take into consideration not only the stock owned by himself but also constructively owned.[24] In other words, direct and indirect ownership, i.e., stock owned by the stockholder's spouse, his children, grandchildren, parents, and, in some cases, a partnership, trust or corporation.

The distribution is substantially disproportionate if:

(a) the ratio which the voting stock of the corporation owned by the stockholder immediately after the redemption bears to all of the voting stock of the corporation at that time

is less than 80 per cent of

(b) the ratio which the voting stock of the corporation owned by the stockholder immediately before the redemption bears to all of the voting stock of the corporation at such time.[25]

Example: A corporation has 400 shares of common stock outstanding which is owned 25 per cent (100 shares) by each A, B, C, and D. The stockholders are unrelated. The corporation redeems 100 shares—55 shares from A, 25 shares from B, and 20 shares from C.

Stockholders	Ownership Before Redemption	Redeemed	Ownership After Redemption	80% of 25% = 20%*
A.	100 shares	55 shares	45 shares	15%
B.	100 shares	25 shares	75 shares	25%
C.	100 shares	20 shares	80 shares	26 2/3%
D.	100 shares	—	100 shares	—
	400 shares	100 shares	300 shares	

No distribution under the rule shall be treated as substantially disproportionate unless the stockholder's ownership of the common stock of the corporation (whether voting or non-voting) after and before also meets the 80 per cent requirement explained above. If there is more than one class of common stock, the determination is based upon the fair market value of the stock.

---

*To be substantially disproportionate each shareholder must own less than 20 per cent of the 300 shares of stock outstanding after the redemption (80 per cent of 25 per cent). Thus, only A's redemption qualifies as an exchange taxable as a capital gain.[26]

Example: A corporation has two classes of stock (common voting and preferred non-voting). Before the redemption, a stockholder owned 40 per cent of the common and 25 per cent of the preferred. After the redemption, stockholder owned 40 per cent of the common and no preferred. The stockholder does not meet the disproportionate rule (40 per cent divided by 40 per cent is not less than 80 per cent).

The disproportionate test cannot be avoided by a plan of yearly redemptions, i.e., a series of redemptions over a period of several tax years. The redemptions each year are aggregated for each stockholder in applying the 80 per cent test.[27]

TERMINATION OF SHAREHOLDER'S INTEREST.

If a shareholder redeems all of the stock he owns in the corporation, the redemption is treated as an exchange, taxable as a capital gain or loss.[28] The construction ownership rules (direct and indirect) apply to such redemptions.[29] Thus, for example, the stock owned by the wife of the stockholder taxpayer must also be redeemed, if the stockholder taxpayer wants the favorable capital gain treatment.

The statute makes an exception to the constructive ownership rule provided all of the following five conditions are met. In other words, if these conditions are met, the stock interest of the taxpayer stockholder's wife does not have to be redeemed in order to consider the transaction an exchange, taxable as a capital gain or loss.

The fact that there was a family dispute is immaterial under the constructive ownership rules, where stock of one of the parties is redeemed. The redemption in such a case results in ordinary income.[30]

Example: The stockholders were members of two families who were related by marriage. The individual stockholders set up trusts for the children of the two families. As a result of a dispute between the families which resulted in divorce, the stock owned by one of the trusts was completely redeemed. However, due to the constructive ownership rule, there was no "complete" redemption. It should be noted that no ten year letter was filed. This would have changed the tax result, i.e. to capital gain.

The five conditions are:

1. Immediately after the redemption the redeeming stockholder must have no interest in the corporation as an officer, other employee, or director, other than as a creditor.[31] The status of a creditor is defined as follows—a person will be considered a creditor only if his rights with respect to the corporation are not broader or greater in scope than necessary to enforce the payment of a claim. The claim may not be in any sense proprietary in nature. It must not be subordinate to the claims of general creditors. It must not be a debt which is dependent upon the corporate earnings as to payment of the principal or of the interest. However, if a stockholder redeems his total stock interest on the basis of a cash payment and a series of notes payable over a period of years collateralized by corporate assets, the stockholder will not be considered a creditor of the type which would defeat this condition.[32]

Example: Stockholder owning 60 per cent of the issued and outstanding stock of a corporation redeems such stock on the basis of $50,000 cash plus a series of ten notes of $20,000 each, payable over the next ten years, secured by the assets of the corporation. The creditor position satisfies the required condition.

With exception of the bare statement in the Code and the Regulations which states that an interested party is an officer, other employee, or a director, there is no overall definition. What about a redeeming stockholder who becomes a "consultant" for the corporation? The Internal Revenue Service holds that a redeeming stockholder who becomes a consultant for the corporation is an "interested" party and, therefore, the redemption results in ordinary income.[33]

Example: X and his family own all of the stock of the Z Corporation. X redeemed all of his stock interest in the corporation. He filed the proper ten year letter. However, after the redemption X entered into a five year contract with the corporation to act as a consultant to the corporation at X dollars a year. He is an interested party. Therefore, the capital gain redemption becomes ordinary income.

Comment: A very important problem. Yet there are no Court decisions on the subject. Would the redeeming stockholder be an "interested party" if (a) there was no contract in the above example or (b) if no consideration was paid for the consulting service?

2. The redeeming stockholder must not acquire an interest in the corporation, other than as a creditor and other than by bequest or inheritance within ten years. An interest includes the position as an officer, employee or director. For example, if within the ten-year period measured from the date of redemption, the former stockholder acquires stock by bequest, such acquisition is allowable and will not defeat this condition. But if the acquisition is by gift or purchase, the redemption will be treated as an ordinary dividend.[34]

3. The redeeming stockholder must agree that he will notify the Commissioner if he acquires an interest in the corporation within ten years of the date of redemption, other than as a creditor or by bequest or inheritance.[35]

The agreement must be in the form of a separate statement in duplicate signed by the redeeming stockholder and attached to a timely filed return for the year in which the redemption occurred.[36] Although the Courts have rendered decisions to the effect that only substantial compliance with the Regulations is necessary with respect to the attachment of the statement to the tax return, the Internal Revenue Service disagrees with these decisions.[37] In these cases, the statement was not attached to the individual income tax return but was filed with the Examining Agent at the time of the audit (within the statutory period).[38]

The agreement must state that the stockholder has not acquired an interest in the corporation as defined above (*see 2*) since the redemption. Further that he will, within 30 days after acquisition of an interest, notify the District Director of Internal Revenue for the district in which he filed his return showing redemption that he has acquired an interest in the corporation. The period of time during which the stockholder must notify the District Director of the acquisition of the interest is within ten years from the date of redemption.[39]

Example 1: Stockholder A, the owner of 65 per cent of the capital stock of the X Corporation, redeems his entire interest for $100,000 on July 15, 1969. The cost of the stock to A six years previously was $30,000. A will report in his calendar year 1969 individual tax return a recognized capital gain of $70,000 and, since the stock was held for more than six months, the gain is a long-term capital gain of $35,000 (50% of $70,000). If the stockholder acquires an interest in the corporation, i.e., as a director, officer or employee, within ten years from July 15, 1969, he must notify the District Director within thirty days of such interest.

If a redeeming stockholder acquires an interest within the ten-year period, the notification to the District Director will result in an audit and the assessment of a tax based upon ordinary dividend on the redemption instead of the capital gain reported on the stockholder's return for the year of redemption. In order to allow the Commissioner to assess such deficiency the statute of limitations is extended.

Example 2: If the stockholder in Example 1 acquires an interest, as defined above, in 1970, the District Director will assess a deficiency based upon an ordinary dividend of $70,000 instead of the capital gain reported of $35,000. The assessment will bear interest at six per cent from the year of the reported redemption (1969).

A suggested form of agreement is as follows:

Mr. John Smith
District Director of Internal Revenue
Internal Revenue Service
Capital Street,
City and State

Dear Sir:

Re: Sec. 302 (c) (2) (iii), IRC 1954
Reg. Sec. 1.302—4 (a)

I was the owner of 65 shares (Certificate No. 5) of the capital stock of the X Corporation, Main Street, City and State, which stock was acquired by me at date of organization of the corporation on January 2, 1964 for cash. The 65 shares represented an interest of 65 per cent of the total issued and outstanding stock of the corporation.

On July 15, 1969, the corporation redeemed the 65 shares for a total payment of $100,000. The cost to me at organization was $30,000. The recognized capital gain of $70,000 is reported on the Form 1040 attached hereto.

Since July 15, 1969, I have not acquired an interest in the corporation as a director, employee or officer and, if I acquire such interest within a period of ten years from July 15, 1969, I will, within thirty days after such acquisition, notify the District Director of Internal Revenue of such acquisition.

Respectfully,

A. Stockholder

A. Stockholder
100 Terrace Drive
City, State

The stockholder is required to retain copies of his income tax returns and any other data or records indicating the amount of the tax which would have been payable had the redemption been taxable as an ordinary dividend, instead of a capital gain. Thus, the stockholder should retain as part of his records the corporate tax return or financial statements showing the balance sheet, the profit and loss statement and other financial data to measure the amount of the capital and surplus, particularly for the year in which the redemption took place.[40]

4. The stockholder must not, within ten years before the redemption, acquire from any person stock which would be considered constructively attributable to the stockholder for the purpose of avoiding the Federal income tax. Thus, any attempt to redeem stock indirectly owned by the stockholder where the purpose is for the avoidance of income tax will cause the redemption to be considered an ordinary dividend.[41]

5. The stockholder must not, within ten years before the redemption, transfer to a person who owns at the time of redemption stock which is attributable to the stockholder under the rules of constructive ownership.[42]

With respect to Conditions 2 and 3 above, these conditions do not apply if the redemption was not essentially equivalent to a dividend or was proportionate. Thus, if the redemption was essentially equivalent to a dividend or proportionate, a complete redemption at capital gain would be accomplished if, in addition, the stockholder had no interest in the corporation and the stockholder did not acquire or transfer stock under the constructive ownership rule.[43]

A sale to a related party within the ten year period by the redeeming stockholder who filed the ten year letter does not void the complete termination rule.[44]

Example: A and his son B each owned 50 per cent of the stock of the corporation. A redeemed all of his stock interest and filed a ten year letter. Within the ten year period, C, another son and brother of B purchased from B a part of his stock interest. The sale from B to C does not affect A's redemption of his interest, i.e., capital gain.

RECAPTURE OF DEPRECIATION.

The distribution of depreciable personal and/or real property in redemption of the corporate capital stock where the value of such property is in excess of the adjusted basis of such assets at the time of distribution is subject to the recapture provisions under the rules explained in Chapters 3 and 4.[45] Thus, the corporation will be required to compute the amount of depreciation recaptured and include this amount as ordinary income in the year of redemption of the capital stock. The stockholders will report a capital gain based upon the fair market value as described in previous paragraphs of this chapter.

INVESTMENT CREDIT RECAPTURE.

In the same way, the corporation will be required to repay the 7% investment credit as the result of an "early disposition" of the Section 38 Asset. The distribution of the property in redemption of the capital stock is the event which marks the disposition requiring the recomputation and repayment of the previously allowed investment credit.[46]

REDEMPTION OF STOCK WITH ACCUMULATED DIVIDENDS.

The redemption rules apply to a total redemption of the preferred stock with accumulated dividends provided all of the prerequisites of Section 302 are met. The total amount received in redemption, including the accumulated dividend, is taxed as capital gain.[47]

DISTRIBUTION OF PROPERTY IN REDEMPTION OF STOCK.

Under the general rule, a corporation realizes no gain when it distributes appreciated property as a dividend or in redemption of its stock. Gain was realized under the following three conditions:

1. a distribution of inventory valued under the life method by the corporation;
2. a distribution of corporate property subject a debt in excess of its basis; and
3. recapture income under Section 1245 and 1250.

The Tax Reform Act of 1969 added a fourth exception to the above three. A corporation will realize gain when it distributes appreciate property in redemption of its own stock. The gain is ordinary or capital depending upon the type of the property as defined for capital gain or loss purposes. However, this was a general rule and subject to certain prerequisites as discussed below.

No gain is recognized under the following conditions:

1. A distribution in complete redemption of all of the stock and complete termination of the interest of a shareholder who, at all times within the 12 month period ending on the date of such distribution, owns at least 10 per cent in value of the outstanding stock of the distributing corporation;

2. A distribution of stock of a subsidiary. For this purpose, a subsidiary is defined as a corporation which is owned 50 per cent or more by another corporation;

3. A redemption to pay death taxes as provided in Section 303;

4. A distribution in redemption of stock owned by certain private foundations; and

5. A distribution of stock of a regulated investment company upon the demand of the stockholder.

There are three additional conditions which are not associated with the general liquidation of corporation.[48]

REDEMPTION OF STOCK—ESTATE TAXES.

Under certain conditions, a redemption of stock to pay estate taxes will be treated as an exchange, taxable as a capital gain or loss, not as an ordinary dividend.[49] The amount to be treated as a redemption, taxable as a capital gain or loss, cannot exceed the total of

(a) the amount of the estate, inheritance or succession taxes, including interest;

(b) the funeral expenses; and

(c) the administration expenses claimed as a deduction in computing the estate tax.

The three conditions, all of which must exist, are as follows:

(1) The corporate stock must be either (a) stock which was included in the gross estate or (b) stock whose basis is determined by reference to stock included in the estate, including Sec. 306 stock.

(2) The value of the stock for Federal estate tax purposes must represent either (a) more than 35 per cent of the gross estate or (b) more than 50 per cent of the taxable estate. For the purpose of this rule, the stock of more than one corporation may be treated as one corporation provided more than 75 per cent in value of the outstanding stock of each is included in the gross estate.

(3) The redemption must take place after the death of the taxpayer stockholder and within the statutory period for the assessment of the Federal estate tax or within 90 days thereafter or if a petition was filed with the Tax Court of the United States within 60 days after the decision of the Court becomes final.[50]

The stock may be redeemed by a person who received the stock as an heir or distributee but not by a stockholder who acquired the stock from the executor in satisfaction of a specific bequest of money.[51]

The redemption of stock for estate tax apparently will not cause a recapture of depreciation or of the 7% investment credit. Each of the sections of the Code applicable to recapture eliminates a transfer by reason of death.[52]

If an estate redeems the stock of a corporation and the proceeds of the redemption is greater than the aggregate of the estate tax and the administration expenses, the excess is essentially equivalent to the dividend and is taxable as ordinary income under Section 302 (b) (1).[53]

CITATIONS

[1] Sec. 317 (b), IRC 1954.

[2] Sec. 346, IRC 1954.

[3] Flanagan v Helvering, 116 F 2d 937; McGuire, 32 BTA 1075, aff. 84 F 2d 431.

[4] Sec. 302 (b) (1) (2) (3), IRC 1954.

[5] Sec. 302 (b) (2) (3), IRC 1954.

[6] Flanagan v Helvering, 116 F 2d 937; McGuire, 32 BTA 1075, aff. 84 F 2d 431; Reg. Sec. 1.302–2.

[7] W. & K. Holding Corp., et al., 38 BTA 803 NA.

[8] Annie Watts Hill, 27 BTA 73, aff. 66 F 2d 45.

[9] McGuire v Comm., 84 F 2d 431, aff. 32 BTA 1075; George Hyman, 28 BTA 1231, aff. 71 F 2d 342.

[10] J. Natwick, 36 BTA 866.

[11] Joseph W. Imler, 11 TC 836; Heber Scowcroft Investment Co., et al., Memo TC 1945; Rev. Rul. 60–232, CB 1960–2, pg. 115; see also Chapter 12.

[12] Flanagan v Helvering, 116 F 2d 937; Robinson v Comm., 69 F 2d 972, aff. 27 BTA 1018; Moore, Memo TC 1964–20; see also Chapter 12.

[13] Rev. Rul. 56–485, CB 1956–2, pg. 176.

[14] Sec. 331 (a) (2), IRC 1954. See Chapter 10 for complete discussion.

[15] South Atlantic Steamship Line, 42 BTA 705; Fox v Hanison, 145 F 2d 531.

[16] Ward M. Canaday, Inc., 29 BTA 355, aff. 76 F 2d 278.

[17] Summerfield v U.S., 145 F. Supp. 104, aff. 249 F 2d 446; Zenz v Quinlivan, 213 F 2d 914; Rev. Rul. 54–458, CB 1954–2, pg. 167.

[18] Sec. 302 (b) (3), IRC 1954.

[19] Holsey v Comm., 258 F 2d 865, rev. 28 TC 962.

[20] Rev. Rul. 58–614, CB 1958–2, pg. 920; Wall v U.S., 164 F 2d 462; Zipp v Comm., 259 F 2d 119, aff. 28 TC 314. See also Niederkrome, et al. v Comm., 266 F 2d 238 and Fred C. Niederkrome, et al., Memo TC 1960.

[21] Jones, DC, N.J., 4/4/72.

[22] Sec. 302 (b) (2) (A) (B), IRC 1954.

[23] Reg. Sec. 1.302–3.

[24] Sec. 318, IRC 1954; Reg. Sec. 1.318–1; 1.318–2.

[25] Sec. 302 (b) (2) (C), IRC 1954.

[26] Reg. Sec. 1.302–3.

[27] Sec. 302 (b) (2) (D), IRC 1954.

[28] Sec. 302 (b) (3), IRC 1954.

[29]Sec. 302 (c) (2) (A) (ii), IRC 1954.

[30]Heft, Tr., 61 TC No. 45.

[31]*Ibid.*

[32]Reg. 1.302–4 (d) (e).

[33]Rev. Rul. 70–104.

[34]Sec. 302 (c) (2) (A) (ii), IRC 1954.

[35]Sec. 302 (c) (2) (iii), IRC 1954.

[36]Archbold, DC, N.J., January 1962.

[37]Cary, 41 TC 214, non acq.

[38]Cary, supra, Van Keppel v U.S., 321 F 2d 717; Pearce, 226 F. Supp. 702.

[39]Reg. Sec. 1.302–4 (a).

[40]Reg. Sec. 1.302–4 (b).

[41]Sec. 302 (c) (2) (B) (i), IRC 1954; Sec. 318 (a), IRC 1954.

[42]Sec. 302 (c) (2) (B) (ii), IRC 1954; Sec. 318 (a), IRC 1954.

[43]Sec. 302 (b) (5), IRC 1954.

[44]Rev. Rul. 71–562.

[45]Sec. 1245; 1250, IRC 1954; Reg. Sec. 1.1245–1 (c).

[46]Sec. 47 (a), IRC 1954, Committee Report, Rev. Act 1962.

[47]Cummins Diesel Sales Corp. v U.S., CA–7, 4/28/72, aff. 323 F. Supp. 1114.

[48]Section 311, IRC 1954.

[49]Sec. 303, IRC 1954.

[50]Reg. Sec. 1.303–2.

[51]Reg. Sec. 1.303–2 (f).

[52]Sec. 47 (b) (1); 1245 (b) (1); 1250 (d) (2); Reg. Sec. 1.1245–1.

[53]Rev. Rul. 71–261.

FOURTEEN

Complete Liquidation of Subsidiary – Section 332, IRC 1954

INTRODUCTION.

Section 332, IRC 1954 provides certain rules for the nonrecognition of gain to the parent corporation upon the receipt of the property in complete liquidation of the subsidiary. This section is not wholly an elective section. It can operate to the disadvantage of the parent, particularly where the subsidiary's assets have appreciated in value. Under the general rule, the parent takes the basis of the subsidiary's assets—a substituted basis.[1]

CONDITIONS OF NONRECOGNITION OF GAIN.

In order to have a tax-free liquidation of the subsidiary into its parent, all of the following conditions must be met.[2]

(a) The parent corporation owns capital stock of the subsidiary possessing at least 80 per cent of the total voting power of all classes of stock entitled to vote, and owns at least 80 per cent of the total number of shares of all other classes of stock (except non-voting stock which is limited and preferred as to dividends). Both percentages must apply.

(b) The ownership of the stock as provided for in (a) above must be in effect at the date of the adoption of the plan and at all times until the receipt of the subsidiary's property in liquidation.

(c) The distribution of the subsidiary's property must fit into either of the two following plans: (1) the distribution by the subsidiary is in complete cancellation or redemption of all its stock and the transfer of the property occurs within the taxable year during which the plan was adopted; and (2) the distribution by the subsidiary is one of a series of distributions in complete cancellation or redemption of all of its capital stock in accordance with a plan of liquidation under which the transfer of all of the property is to be completed within three years from the close of the taxable year during which the first distribution was made.

Warning: If, under the second method, the distribution of the subsidiary's property is not completed within the three-year period or if the parent does not continue to meet the 80% stock ownership requirements, then one of the distributions will be considered a distribution in complete liquidation.

Warning: If the liquidation is not completed within the taxable year during which the plan was adopted, the Commissioner of Internal Revenue has the right to require either a bond or a waiver of the statute of limitation or both.[3]

MINORITY STOCKHOLDERS.

The rule of nonrecognition of gain under Section 332 does not apply to the minority stockholders, i.e., the other 20% or lesser per cent. Therefore, to the minority stockholder the liquidation is taxable. The Internal Revenue Code of 1954, has, however, provided some relief to such stockholders.[4]

PLAN OF LIQUIDATION.

The use of Section 332 is predicated upon the adoption of a plan of liquidation. This plan must be adopted by both corporation and the minority stockholders, if any. Thus, both corporations are required to call special joint or separate meetings of the stockholders and directors to adopt and approve the liquidation. The plan should be incorporated with the minutes and adopted by resolution. If the plan provides for a series of distributions extending over more than one year, the plan must include a statement showing the period within which the transfer of the property to the parent is to be completed.

Exception: If, however, the property of the subsidiary will be distributed to the parent within the taxable year, it is necessary only for the stockholders to adopt a resolution providing for the distribution of the assets. The resolution need not specify the time for the completion of the transfer of the property.

MONEY.

The term "property" as used in Section 332 includes money. Hence, the receipt of money by the parent from the subsidiary is a transaction in which no gain or loss is recognized.[5]

INDEBTEDNESS OF SUBSIDIARY TO PARENT.

If the subsidiary is indebted to the parent and the subsidiary's assets are applied in cancellation or redemption of the indebtedness upon liquidation, there is a tax-effect to both the subsidiary and the parent.[6]

(a) Subsidiary: A new rule was introduced by the Internal Revenue Code of 1954, applicable to Section 332. If a subsidiary is liquidated in a non-taxable liquidation to its parent corporation and on the date of the adoption of the plan the subsidiary was indebted to the parent, then no gain or loss will be recognized to the subsidiary because of the transfer of the property in satisfaction of the debt. Thus, it is immaterial whether the fair market value of the subsidiary's property is greater or less than its cost or other basis to the subsidiary. No gain or loss will be recognized to the subsidiary.

(b) Parent: However, in the hands of the parent, the fair market value of the property received from the subsidiary in satisfaction of the subsidiary's debt is important. If the fair market value of the assets transferred (in excess of the subsidiary's other assets) is less than the amount of the debt, the parent is entitled to a bad debt deduction and a loss for worthless stock. The basis for this section is due to the fact that the application of assets against the debt is not considered a distribution in liquidation under Section 332.[7] The same rule was applied where the preferred stock took all of the assets of the subsidiary (parent owned both common and preferred).[8]

If fair market value of the assets exceeds the indebtedness, the assets are first applied against the indebtedness and the excess constitutes the Section 332 liquidating distribution. On such excess, no gain or loss is recognized under the Code.[9]

INDEBTEDNESS OF PARENT TO SUBSIDIARY.

A parent corporation which is indebted to a subsidiary has no recognized gain or loss upon the receipt of its note on the liquidation of the subsidiary.[10] Gain or loss is not recognized upon the receipt of property. The parent's note in the hands of the subsidiary constitutes property.[11]

Example: Corporation P owned 100 per cent of Corporation S. Both corporations were engaged in manufacturing. P borrowed 2000 X dollars from S. P gave S a note for the loan which was payable in five equal installments. After three installments had been paid by P, a plan of complete liquidation under Section 332 was adopted. S distributed all of its assets, including P's note, to P. P realizes no income, gain or loss upon the receipt of the note.

DEBT v EQUITY.

The Court in one case found that where the "debt" was really advances similar to risk capital, the transfer of the assets resulted in no recognized gain or loss to parent or subsidiary. Since the "debt" was really capital, the distribution was a liquidating dividend under Section 332.[12]

INSTALLMENT OBLIGATIONS.

No gain or loss is recognized to the subsidiary upon the transfer of installment obligations in liquidation to the parent under Section 332.[13]

LIQUIDATION INVOLVING SECTION 337.

Section 337 (a) of the Internal Revenue Code of 1954 provides in general that if a corporation adopts a plan of complete liquidation and, within a 12-month period beginning on the date of the adoption of the plan, all of the assets of the corporation are distributed in complete liquidation, less those retained to meet claims, then no gain or loss will be recognized to such corporation from the sale or exchange by it of property within such 12-month period.

Section 337 (c) (2) of the Code provides that Section 337 of the Code will not apply in the case of a sale or exchange following adoption of a plan of complete liquidation, if Section 332 of the Code applies with respect to such liquidation and the basis of the property of the liquidating corporation in the hands of the distributee is determined under Section 334 (b) (1) of the Code. Thus, the transaction is treated as a sale and the basis of the assets acquired is the cost.

The Supreme Court of the United States held that a sale of property by the shareholders of a corporation after receipt of the property as a liquidating distribution was taxable to the corporation when the corporation had in fact conducted all the negotiations and the terms of the sale had been agreed upon prior to the distribution of the property.[14]

Thus, it seems that there is a conflict between the various sections of the Code and the Supreme Court decision.[15] The following examples illustrate the application of the Code to a liquidation under Section 332 where there is a sale of assets under Section 337. In the examples P indicates parent corporation and S indicates subsidiary corporation.

Example: The shareholders of P adopted a plan of complete liquidation under Section 337. P sold its assets, except for the capital stock of S to an unrelated party. P distributed to its stockholders in complete liquidation the proceeds from the sale of the assets and the stock of S. The shareholders then adopted a plan of liquidation under Section 337. S then sold its assets to an unrelated party. S then distributed to its shareholders in complete liquidation the proceeds of the sale. No gain or loss is recognized to either P or S since all of the requirements of Section 337 were met.

Example: P adopted a plan of complete liquidation of S pursuant to Section 332. S sold all of its assets to an unrelated party pursuant to negotiations conducted by S, and distributed the proceeds to P in complete liquidation. The shareholders of P then adopted a plan of complete liquidation under Section 337 and P thereafter sold its assets to an unrelated party. P distributed to its shareholders in complete liquidation the proceeds from the sale and the proceeds from the sale of the assets of S received in the liquidation of S.

Section 337 is not applicable to the sale by S of all of its assets. Gain or loss is recognized to S because Section 332 of the Code applied to the liquidation of S and the basis of the property of S in the hands of P is determined under Section 334 (b) (1). However, no gain or loss is recognized to P on the sale of its assets because all the other requirements of Section 337 of the Code were met.

Example: Plans of complete liquidation were adopted for P and S. During the past several years, S had received numerous offers from an unrelated party to purchase its assets. S had consistently rejected these offers. All of the assets of S were distributed to P pursuant to Section 332 of the Code. Thereafter, the assets of P (which included the assets of S) were sold to the unrelated party, and the proceeds were distributed to the shareholders of P in complete liquidation. Negotiations for the sale of the assets, including the assets of S, were in fact conducted and agreed upon by P.

Under these circumstances, because the facts establish that the assets were sold by P, and S had rejected all offers to sell, no gain or loss is recognized to P or S assuming that all of the other requirements of Section 337 of the Code are met.

Example: Plans of complete liquidation were adopted for P and S. Prior to this time, S had entered into preliminary negotiations for the sale of its assets with an unrelated purchaser, Z, and both agreed in general to the terms of the sale. It was mutually agreed that the assets of S should be distributed to P pursuant to Section 332 of the Code, and thereafter P would sell its assets (including the assets of S) to Z. The part of the sales agreement between P and Z that pertained to the assets of S closely paralleled the terms previously agreed to by S and Z. The transaction between P and Z was consummated and the proceeds were distributed to the shareholders of P.

Under these circumstances, because the facts establish that S had conducted the negotiations for and agreed in general to the terms of the sale of its assets and then transferred them to Z through P, gain or loss is recognized to S on the sale of its assets even though in form the assets were sold by P. No gain or loss is recognized to P on the sale of its assets assuming all of the other requirements of Section 337 of the Code are met.

BASIS OF PROPERTY—PARENT.

Under the general rule, the basis of the property received by the parent in liquidation of its subsidiary under Section 332 is the same as in the hands of the subsidiary.[16] However, the general rule is subject to an important exception.

Exception: If a parent corporation purchases the stock of another corporation and adopts a plan of liquidation within two years, the basis of the assets of the subsidiary in the hands of the parent after the liquidation will be the amount the parent paid for the stock.[17]

The following conditions must be met:

(a) the plan of liquidation must have been adopted on or after 6/22/54, and not more than 2 years after the acquisition of the stock of the corporation described in (b) below;

(b) the parent corporation must have acquired by purchase, during a period of not more than 12 months, stock of the subsidiary corporation. This stock must possess at least 80% of the total combined voting power of all classes of stock entitled to vote and at least 80% of the total number of shares of all other classes of stock (except non-voting stock which is limited and preferred as to dividends).

"Purchase" is specifically defined in the Code.[18] The acquisition of the stock of the subsidiary by the parent must be through a taxable transaction—a purchase by the parent and a sale by the previous owner. The stock cannot be acquired in any tax-free exchange whereby the purchaser looks to the basis of the stock in the hands of the seller. Neither can the stock be acquired from a decedent by inheritance or by a tax-free transfer from a controlled corporation.[19] Also the corporation may not acquire for this purpose the stock from a person whose stock the parent corporation constructively owns.[20] Under certain conditions, an acquiring corporation can acquire the stock of another corporation by purchasing from the stockholders of the corporation to be acquired their stock options to purchase such stock. However, the purchase of the option must be from an individual who is not related to the acquiring corporation under the rules of constructive ownership.[21] Further, the option is considered to be acquired on the date of purchase and it must be exercised on or before the last day of the 12 month period.[22] The basis of the provision, which was enacted into the Code in 1954, was a long time of decisions which corrected the unfavorable features of the Internal Revenue Code of 1939.[23]

The basis of the stock for the purpose of determining the basis of the property in the hands of the parent is adjusted by the transactions occurring after the acquisition of the capital stock. Chief among these adjustments are (a) dividend distributions made to parent by subsidiary; (b) money received by parent corporation; (c) liabilities assumed or subject to on property received; and (d) the portion of the earnings since acquisition of the capital stock.[24]

Example: Corporation A bought all of the capital stock of Corporation B for $1,000 on 1/1/55. The only asset of Corporation B was a building having a basis of $100. On 7/1/55, the building was sold for $1,050 and the proceeds were invested in another building. On 12/30/55, Corporation B was liquidated into Corporation A under Section 332. The basis of the building in the hands of Corporation A upon receipt if $1,050 (cost of stock $1,000 plus excess selling price of building over cost of stock).

Records: The parent corporation must maintain complete records in permanent form of every distribution received in liquidation as to the date or dates, basis and the fair market value and other pertinent data.[25]

INVESTMENT CREDIT ALLOWED ON LIQUIDATION.

An investment credit is allowable on the liquidation of a wholly owned subsidiary under Section 332 provided there is a purchase and the parent corporation elects the use of Section 334 (b) (2) as previously discussed. No investment credit is allowable if there is no purchase as defined in Section 334 (b) (2).[26] Thus, if the liquidation is consummated under Section 332 and Section 334 (b) (1), no investment credit will be allowed.

RECAPTURE OF DEPRECIATION.

As already explained, the liquidation of a subsidiary may fall under the general rule whereby the parent takes over the subsidiary's assets at the same basis as in the hands of the subsidiary, i.e., a carryover basis. Under this general rule, there is no recapture of depreciation as it applies to both depreciable personal and real property.[27] However, if the liquidation is accomplished under the exception which, in effect, is a purchase and allows a stepped-up basis in the hands of the parent, the recapture provisions apply. Thus, the subsidiary will be required to compute the recaptured depreciation and include such amount as ordinary income.[28]

INVESTMENT CREDIT RECAPTURE.

There is no specific provision for recapture of the 7% investment credit.[29] However, based upon the general provision that the same business is continued, there would be no recapture of the investment credit upon the liquidation of the subsidiary.

Form 1120: For each year in which the corporation receives a distribution from the subsidiary, there must be attached to the income tax return the following: (a) a certified copy of the plan and the resolution adopting such plan and a statement under oath showing all of the transactions incident to or pursuant to the plan; (b) a list of all the assets received as to their cost or other basis, the fair market value and the date or dates distributed; (c) a statement of any indebtedness of the subsidiary to the parent and the assets received in satisfaction thereof, together with the value and the basis; (d) the ownership of each class of stock, percentage owned, number of shares, voting power of each at adoption of the plan and at all times up to the date of distribution, and the cost or other basis and dates of purchase.

Form 966: Form 966, together with the plan and the resolution certified to by the secretary, must be filed within 30 days after the adoption of the plan. Any amendment of the original plan requires the filing of another Form 966 with a certified copy of the amendments. Form 966 is filed at the office of the Internal Revenue Service Center for the area in which the corporation files its income tax returns.

CITATIONS

[1] Reg. Sec. 1.332–1.

[2] Sec. 332 (b), IRC 1954; Reg. Sec. 1.332–2.

[3] Reg. Sec. 1.332–4.

[4] Sec. 337 (d), IRC 1954. See Explanation and Example in Chapter 8.

[5] GCM 19435, CB 1938–1, pg. 176; International Inv. Corp., 11 TC 678, aff. 175 F 2d 772.

[6] Sec. 332 (c), IRC 1954; Reg. Sec. 1.332–7.

[7] Iron Fireman Mfg. Co., 5 TC 452; American Zinc, Lead & Smelting Co., Memo TC 1943; H.G. Hill Stores, Inc., 44 BTA 1182.

[8] Spaulding Bakeries, Inc., 27 TC 684, aff. 252 F 2d 693.

[9] Reg. Sec. 1.332–7; IT 4109, CB 1952–2, pg. 138. See also Houston Natural Gas Corp., 9 TC 570, aff. 173 F 2d 461.

[10] Rev. Rul. 74–54.

[11] Sec. 332 (b), IRC 1954.

[12] Byerlite Corporation v Williams, 170 F. Supp. 48, 286 F 2d 285.

[13] Sec. 453 (d) (4), IRC 1954; Advance Aluminum Casting Corp. v Harrison, 158 F 2d 922.

[14] Comm. v Court Holding Co., 324 U.S. 331. See also U.S. v Cumberland Public Service Co., 338 U.S. 451.

[15] Rev. Rul. 69–172.

[16] Sec. 334 (b) (1), IRC 1954; Reg. Sec. 1.334–1.

[17] Sec. 334 (b) (2), IRC 1954; Reg. Sec. 1.334–1.

[18] Sec. 334 (b) (3), IRC 1954.

[19] Sec. 1014 (a); 351, IRC 1954.

[20] Sec. 318 (a), IRC 1954.

[21] Sec. 318 (a), IRC 1954.

[22] Rev. Rul. 74–295.

[23] Kimball–Diamond Co., 14 TC 749, aff. 187 F 2d 718.

[24] Reg. Sec. 1.334–1 (c) (4).

[25] Reg. Sec. 1.332–6.

[26] Rev. Rul. 73–461.

[27] Sec. 1245 (b) (3); 1250 (d) (3); 334 (b) (1); IRC 1954; Committee Report, Rev. Act 1962 & 1964.

[28] Sec. 334 (b) (2), IRC 1954.

[29] Sec. 47 (a), IRC 1954.

FIFTEEN

Liquidations of Corporations — Sections 1361 and 1371 Elections

INTRODUCTION.

Section 1361 of the Internal Revenue Code of 1954 allowed partnerships and sole proprietors to elect to be taxed as corporations instead of as a partnership and as an individual. Thus, for taxable years beginning after December 31, 1953, an unincorporated business entity in the form of a partnership or sole proprietorship would be treated as it if were a corporation for Federal income tax purposes.

The Technical Amendment Act of 1958 provided the reverse election. Under Section 1371 *et seq.*, a corporation could elect to be taxed as a sole proprietorship (corporation with one stockholder) or as a partnership (corporation with more than one stockholder). This election was available only for taxable years beginning after December 31, 1957 and ending after September 2, 1958.

Under either of the two elections, the electing original entity does not lose its actual legal status. Thus, under Section 1371 *et seq.*, the corporation remains a corporation under the state statutes. It is merely subject to a tax as if it were a proprietorship or a partnership. The corporation would be subject to no corporate income tax, but the income would be taxed directly to the stockholders as individuals. The same is true if a sole proprietor or a partnership elected to be taxed as a corporation under Section 1361, IRC 1954. The entity despite paying a corporate income tax remains for all purposes a proprietorship or a partnership.

SECTION 1361 ELECTION.

An unincorporated business, whether it be a sole proprietorship or a partnership, will be treated as a corporation with respect to the operation, distributions, sale of an interest, and for any other purpose. Each owner of an interest in such an unincorporated business will be considered a stockholder in proportion to his interest.[1]

This election was effective from 1954 through April 14, 1966. However, all elections terminated on January 1, 1969. This chapter is retained in the text since the statute of limitations, and in some cases extensions, have been granted on the applicable years.

Example: A proprietor elects Section 1361. The net income of the "corporation" in its first year of election before "officer's salary" is $50,000. The proprietor sets up as "officer's salary" $20,000, leaving $30,000 as the net income of the corporation. Since the "corporate tax" on $30,000 is $10,100, the "corporation" will have an "earned surplus" at the end of the first year of $19,900 ($30,000 − $10,100).[2]

The balance sheet of the "corporation" will show an earned surplus of $19,900. The "capital stock" is equal to the net worth of the proprietorship at the beginning of the first year of the election. Any "distribution" from the "earned surplus" is taxable to the "shareholder" as an ordinary dividend paid by a corporation.[3]

"CORPORATE" LIQUIDATION.

An unincorporated entity electing under Section 1361 may liquidate under Section 331 (a) (1)–Complete Liquidation; Section 331 (a) (2)–Partial Liquidation; Section 333–Calendar Month Liquidation; and Section 337–Twelve Month Liquidations.[4]

CEASING BUSINESS.

If the proprietor or partnership ceases to conduct its business in an unincorporated form, the Sec. 1361 election terminates and the entity is considered to have made a complete distribution of its assets under Sec. 331 (a) (1), IRC 1954.[5]

Thus, if a partnership elected Sec. 1361, IRC 1954 and, after operating under this election for several years, organized a corporation under the state statute to which the unincorporated partnership transferred all or a part of its assets, the distribution of the assets to the corporation would be a liquidating dividend to each partner in proportion to his interest.

Specimen Example: The AB Partnership was formed in 1950 by A and B, who were equal partners. In 1955, the partnership elected under Sec. 1361, IRC 1954. The balance sheet of the partnership as of December 31, 1954 was as follows:

ASSETS

Cash		$ 5,000
Accounts Receivable	$ 20,000	
Less: Reserve for Doubtful Accounts	1,500	18,500
Machinery and Equipment	$100,000	
Less: Reserve for Depreciation	20,000	$ 80,000
Other Assets		2,500
Total Assets		$106,000

LIABILITIES AND CAPITAL

Accounts Payable	$ 8,000
Bank Loan Payable	30,000
Capital A	34,000
B	34,000
Total Liabilities and Capital	$106,000

As of January 1, 1961, the partners decided to organize a corporation under the laws of their state. The balance sheet per the books on December 31, 1960 was as follows:

ASSETS

Cash		$ 20,000.00
Accounts Receivable	$ 60,000.00	
Less: Reserve for Doubtful Accounts	4,000.00	56,000.00
Machinery and Equipment	125,000.00	
Less: Reserve for Depreciation	35,000.00	90,000.00
Other Assets		2,000.00
Total Assets		$168,000.00

LIABILITIES AND CAPITAL

Accounts Payable	$ 15,000.00
Bank Loan Payable	25,000.00
Earned Surplus	60,000.00
Capital Stock (A and B)	68,000.00
Total Liabilities and Capital	$168,000.00

The fair market value of the assets on December 31, 1960 was:

Cash	$ 20,000.00
Accounts Receivable (Net)	56,000.00

Machinery and Equipment (Net)		140,000.00
Other Assets		2,000.00
Total		$218,000.00

COMPUTATION OF RECOGNIZED GAIN ON LIQUIDATION

Fair Market Value of Assets		$218,000.00
Less: Liabilities—		
Accounts Payable	$15,000.00	
Bank Loan Payable	25,000.00	40,000.00
Net Fair Market Value of Assets		$178,000.00
Less: Capital Stock		68,000.00
Recognized Capital Gain on Liquidation		$110,000.00
Recognized Capital Gain to		
A		$ 55,000.00
B		55,000.00
		$110,000.00

LIQUIDATION OF UNINCORPORATED ENTITY.

If the unincorporated entity after electing Sec. 1361, IRC 1954 decides to discontinue the business, the distribution is taxable as a liquidating dividend. For this purpose, the entity and its "stockholders" may elect Sec. 331 (a) (1) or Sec. 333, IRC 1954. The selection will, of course, depend upon the tax consequences under each method as described in previous chapters.[6]

SALE OF CORPORATE ASSETS.

Sec. 337, IRC 1954 may be elected by the entity and its "stockholders" if the entity anticipates a sale of its assets or business. Under this method, a double tax is avoided on the sale of the assets and subsequent liquidation of the proceeds of the sale and other assets.[7]

PARTIAL LIQUIDATION.

Under the prerequisites provided in Sec. 331 (a) (2), IRC 1954, the entity may elect a partial liquidation of its "stock." As discussed in a previous chapter, this method is generally limited to genuine contraction of the business.[8]

FAILURE TO RE-ELECT—CHANGE OF OWNERSHIP.

If an electing entity changes its ownership by 20 per cent or more, a new election under Sec. 1361, IRC 1954 must be made.[9] If a timely new election is not made, the entity is considered to have liquidated under Sec. 331 (a) (1), IRC 1954 and the "stockholders" will be required to include the recognized gain in their individual returns at that time.

COLLAPSIBLE CORPORATIONS.

If the "corporation" is a collapsible entity as defined in Sec. 341, IRC 1954, the gain on the liquidation will be treated as ordinary gain instead of capital gain.

PROCEDURE.

An unincorporated entity electing under Sec. 161, IRC 1954 must follow the same procedure of liquidation as provided for a corporation which was duly organized under the state law.[10] Thus, the "stockholders" are required to hold a meeting and adopt a plan of liquidation under a specific section of the Code. The meeting would be similar to a joint meeting of the stockholders and directors, including the adoption of a resolution to liquidate.[11]

If Sec. 331 (a) (1) or Sec. 337, IRC 1954 is adopted as the method of liquidation, Form 966 must be filed within thirty days after the adoption of the resolution to liquidate. If Sec. 333, IRC 1954 is adopted, Form 964, in addition to Form 966, must be filed by each "stockholder" within the thirty-day period and the liquidation must be completed within the calendar month selected.

In addition, Form 1096 and the liquidation information form, Form 1099 L must be filed on or before February 28 of the year following the distribution in liquidation.

SECTION 1371 ELECTION.

A corporation may, under certain conditions, elect to be taxed as a sole proprietorship (one stockholder) or as a partnership (more than one stockholder but not more than ten).[12] Although taxed as a sole proprietorship or as a partnership, the corporation continues its corporate status under the laws of the state in which it was incorporated. Hence, for purposes of liquidation and dissolution, all of the Internal Revenue Code provisions apply.

CORPORATE LIQUIDATION.

A corporation which has elected to be taxed under Sec. 1371 *et seq.*, IRC 1954 may adopt any one of the methods available, i.e., Sec. 331 (a) (1), Sec. 333, or Sec. 337, IRC 1954. The methods used will, of course, depend upon the tax results under each method as applied to each particular set of facts. In addition, a partial liquidation may be adopted under Sec. 331 (a) (2), IRC 1954.

EFFECT OF THE 1371 ELECTION.

Each stockholder will include in his individual income tax return his share of the corporate net income, whether or not distributed. However, if the corporation incurred a net loss, each shareholder is entitled to his share of such loss. Also, if the corporation had a net long-term capital gain, the gain is passed through the stockholders.[13] As the result of the inclusion in the taxable income of each stockholder of his share of the net income, whether or not actually received, and the share of any net operating loss, the basis of the capital stock and stockholders' loans must be adjusted. The adjustment is important in determining the amount of the recognized gain or loss on liquidating dividend.

BASIS.

The basis of the stock of each shareholder must be adjusted as follows:[14]

(1) Increase the stock basis by the amount of net income which was not actually received by the stockholder-shareholders' undistributable net income on balance sheet of Form 1120-S.

Example: Corporation XY elected Sec. 371 for the calendar year 1961. For the calendar year 1961, the corporation had a net income of $20,000, none of which was paid to the two stockholders. At the organization of the corporation, each stockholder had paid in $5,000 for his capital stock. The basis of the capital stock for each shareholder in the event of a corporate liquidation would be $15,000 ($10,000 shareholders' undistributed net income plus cash paid for the capital stock, $5,000).

(2) Reduce the stock basis by the amount of the corporation's net operating loss.

Example: Corporation AB elected Sec. 371 for the calendar year 1961. For the calendar year 1961, the corporation had a net operating loss of $6,000. At the organization of the corporation, each stockholder paid in $5,000 for capital stock. The basis of the capital stock for each shareholder in the event of a liquidation of the corporation would be $2,000 ($5,000 paid in for the capital stock at organization minus one-half of the loss, $3,000).

(3) Reduce the stock basis by the amount of any subsequent distributions of earnings that were previously taxed to the stockholder or that were not considered dividends (shareholders' undistributed net income per the balance sheet on Form 1120-S).

Example: The balance of the MN Corporation, a corporation electing Sec. 1371, was, as of December 31, 1960:

Assets	$75,000
Current Liabilities	$30,000
Earned Surplus	15,000
Shareholders' Undistributable Net Income	10,000
Capital Stock (Paid in by M and N equally)	20,000
	$75,000

For the calendar year 1961, the corporation showed no income or loss. The corporation elected to pay $2,000 to each shareholder in December, 1961 out of shareholders' undistributable net income. In January 1962, the corporation elected to liquidate. The basis of each stockholder's capital stock will be $13,000 ($10,000 plus $5,000 minus $2,000).

(4) Reduce the basis of any corporate indebtedness to the stockholder by the excess of your share of the corporation's net operating loss over the stock basis.

Example: Corporation OR, a corporation electing Sec. 1371 showed the following assets and liabilities as of December 31, 1960:

Assets	$80,000
Accounts Payable	45,000
Loan Payable–O stockholder	7,500
Loan Payable–R stockholder	7,500
Shareholders' Undistributable Net Income	0
Capital Stock	20,000
Total	$80,000

During the two years of business (1960–1961) the corporation showed net operating losses of $22,000. The basis of the capital stock of each stockholder for purpose of liquidation is $0. In addition, the loans payable to the stockholders are reduced to $6,500 each ($7,500 minus excess net operating loss over capital stock basis, $1,000).

Specimen Example: The PS Corporation was organized in 1952 by P and S, equal shareholders. The corporation elected Sec. 1371 for the calendar year 1959. The stockholders adopted a plan of liquidation under Sec. 331 (a) (1), IRC 1954, effective December 31, 1961. The balance sheet as of December 31, 1961 was as follows:

ASSETS

Cash		$ 6,000.00
Accounts Receivable	$ 20,000.00	
Less: Reserve for Bad Debts	1,500.00	18,500.00
Machinery and Equipment	$100,000.00	
Less: Reserve for Depreciation	25,000.00	75,000.00
Other Assets		3,500.00
Total Assets		$103,000.00

LIABILITIES AND CAPITAL

Accounts Payable	$ 5,000.00
Bank Loan Payable	20,000.00
Earned Surplus	12,000.00
Shareholders' Undistributable Net Income	30,000.00
Capital Stock	36,000.00
Total Liabilities and Capital	$103,000.00

The fair market value of the assets on December 31, 1960 was:

Cash	$ 6,000.00
Accounts Receivable (Net)	18,500.00

Machinery and Equipment (Net)	125,000.00
Other Assets	3,500.00
Total Assets	$153,000.00

COMPUTATION OF RECOGNIZED GAIN ON LIQUIDATION

Fair Market Value of Assets		$153,000.00
Less: Liabilities—		
Accounts Payable	$ 5,000.00	
Bank Loan Payable	20,000.00	25,000.00
Net Fair Market Value of Assets		$128,000.00
Less: Capital Stock	$36,000.00	
Shareholders'		
Undistributable Net		
Income	30,000.00	66,000.00
Recognized Capital Gain on Liquidation		$ 62,000.00
Recognized Capital Gain to:		
P		$ 31,000.00
S		31,000.00
		$ 62,000.00

SECTION 333 LIQUIDATION.

If the corporation elected Section 333, IRC, the two taxpayer stockholders would each have an ordinary dividend of $6,000.00 (one-half of earned surplus of $12,000.00). Since the cash ($6,000.00) does not exceed the earned surplus ($12,000.00), no capital gain will be taxed to either stockholder P or S. In computing the basis of the other assets received in liquidation, the basis of the other assets is based upon the basis of the stock—$66,000.00 (Shareholders' Undistributable Net Income $30,000.00 plus Capital Stock $36,000.00).[15]

SECTION 337 LIQUIDATION.

If the corporation elected Sec. 337, IRC 1954, the basis for the capital stock is $66,000.00 (Shareholders' Undistributable Net Income $30,000.00 plus Capital Stock $36,000.00).[16]

"AUTOMATIC" LIQUIDATION.

If a corporation elects to be taxed under Sec. 1371, IRC 1954, the net income or net loss is taxable to the shareholders, whether or not actually distributed.[17] If a part of the income is derived from a sale of capital assets resulting in a net long-term capital gain, this gain is reflected in the stockholder's individual Form 1040.[18]

Example: Corporation adopted Sec. 1371 for the calendar year 1961. The corporation had a gross income of $35,000.00, including a long-term capital gain of

$10,000.00. The net income on the Form 1120-S was $18,000.00. The sole stockholder of the corporation, whether or not the income was actually distributed, will include in his individual income tax return for the calendar year 1961:

Net Long-Term Capital Gain (Schedule D)	$10,000.00
Undistributable Net Income (Schedule B, Part V—Other Income)	$ 8,000.00

A corporation contemplating liquidation or in the process of liquidation may elect Sec. 1371, IRC 1954.[19] Hence, if during the process of liquidation and sale of its assets, the corporation has a net long-term capital gain, the gain will flow through to the stockholders as if sold by the stockholders as individuals.

However, as in all corporate liquidations, the plan of liquidation must be adopted and certain forms must be timely filed.

RECAPTURE PROVISIONS.

Dependent upon the section of liquidation elected, the recapture provisions applicable to depreciation and the investment credit apply or do not apply as already discussed under each method in prior chapters.

PROCEDURE.

A corporation electing to be taxed under Sec. 1371, IRC 1954 (Subchapter S) must follow the same procedure of liquidation as required for a corporation not electing this section. A meeting of the stockholders and directors must be held at which a resolution is adopted concerning the liquidation.

If Sec. 331 (a) (1) or Sec. 337, IRC 1954 is adopted as the method of liquidation, From 966 must be filed within thirty days after the adoption of the resolution to liquidate. If Sec. 333, IRC 1954 is adopted, Form 964, in addition to Form 966, must be filed by each stockholder within the thirty day period and the liquidation must be completed within the calendar month selected.[20]

In addition, Form 1096 and the liquidation information form, Form 1099 L must be filed on or before February 28 of the year following the distribution in liquidation.[21]

CITATIONS

[1] Sec. 1361 (c), IRC 1954; Reg. Sec. 1.1361–3 (a) (2).

[2] Reg. Sec. 1.1361–3 (c) (2) (3).

[3] Sec. 1361 (k), IRC 1954; Reg. Sec. 1.1361–10.

[4] Sec. 1361 (l), IRC 1954; Reg. Sec. 1.1361–11.

[5] Reg. Sec. 1.1361–5 (b).

[6] Chapters 3 and 6.

[7] Chapter 8.

[8] Chapter 10.

[9] Sec. 1361 (f), IRC 1954; Reg. Sec. 1.1361–6.

[10] Reg. Sec. 1.1361–11 (b).

[11] Chapters 4, 7 and 9.

[12] Sec. 1371 *et seq.*, IRC 1954.

[13] Sec. 1373–1375, IRC 1954.

[14] Sec. 1376, IRC 1954; Reg. Sec. 1.1376–1.

[15] Chapter 6.

[16] Chapter 8.

[17] Sec. 1373, IRC 1954; Reg. Sec. 1.1373–1.

[18] Sec. 1375, IRC 1954; Reg. Sec. 1.1375–1.

[19] Sec. 1372, IRC 1954; Reg. Sec. 1.1372–1.

[20] Chapters 3, 6 and 8.

[21] *Ibid.*

SIXTEEN

Subchapter S Corporations – Basic Rules

INTRODUCTION.

A Subchapter S corporation is a regular corporation which has elected under Section 1372 (a) of the Internal Revenue Code. Under such an election, the corporation is treated in many ways like a partnership rather than a corporation for tax purposes.

In general, the corporation is exempt from all Federal corporate income taxes. However, under certain limited conditions, such a corporation may be subject to a tax on long-term capital gains. The corporate income is taxed to the shareholders whether or not actually distributed to the shareholders. Such income, in most instances, is taxed as ordinary income, although if the corporation realized any net long-term capital gain, the gain passes through to the shareholder and is taxed as long-term capital gain on the individual shareholder's income tax return. A corporate loss, on the other hand, is deducted by the shareholders on their individual income tax returns as a business loss within certain limitations.

As already indicated, the corporate income is taxable to the shareholders whether or not distributed. That part of the income which is not distributed is accumulated in the corporation and can be distributed in a later year without further tax. While the income is retained by the corporation, it becomes part of the shareholders' investment in the capital of the corporation. In order to understand the liquidation of a Subchapter S corporation, it is necessary to understand thoroughly the rules applicable to the method of reporting the income and loss of such a corporation.

CORPORATE TAXABLE INCOME.

Taxable Income of a Subchapter S corporation is computed in the same way as the Taxable Income of a regular corporation (one not electing the provisions of Subchapter S),[1] with two exceptions:

    1. The special corporation deductions are not allowed. These deductions are (a) interest on partially tax-exempt interest received on obligations issued by the United States or any instrumentality thereof;[2] (b) dividends received deduction;[3] (c) dividends received on certain preferred stock;[4] (d) dividends received from certain foreign corporations;[5] (e) dividends received on certain preferred stock of public utilities.[6]

    2. A net operating loss deduction is not allowed.[7] As explained more fully below, a corporate net operating loss passes through to the stockholders in proportion to their stock ownership rates (with certain limitations.)

BASIC RULES OF TAXATION.

Under the general rule, a corporation which has elected the provisions of Subchapter S is exempt from corporate income taxes. The taxes from which the corporation is exempt are the normal tax, the surtax, the surcharge, the capital gains tax, the tax on unreasonable accumulated surplus, and the tax on undistributed personal holding company income. Thus, under the general rule, the only tax on the corporate Taxable Income is upon the shareholders, whether or not distributed. Under certain conditions, a Subchapter S corporation is liable for a tax on capital gains.

CORPORATE CAPITAL GAINS TAX.

A corporation which has elected the provisions of Subchapter S is liable for a capital gains tax only if the taxable income of the corporation for the tax year is more than $25,000, and the excess of net long-term capital gain over net short-term capital loss is both more than $25,000 and more than 50 per cent of taxable income and the transaction occurred within the first three years under the election. Thus, the capital gains tax does not apply if the corporation has completed three tax years under the election. This rule is further modified. The capital gains tax does not apply if the corporation is a new corporation in existence for less than four years and was a duly elected Subchapter S corporation since its incorporation.[8]

CORPORATE INCOME AND EARNINGS AND PROFITS—BASIC RULES.

A corporation under Subchapter S is required to file Form 1120-S. It is, under the general rule, merely an information return. It is an information return and a tax return only if the capital gains tax applies. The important sections of Form 1120-S for the purpose of a corporate liquidation are illustrated by the following various examples.

FORM 1120—S

Line		
1–3	Gross Profit	$xxxx

4–8; 9 (a) (c)	Dividends, Interest, Rents, Royalties, Net short-term capital gain reduced by any net long-term capital loss, ordinary gain or loss	xxxx
9 (b)	Net long-term capital gain reduced by any net short-term capital loss	xxxx
10	Other income	xxxx
11	Total Income	$xxxx
12	Compensation of officers	xxxx
13–26	Other deductions	xxxx
27	Total deductions	$xxxx
28	Taxable Income	$xxxx

SCHEDULE K

COMPUTATION OF CORPORATION'S UNDISTRIBUTED TAXABLE INCOME

1. Taxable Income (line 28 above)			$xxxx
2. Less: (a) Money distributed as dividends out of earnings and profits of the taxable year	$xxx		
(b) Tax imposed on certain capital gains	$xxx	xxx	
3. Corporation's Undistributed Taxable Income			$xxxx

SUMMARY OF DISTRIBUTIONS AND OTHER ITEMS

Compensation	$xxxx
4. Actual dividend distributions taxable as ordinary income.	$xxxx
5. Actual dividend distributions taxable as long-term capital gains (after tax)	xxxx
6. Actual dividend distributions taxable as ordinary income and qualifying for the dividends exclusion	xxxx
7. Nontaxable distributions	xxxx
8. Undistributed taxable income—taxable as ordinary income or loss	xxxx
9. Undistributed taxable income—taxable as long-term capital gain (after tax)	xxxx
10. Interest on investment indebtedness	xxxx
11. Items of tax preference	xxxx
12. Investment credit property	xxxx

Example 1: The A Corporation was organized in January, 1973 and immediately elected Subchapter S. A owned all of the corporate stock and reported for tax purposes on the calendar year basis. A drew an officer's salary of $15,000. The

corporation had a Taxable Income of $20,000 for the calendar year 1973, consisting entirely of ordinary income. The Taxable Income of $20,000 was distributed timely (as later defined) on January 15, 1974. Since the entire Taxable Income was distributed to the stockholder, there would be no Undistributed Taxable Income for the tax year. Thus, the Schedule of Distribution would show compensation $15,000 in Column (a), dividends $20,000 in Column (b) and the amount taxable as ordinary income in Column (f) $20,000.

Example 2: Assume the same facts as in Example 1, except that none of the Taxable Income was paid out. The Distribution Schedule will show the compensation in Column (a)–$15,000; the Undistributed Taxable Income in Column (c) and Column (f)–$20,000. Although not distributed, the $20,000 Taxable Income is taxable to A for the calendar year 1973.

Example 3: Assume the same facts as in Example 1, except that the Total Income (Line 11 above) included a long-term capital gain of $5,000 (Line 9 (a)). The $20,000 distribution will be reported in Column (b); $5,000 will be entered in Column (d)–long-term capital gain; and $15,000 in Column (f)–ordinary income. Thus, A on his Form 1040, will report $5,000 as a long-term capital gain and $15,000 as ordinary income from the Subchapter S corporation.

Example 4: Assume the same facts as in Example 1 and 3 except that no part of the Taxable Income was distributed. In such a case, the $20,000 Undistributed Taxable Income will be entered in Column (c); $5,000 in Column (d)–long-term capital gain and $15,000 in Column (f)–ordinary income. Despite the fact that no distribution was made, the taxpayer reports for the calendar year $5,000 as a long-term capital gain and $15,000 as ordinary income from a Subchapter S corporation.

Example 5: Assume the same facts as in Example 1 except that the corporation sustained a net loss of $4,000. The net operating loss (within certain limitations)[9] passes through to the stockholder who includes the loss on his Form 1040 as a Net Loss from a Subchapter S corporation. The loss affects the basis of the stock and loans as later discussed.

EARNINGS AND PROFITS.

Where a corporation was in existence prior to its election under the provision of Subchapter S, the corporation may have earned surplus or an accumulated deficit. The stockholders' equity section of the balance sheet on Form 1120 is as follows:

Capital stock	$xxxx
Paid in or capital surplus	xxxx
Retained earnings—appropriated	xxxx
Retained earnings—unappropriated	xxxx

It is necessary to understand what effect the Subchapter S election has upon the prior accumulated earnings and profits (or deficit) in order to fully understand the application of the rules of corporate liquidation. The stockholders' equity section of the balance sheet on Form 1120-S is as follows:

Capital stock . . . . $xxxx
Paid-in or capital surplus xxxx
Retained earnings–appropriated xxxx
Retained earnings–unappropriated xxxx
Stockholders undistributed taxable income xxxx

The Rules are illustrated by the following example.

Example 1: The B Corporation was organized on January 2, 1973 and adopted the calendar year for reporting its income. As of December 31, 1973 the corporation had earned surplus of $10,000. On January 2, 1974, it adopted the provisions of Subchapter S. For the calendar year 1974, the corporation had a Taxable Income of $15,000. The corporation made no distribution of its 1974 Taxable Income. However, the stockholders will report the $15,000 Taxable Income for tax purposes. The balance sheet at December 31, 1974 will show the following–

Retained earnings $10,000
Shareholders' undistributed taxable income   15,000

Example 2: Assume the same facts as in Example 1 except that the Taxable Income of $15,000 was distributed to the shareholders (timely). The balance sheet will reflect only the retained earnings of $10,000.

Example 3: The C Corporation was in existence for two years before electing Subchapter S. As of December 31, 1973, the earned surplus was $10,000. In January 1974, the corporation elected Subchapter S. In the calendar year 1974, the corporation sustained a net loss of $6,000. The net loss which passed through to the stockholders was fully deductible assuming the limitation—capital stock and debts—applicable to losses was $8,000. The balance sheet will show the earned surplus of $10,000.

Example 4: Assume the same facts as in Example 3 except that the stockholders' limitation on their net loss deduction is $4,000. The earned surplus of $10,000 is not affected by the fact that the net loss of $6,000 is passed through only to the extent of $4,000.

Example 5: The D Corporation had a net long-term capital loss of $2,000 (or some other nondeductible item). At the beginning of the taxable year, the corporation had an earned surplus of $10,000. The corporation had a current year Taxable Income of $7,000. Whether or not distributed, the shareholder will report income of $7,000. At the beginning of the following year, the earned surplus will be reduced to $8,000 ($10,000 – $2,000).

Example 6: Assume the same facts as in Example 5 except that at the close of the tax year, the corporation distributed $17,000 to its stockholder ($10,000 plus

$7,000). The total $17,000 will be taxed to the stockholder—$7,000 as ordinary income and $10,000 as a dividend distribution subject to the dividend exclusion allowable to individual taxpayers.

If a Subchapter S corporation is subject to a capital gains tax, the amount of the tax reduces the earned surplus and if there is none, creates a deficit.

DISTRIBUTIONS TO STOCKHOLDERS—ADDITIONAL RULES—CASH:

As already explained an actual dividend distribution is taxed to the stockholder who receives the distribution. This rule applies even though the stockholder has disposed of his stock prior to the close of the corporate tax year. When the taxable income is not distributed to the shareholder, the shareholder still receives taxable income which is called a constructive dividend. Unlike an actual dividend distribution, a constructive dividend is taxable only to those stockholders who are stockholders at the end of the taxable year of the corporation.

Cash distributions made within two and a half months after the close of the corporate tax year are considered as having been made out of the prior year's Taxable Income.[10] It does not reduce the prior earned surplus (if any). The rule applies even though the corporation lost its Subchapter S status in the year prior to the actual distribution.

Example 1: The M Corporation, a Subchapter S corporation, reported on the basis of a calendar year. For the calendar year 1973, the corporation had a Taxable Income of $12,000. The $12,000 was paid to the sole stockholder on March 1, 1974. The dividend distribution is taxable to the stockholder for the calendar year 1973.

Example 2: Assume the same facts as in Example 1 above except that the distribution on March 1, 1974 was only $10,000. For 1973, the stockholder reports as income $12,000 ($10,000 distributed and $2,000 undistributed). The $2,000 is Shareholders' Undistributed Taxable Income on the balance sheet.

PROPERTY:

Property distributed other than money does not reduce the Undistributed Taxable Income. Current earnings are allocated between the property and constructive dividends. Thus, the dividends are from current earnings.[11]

Example 1: Taxable income for the current tax year was $40,000. During the tax year, corporate property with a fair market value of $20,000 was distributed to the sole stockholder. The Undistributed Taxable Income remains at $40,000. The total distribution (actual and constructive) was $60,000.

(a) Property distribution from current earnings—

$$40,000 \times \frac{20,000}{60,000} = \$13,333.33$$

(b) Constructive dividend of Undistributed Taxable Income–

$$40,000 \times \frac{40,000}{60,000} = \$26,666.67$$

Example 2: Assume the same facts as in the above example except that the corporation distributed $10,000 as a cash dividend during the tax year (out of current earnings). Undistributed Taxable Income is reduced to $30,000 ($40,000 − 10,000). The stockholders taxable income is $40,000 computed as follows–

(a) Cash dividend $10,000
(b) Property distribution

$$30,000 \times \frac{20,000}{50,000} = \qquad\qquad 12,000$$

(c) Constructive distribution

$$30,000 \times \frac{30,000}{50,000} = \qquad\qquad 18,000$$

STOCK REDEMPTIONS AND CORPORATE LIQUIDATIONS.

As explained in the succeeding chapter, a liquidation distribution does not reduce current earnings. Such a distribution is a capital transaction.

The same rule applies to a redemption of stock as described in Chapter Thirteen and to a partial liquidating dividend as described in Chapter Twelve.

Example: A Subchapter S corporation adopted a plan of liquidation in 1974. For the tax year 1974, the earnings were $10,000. A payment of $10,000 was made during the year as a liquidating dividend. The Undistributed Taxable Income remains the same. The stockholder received a constructive dividend of $10,000 which is treated as ordinary income at the time of final liquidation. The basis of the stock is increased by $10,000.

BASIS OF STOCK.

The basis of the stock for the purpose of a sale of the stock or in the event of a corporate liquidation or a stock redemption, is made up of several items. Some of them represent money or property paid in for the capital stock or as paid in or capital surplus while others represent constructive dividends, i.e. undistributed taxable income.

Example 1: A corporation was organized in 1970. The stockholders paid in $15,000 for the capital. For the calendar year 1973, the corporation adopted Subchapter S status. For the calendar years 1973 and 1974, the corporation had Taxable Income of $10,000 and $12,000 respectively. The corporation did not distribute the

Taxable Income of 1973 and 1974. The stockholder included the 1973 and 1974 Taxable Income as undistributed income. The basis of the stockholder's investment in the corporation is $37,000, computed as follows:

Capital Stock	$15,000
Stockholders' Undistributed Taxable Income	22,000
Total	$37,000

Example 2: Assume the same facts as in Example 1, and that the corporation had a Taxable Income in 1975 of $5,000. The corporation distributed the $5,000 Taxable Income and an additional $10,000. The basis of the capital stock at the close of 1975 was $27,000 ($37,000 − $10,000).

Example 3: Assume the same facts as in Example 1 and that the corporation sustained a net loss in 1975 of $5,000. The corporation made no distributions. The basis of the capital stock at the close of 1975 was $32,000 ($15,000 − $5,000 + $22,000).[12]

Example 4: A sole proprietor transferred his business to a corporation tax free.[13] The adjusted basis of the assets in the hands of the proprietorship was $50,000. The proprietor received all of the capital stock of the corporation. The basis of the capital stock is $50,000.

Example 5: Assume the same facts as in Example 4. In the third year of corporate existence, the stockholder transferred an asset having a cost or other basis in his hands of $10,000. He received a capital credit on the corporate books. The basis of the capital is $60,000 ($50,000 paid in capital plus $10,000 paid in or capital surplus).

In summary, the basis of the stockholder's capital for all purposes involving a sale or other disposition of the stock consists of one or more of the following balance sheet items—

Capital Stock
Paid in or Capital Surplus
Shareholders' Undistributed Taxable Income

LIQUIDATION CAN ELIMINATE SUB S STATUS.

The receipt of a liquidating dividend by a Subchapter S corporation could cause the loss of a Sub S election.[14]

Example: The X corporation properly elected under Section 1372. One of its assets was an investment in the Y Corporation. The Y Corporation sold its assets, adopting a plan of liquidation under Section 337. As a result of the liquidation of Y, X Corporation received a liquidating dividend which resulted in a long-term capital gain. The gross liquidating dividend was more than 20 per cent of the corporation's gross receipts for the tax year. In the year of receipt of the liquidating dividend from the Y Corporation, the X Corporation lost its status as a Subchapter S Corporation.

CITATIONS

[1]Section 1371–1378, incl.

[2]Section 242.

[3]Section 243.

[4]Section 244.

[5]Section 245.

[6]Section 247.

[7]Section 172.

[8]Section 1378; Reg. Sec. 1.1378–1; 1.1378–2.

[9]Section 1374 (c) (2).

[10]Section 1375 (f); P.L. 89–389, effective for distributions after 4/14/66.

[11]Reg. Sec. 1.1373–1.

[12]Section 1374 (c).

[13]Section 351.

[14]Lansing Broadcasting Company v Comm., 52 TC 299, aff. 427 F 2d 1014.

SEVENTEEN

Liquidation of Subchapter S Corporations

INTRODUCTION.

It is important to remember that although a corporation as a result of its election to be taxed under Subchapter S is taxed much the same as a partnership, the entity is still a corporation for tax purposes. Thus, a Subchapter S corporation is subject to all of the following liquidation and redemption provisions:

1. Section 331 (a) (1)–the general method of liquidation;
2. Section 333–the calendar month liquidation;
3. Section 337–the twelve-month liquidation;
4. Section 331 (a) (2)–the partial liquidation; and
5. Section 302–the redemption of stock.

TAX IMPACT.

As in the case of the regular corporation, the basic methods of liquidation must be applied in order to determine the tax impact on the corporation and on the shareholders of each method of liquidation. In making this comparison, the basic difference between the regular and the Subchapter S corporation must be taken into account. These differences fall into four basic areas–

(1) the cost of the adjusted basis to the stockholders of the capital stock;
(2) the paid-in or capital surplus;

(3) the shareholders undistributed taxable income; and

(4) the loans payable to shareholders.

Further, these items are affected by the distributions of a Subchapter S corporation and by the net operating loss of such a corporation which passes through to the stockholders.

ADJUSTMENT TO STOCKHOLDER'S LOANS TO CORPORATION.

In addition to the adjustment to the cost or other basis of the capital stock as explained in detail in Chapter 15, the method of liquidation selected may be affected by the adjustment in the Loans Payable (Stockholders) account.

If a Subchapter S corporation sustains a net loss, each shareholder is allowed to deduct his proportionate share on his individual return. However, the deduction for the loss is limited to the basis of the shareholder's capital stock plus the basis of his loans to the corporation. The loss is first applied to the basis of the stock and then to the basis of the loans.[1]

The stockholder's capital basis, after its reduction by a net loss, can be increased by an additional investment by the stockholder or by leaving in the corporation its net income, i.e. shareholders undistributed taxable income. The basis of the shareholder's loan cannot be increased after its reduction by any net loss. Any additional money loaned to the corporation by the shareholder constitutes a new loan and has no effect on the prior loan.

Warning: If the corporation repays the stockholder's loan, represented by an open account, after its reduction by a net loss, the shareholder has ordinary income to the extent that the basis was reduced.[2]

The basis of the capital stock and the loan cannot be reduced below zero.[3]

The distribution of the shareholders undistributed taxable income reduces the basis of the stock but does not reduce the earned surplus. The excess is a partial liquidating dividend and taxed as a capital gain.[4]

GENERAL METHOD OF LIQUIDATION[5]

SUMMARY.

Under the general method, the assets are valued at their fair market value at the date of liquidation. The following outline illustrates the general method:

Fair Market Value of All Assets

minus

Liabilities

equals

Net Fair Market Value of Assets

minus

Cost or Other Basis of Capital Stock

equals

Capital Gain or Loss

The complete explanation of this method of liquidating a corporation applies to Subchapter S corporations with the additional adjustments explained below.[6]

Example: The ABC Corporation was organized on May 2, 1960 by A. Adams, B. Black and C. Charles. Each of the three shareholders paid in $20,000 and received 100 shares of stock. In 1962, each shareholder returned $3,000 of their officers' salary in order to increase the working capital. In 1974, Adams loaned the corporation $30,000. On January 1, 1969, the corporation elected under Section 1372 (a). The following schedule shows the net income or loss since the Subchapter S election.

1969	$15,000 (distributed)
1970	20,000 (distributed)
1971	10,000 (distributed)
1972	(30,000) (loss)
1973	3,000 (not distributed)
1974 (to 8/31/74)	$6,000 (distributed)

ABC CORPORATION

Balance Sheet as of August 31, 1974

ASSETS:

Cash		$ 5,000
Accounts Receivable	$ 60,000	
Less: Reserve for Bad Debts	3,000	57,000
Notes Receivable		12,000
Inventory		36,000
Land		25,000
Factory Building	150,000	
Less: Reserve for Depreciation	30,000	120,000
Machinery	80,000	
Less: Reserve for Depreciation	36,000	44,000
Deferred Assets		1,000
Total Assets		$300,000

LIABILITIES & CAPITAL

Accounts Payable	$ 63,000
Mortgage Payable	100,000
Loan Payable—A. Adams	30,000
Capital Stock	60,000
Capital Surplus (Paid-in)	9,000
Earned Surplus (Prior to election)	35,000
Shareholders Undistributed Taxable Income	3,000
Total Liabilities & Capital	$300,000

ABC CORPORATION

Fair Market Value of Assets as of 8/31/74

Cash	$ 5,000
Accounts Receivable	55,000
Notes Receivable	12,000
Inventory	36,000
Land	40,000
Factory Building	195,000
Machinery	84,000
Deferred Assets	1,000
	$428,000

COMPUTATION OF NET FAIR MARKET
VALUE OF ASSETS

Fair Market Value of Assets		$428,000
Less: Liabilities–		
Accounts Payable	$ 63,000	
Mortgage Payable	100,000	
Loan Payable–A. Adams	30,000	193,000
Net Fair Market Value		$235,000

COMPUTATION OF STOCKHOLDER'S BASIS

Capital Stock	$60,000
Capital Surplus	9,000
	$69,000
Plus: SUTI	3,000
	$72,000
Less: Net Loss Adjusted	30,000
Adjusted Basis	$42,000

BASIS OF CAPITAL STOCK TO SHAREHOLDERS

Stockholders	*Adjusted Basis*
Adams	$14,000
Black	14,000
Charles	14,000
	$42,000

COMPUTATION OF RECOGNIZED STOCKHOLDER'S GAIN

	Adams	*Black*	*Charles*
Net Fair Market Value of Assets	$78,334	$78,333	$78,333
Basis of Stock	14,000	14,000	14,000
Recognized Gain	$64,334	$64,333	$64,333

Note: If the net loss was in excess of the capital stock and the capital surplus, the loss would reduce the basis to zero which would then be the basis for computing gain on liquidation.

CALENDAR MONTH LIQUIDATION[7]

SUMMARY.

Under Section 333, the stockholders may receive, in complete liquidation of the corporation, the property that has appreciated in value without the recognition of gain. However, if the liquidating corporation has an earned surplus, the surplus is taxed to the stockholders as an ordinary dividend. The cash which is distributed in liquidation to the extent that it exceeds the earned surplus (if any) is taxed as a capital gain. The basis of the property distributed in complete liquidation is based upon the basis of the stock in the hands of the stockholders.

The basic rules which apply to the regular corporation also apply to a corporation which has elected under the Subchapter S provisions. In addition to the nature of the surplus and undistributed earnings, additional adjustments to the basis are required.

Example: The XYZ Corporation was organized on June 16, 1951 by E. Davis and F. Factor. Davis paid in $2,500 for 250 shares and Factor $7,500 for 750 shares. On January 1, 1971, the shareholders elected Section 1372 (a). The corporation and the shareholders elected to liquidate during the calendar month of August, 1974. The earnings from 1/1/71 to 12/31/73 were not distributed. The earnings for the fractional year ending August 31, 1974 were distributed timely. The balance sheet as of the date of liquidation in August 1974 was as follows:

XYZ CORPORATION

ASSETS		
Cash		$ 8,000
Land		20,000
Building	$185,000	
Less: Reserve for Depreciation	33,000	152,000
Total Assets		$180,000

LIABILITIES & CAPITAL

Accounts Payable	$ 12,000
Mortgage Payable	140,000
Capital Stock	10,000
Earned Surplus (Prior to election)	6,000
Shareholders' Undistributed Taxable Income	12,000
Total Liabilities & Capital	$180,000

Based upon expert appraisals, the assets of the corporation for purposes of liquidation were valued as follows:

**Fair Market Value of Assets
as of August 1974**

Cash	$ 8,000
Land	40,000
Buildings	270,000
Total	$318,000

COMPUTATION OF STOCKHOLDERS BASIS OF CAPITAL STOCK

	E. Davis	F. Factor	Total
Capital Stock	$2,500	$ 7,500	$10,000
Shareholders' Undistributed Taxable Income	3,000	9,000	12,000
Total	$5,500	$16,500	$22,000

COMPUTATION OF RECOGNIZED GAIN ON LIQUIDATION

Distribution to Stockholders	E. Davis	F. Factor	Total
Money	$ 2,000	$ 6,000	$ 8,000
Securities acquired after 12/31/53	0	0	0
	$ 2,000	$ 6,000	$ 8,000
Other Property	77,500	232,500	310,000
Total Distributions	$79,500	$238,500	$318,000

Basis of Stockholder's Stock	5,500	16,500	22,000
Actual Gain	$74,000	$222,000	$296,000
Earned Surplus	$ 1,500	$ 4,500	$ 6,000

Application of Section 333:

Ordinary Dividend	$ 1,500	$ 4,500	$ 6,000
Capital gain	500	1,500	2,000
Non-recognized gain	72,000	216,000	288,000

COMPUTATION OF BASIS OF OTHER PROPERTY

Adjusted Basis of Stock Cancelled		$ 22,000
Less: Money Received		8,000
		$ 14,000
Add: Liabilities assumed (a/c's Payable)	$ 12,000	
Specific liens against property	140,000	
Gain Recognized (ordinary and necessary)	8,000	160,000
Basis of Assets (subject to apportionment)		$174,000
Basis of Assets subject to apportionment		$174,000
Minus: Specific liens		140,000
Basis to be apportioned		$ 34,000
Land and buildings		$310,000
Less: Specific liens		140,000
		$170,000
170,000/170,000 × $34,000 = 34,000 plus 140,000 =		$174,000

LIQUIDATION UNDER SECTION 337[8]

SUMMARY.

Where a corporation sells its assets, the gain is taxed to the corporation. However, if the corporation meets the requirements of the provisions of Section 337, the gain will be recognized not to the corporation but to the stockholders. The basic rules of Section 337 may be summarized as follows:

(a) if a corporation adopts a plan of liquidation; and

(b) within the 12-month period beginning on the date of adoption of the plan of liquidation, all of the assets of the corporation are distributed in complete liquidation (less assets retained to meet claims); then

(c) no gain or loss will be recognized to such corporation from the sale or exchange by the corporation of its property within the 12-month period.

SUBCHAPTER S CORPORATION AND SECTION 337.

Before considering the provisions of Section 337, a Subchapter S corporation must consider several important factors which have a tax impact on the stockholders and the corporation itself.

(a) Installment Sale Method: If a Subchapter S corporation elects under Section 337 and sells its assets on a deferred payment plan, the installment method cannot be elected.[9] Thus, under Section 337, the stockholders must report the recognized gain at the date of the liquidating distribution. This is accomplished by taking into account the face value of the mortgage receivable or its fair market value. The tax impact on the stockholder under these conditions would result in a full tax payable on the sale and liquidation of the corporation despite the fact that only a portion of the sale price was received.[10]

(b) Capital Gains Tax: Under certain conditions, a Subchapter S corporation is subject to a capital gains tax on the sale of its assets. The tax applies where the taxable income is more than $25,000 and where the excess of the long-term capital gain over the net short-term capital loss (if any) is both more than $25,000 and more than 50 per cent of the taxable income and the transaction occurred within the first three years under the election.[11] Under such conditions, the corporation will pay a tax on the amount of the recognized long-term capital gain in the tax year of the sale of the corporate property. The corporation can elect the installment sale method, assuming its prerequisites are met. In such a case, the capital gain tax will be based only upon the recognized gain on the initial payment. Thus, if the recognized gain is less than $25,000 as described above, the corporation will not be liable for the capital gains tax.

(c) Pass-through of Capital Gain: If a Subchapter S corporation sells its assets and does not meet the requirements of Section 337, the corporation's capital gain on the sale will be passed through to the shareholders and taxed to them as capital gains on their individual income tax return.

Comment: Before making an election, the tax impact under each method should be computed.

REDEMPTION OF STOCK.[12]

The provisions of Section 302 apply to a Subchapter S corporation as well as to a regular corporation. The basis of the capital stock to be redeemed must be adjusted under the rules applicable to a Subchapter S corporation.

PARTIAL LIQUIDATION.[13]

A Subchapter S corporation may elect a partial liquidation under Section 331 (a) (2). As in the case of the regular corporation, the Code and the Regulations apply to a very limited number of transactions.

In addition to the election under Section 331 (a) (2), a Subchapter S corporation shareholder may involuntarily fall into a partial liquidation situation.

Example: A corporation was organized in 1960. Its paid-in capital was $15,000. In 1970, it elected Subchapter S status. At the date of the election it had no earned surplus. Taxable income amounting to $10,000 was not distributed from 1970 through 1973. In 1974, the corporation had a Taxable Income of $3,000. The corporation distributed $30,000 to the shareholders.

The shareholders had a Taxable Income from the Subchapter S corporation of $3,000; a non-taxable distribution of $10,000; a return of capital of $15,000 and a partial liquidation distribution of $2,000.[14]

CITATIONS

[1]Section 1374 (c); 1376 (b).
[2]Rev. Rul. 64–162.
[3]Reg. Sec. 1.1376–1; 1.1376–2.
[4]Reg. Sec. 1.1375–4.
[5]Section 331 (a) (1).
[6]Chapter 6.
[7]Chapter 8.
[8]Chapter 10.
[9]Section 453.
[10]Chapter 10.
[11]Chapter 16.
[12]Chapter 13.
[13]Chapter 12.
[14]Reg. Sec. 1.1375–4.

Index To Code and Regulations

TABLE OF DECISIONS AND RULINGS

D

E

F

G

H

Index

A

Accounting
  expenses, 33
  journal entry
    liquidation, 92
    new entity after liquidation, 93
Accounting expenses
  calendar year liquidation, 153
Accounts receivable
  collection on, 79
  no value at liquidation, 78
  valuation of, 40
Accrual basis
  complete liquidation, 72
  when gain recognized, 28
Acquisition
  stock
    different dates, 29
Allocation
  calendar month liquidation, 106
Apportionment
  calendar month liquidation, 108
Assets
  accounts and notes receivable, 40
  appointment of basis, 109
  appreciated-liquidated, 35
  building, 39
  claims
    no value at liquidation, 28
  contracts, 40
  copyrights, 38
  creditors, distributed to, 149
  depreciated-liquidation, 29
  depreciated, sale of, 28
  fair market value, 35
  goodwill, 36
  indebtedness, excess of, 192
  intangible, 36
    goodwill, 36
  inventory, 40
  land, 39
  leaseholds, 39
  life insurance, 40

Assets Cont.

  mortgages, 42
    no value at liquidation, 78
  non-depreciable, 40
  patents, 38
  receivables
    no value at liquidation, 78
  retained, 107
  retention of, 29
  sale by corporation
    partial liquidation, 174
  sale by stockholders
    partial liquidation, 175
  sale of, in liquidation, 133
  securities, 41
  sold, 21
    retention of charter, 71, 176
  transfer to another entity, 70
  valuation of, 35
Automatic liquidation, 205

B

Balance sheet
  calendar month liquidation, 116
  complete liquidation, 85
Basis
  appreciated assets, 68
  assets
    calendar month liquidation, 116
  installment obligation
    12 month liquidation, 140
  mortgage receivable, 142
  stock
    pseudo-corporation, 202
    Subchapter S Corp., 208
  subsidiary's assets, 191
  subsidiary's property, 193
Buildings
  valuation of, 39
Bulk sale
  inventory, 139
  replaced, 140

237